On the Seventh Day

40 SCIENTISTS AND ACADEMICS EXPLAIN
WHY THEY BELIEVE IN GOD

edited by

JOHN F. ASHTON

First printing: June 2002

ISBN: 0-89051-376-7
Library of Congress Card Number: 2002105380

Printed in the United States of America

For information regarding author interviews, please contact the publicity department at (870) 438-5288.

Please visit our website for other great titles:
www.masterbooks.net

CONTENTS

FAITH AND EXPERIENCE

EDITOR'S PREFACE

Millions of people around the world still believe in and pray to the God of the Bible. The Bible tells of an all-powerful, all-knowing being who exists outside space and time as we know it and who created the universe. This God is supernatural — that is, above nature — yet has personality and can intellectually communicate with humans, giving instruction, guidance, wisdom, and comfort. His power sustains all the processes of the universe, including life, and even the laws of nature are subject to his will. Miracles can be wrought in our world by His power — that is, He can cause outcomes contrary to those predicted by the observed laws of science.

The Bible records many examples of miracles that occurred down through history which served to demonstrate that this supernatural power exists. In a number of instances the miracles occurred before a multitude of witnesses, such as the parting of the Red Sea by Moses and the raising of Lazarus four days after he died by Jesus.

The Bible also tells of the Creator's guidelines for how humans are to live (standards for morality). For example, we are told it is wrong to murder, to steal, to bear false witness, or to have sex outside a vowed, lifelong, loving relationship with a member of the opposite sex. We are also told that God is seeking to have a personal, loving, intellectual relationship with each one of us and that those who respond affirmatively to this invitation will live forever and enjoy fellowship with their Creator. Such an offer must surely be considered the most important matter we will ever have to decide in our lives.

Many scientists and academics, however, now teach that there is no supernatural God and that everything, including life, exists as a result of natural forces. In fact, there is a prevailing idea that this naturalism is part and parcel of science. This leaves no room for a supernatural God in our understanding of our existence. There is no God factor in our daily lives and no hope of having eternal life with God in heaven.

A few years ago, Oxford University professor Dr. Richard Dawkins, in his Voltaire Lectures to the British Humanist Association, talked about religious belief as being a kind of virus in the human software. Dr. Dawkins argued that belief in a supernatural God is essentially irrational.

Recently I picked up a book called *Think Big,* written by Dr. Ben Carson, director of Pediatric Neurosurgery at Johns Hopkins University Hospital in Baltimore. Near the end of the book this highly successful brain surgeon writes of an answer to prayer during difficult surgery. While operating deep inside a patient's brain, an artery broke loose in an area he couldn't see. This resulted in vigorous bleeding. Because no one could see where the bleeding was coming from, it looked as though the patient might be lost. Dr. Carson started praying for God's help. Just then he did something that later seemed irrational. He placed the bipolar forceps into the pool of blood where the bleeding might be coming from and the blood started being sucked away. He prayed earnestly, "God, you've got to stop this bleeding. Please, God, I cannot control it." Dr. Carson reports that, as strange as it may seem, at that instant the bleeding stopped without his ever being able to locate the cause. Afterwards the patient awakened and recovered fully.[1]

Dr. Dawkins argues that religion is irrational, but Dr. Carson's irrational action and the unexplainable event which followed saved the life of the patient. Dr. Carson prayed because he could see no natural way of stopping the bleeding. When the natural means were exhausted he called on supernatural means — the God factor. While experiences such as this do not necessarily prove that God exists, the fact that a highly educated and eminently respected surgeon such as Dr. Carson believes in God suggests that such a belief is not excluded by the findings of science.

In 1997 the leading science journal *Nature* published a survey of religious belief among scientists in the United States.[2] The authors found that nearly 40 percent of the 1,000 scientists surveyed said they believed in a personal God — "a God in intellectual and effective communication with humankind, i.e., a God to whom one may pray in expectation of receiving an answer." This survey shows that despite a prevailing popular belief to the contrary, many highly educated people do believe there is a personal, supernatural God. However, relatively little is known about the reasons such people believe and the experiences that have resulted from their faith.

Some academics, such as Dr. Carson, reveal personal answers to these questions in books they have written. Others, such as Dr. Robert Herrmann, professor of mathematics at the United States Naval Academy, explain the reasons for their faith in God on their personal Internet sites.[3]

The purpose of this book is to reveal the diversity of reasons why highly educated university academics believe in God. It opens the debate over the existence of God to a wider audience — not with narrow and closed arguments but with a straightforward and wide-ranging analysis of the issues confronting both the scientific community and the general public. In this book, scientists and other academics explain their reasons for believing in a personal God. They include emeritus professors, heads of university departments, physicists, chemists, biologists, psychologists, engineers, medical researchers, and mathematicians. The articles in this book are not exhaustive. The academics who contributed to this effort gave their personal response as to why they choose to believe in the supernatural Creator God of the Bible, in the literal resurrection of Jesus Christ, in miracles, and in answers to prayer.

No one was asked to write on a particular topic or from a particular perspective. However, I have arranged the final papers in two sections to allow for a developing discussion from two key perspectives: (1) Reason and Faith, and (2) Faith and Experience.

In the first section, examples are presented of the reasons why academics choose to believe. The authors describe the facts that sustain their beliefs and state the arguments to justify their faith, confidence, and trust in the ability and goodness of God. They tell of the overwhelming impression of design in nature as evidence of a Creator's mind behind our existence; of the harmony of the mathematical functions that explain the various laws of nature and suggest organization by an all-knowing intelligent mind; of the unique and precise astronomical position of our earth in the solar system which enables life as we know it to continue to exist; of the shortcomings of the theory of evolution such as its inability to account for the development of language capacity in human beings, the complex life cycles of plants and the irreducible complexity of living cells; of the historical evidence of the authenticity of the biblical text; of the accurate fulfilment of biblical prophecy; of the tremendous good achieved in the world by those dedicated to serving others as Jesus instructed us to do (such as the hundreds of mission hospitals that were set up around the world last century by dedicated Christian doctors); of the biblical principles that have underpinned the freedom we enjoy in Western democracies.

Some of the essays in this first section reveal rare intellectual insights by the authors, and arguments not commonly encountered in the wider literature. To do them justice requires time to contemplate the issues they raise.

While all the authors confess a personal experience as a result of their faith in God, I have placed in the second section those chapters which, in my view, present a greater emphasis on the experiences that were a result of their faith in God. The authors tell of putting their faith to the test. They report the actual observations of the facts or events that have taken place because of their faith. These writers present the knowledge of God they have gained as a result of practical demonstrations of God's power in their own lives. They describe experiences of unexplainable healings in answer to prayer; of revelations that solved otherwise unsolvable problems; of experiences with evil spirits; of the blessings of faith that led to highly successful careers in service for God; of personal experiences of God's presence in traumatic situations such as heart bypass surgery; of unusual experiences of providence such as being saved from committing murder; of prayers that changed an abusive father and prayers that changed an adulterous husband; of finding God again after the tragic death of a child.

Throughout the chapters of this book, irrespective of whether I have included them in the "Reason and Faith" or "Faith and Experience" sections, there is a common consensus that faith in the God of the Bible leads to real personal experience of the power and presence of God — empirical evidence that the God factor is real. These essays challenge the overall approach to conventional science education and are essential reading for academics, educators, politicians, parents, and students.

John F. Ashton

REASON

AND

FAITH

John R. de Laeter

Physics

Professor de Laeter is Emeritus Professor of Physics at Curtin University of Technology in Australia, where he was previously Deputy Vice-Chancellor of Research and Development. He holds a B.Sc. in physics and B.Ed. in education, both with first class honors, a Ph.D. in physics and a D.Sc. in physics, all from the University of Western Australia. Professor de Laeter has served as chairman of the International Commission on Atomic Weights and Isotopic Abundances, and presently is the Australian Academy of Science's representative on that commission. He has published approximately 200 research papers and was awarded the Kelvin Medal of the Royal Society of Western Australia in 1993. A minor planet is named after Professor de Laeter in recognition of his contributions to astrophysics. He is an Officer of the Order of Australia.

Can a scientist believe in God? I have been asked that question many times during my professional life as a physicist.

When I studied science at the University of Western Australia (UWA) during the early 1950s the conventional answer to that question was "no." Science and religion were incompatible!

The Australian student Christian movement at UWA attempted to convince people by logical reasoning that science and religion were compatible, but I was not particularly impressed with their approach, in the sense that faith and not logical argument is the way to the kingdom of heaven.

I later studied philosophy in an attempt to see if there were irrefutable arguments to prove the existence of God — but one unit away from a bachelor of arts degree I gave up the study of philosophy because it did not answer my question.

However, there were two incidents at the UWA which had an important impact in my search for God, although, I have to admit, by instinct and upbringing I was always a believer.

The first occurred during my honors year in physics. One of the subjects we had to study was quantum mechanics, and I was struggling to understand the subject. I was getting desperate when I discovered a book on quantum mechanics written by a well-known theoretical physicist/applied mathematician named Professor C.A. Coulson. To my surprise (and delight) I found I could understand Coulson's approach to quantum mechanics and I subsequently passed the subject with flying colors. I then discovered, quite by accident, that Professor Coulson had written a number of books about science and religion in which he declared his Christian faith. So Coulson became, in a sense, my role model.

The second incident occurred when I was carrying out research on nuclear astrophysics for my doctorate in physics. My task was to separate minute amounts of tin from iron meteorites for mass spectrometric analysis. Knowing little about chemical separation procedures, I was directed to a book entitled *Ion Exchange Chemistry*. I had no sooner picked up this specialized treatise when I was amazed to read, in the preface, that the writer claimed that God was the first ion exchange chemist! His assertion was based on a story in the Old Testament covering the bitter springs of Marah (Exod. 15:25). Moses, under instructions from God, told the Israelites to put branches of trees into the bitter water and, lo and behold, the water became drinkable and the children of Israel were saved from dying of thirst. The author of the book went on to argue that early ion exchange materials used for water softening were, in fact, made of cellulose, a major constituent of wood, thus giving an explanation as to how the bitter springs of Marah were made sweet. He concluded by saying that if scientists had taken this Old Testament story seriously, ion exchange chemistry would have been developed much earlier than the 20th century.

This incident had a deep impact on me because it answered — at least in part — one of the criticisms of scientists, and others, that many (or all) of the biblical stories were "fairy tales." I have since studied many of these Old Testament stories and satisfied myself as to their veracity, even down to the smallest detail.

BUT WHY DO I BELIEVE?

Most scientists accept that the universe is a rational place. In fact, the scientific method is based on the assumption that if you perform an experiment today and get a certain outcome, others can repeat the experiment under similar conditions, albeit in other places, and get the same answer.

To me, the Christian story as revealed in the Bible is a convincing account of human nature. As I observe my fellow human beings, the events of history, and the social phenomena of our times, I can perceive the age-old struggle between good and evil, of sin and guilt on the one hand, and the freedom of forgiveness on the other. I see people struggling with their personal demons, and others who have risen above their strife through faith in a personal God.

In some respects I find that being a practicing scientist helps me in my understanding of God. The Trinity, the godhead, the three-in-one, may be a stumbling block for some, but to a physicist, who accepts the concept of the wave-particle duality of matter, the Trinity is a perfectly acceptable concept of the nature of God.

In my own research area of nuclear astrophysics I am struck by the large number of cosmic "coincidences" which have occurred in order for the universe to be as it is and for life to exist on planet Earth. Far from weakening my faith, science has in fact strengthened it.

Why do we as human beings exist in this vast universe? For what purpose are we here? Is it by accident or design? Are we simply part of the flotsam and jetsam of the universe, or is there meaning in life?

My scientific colleagues will accept the rationality of the universe and be prepared to concede that there may well be a "designer." In fact, most people around the globe and from the beginning of human existence have reached the same conclusion. Most of my colleagues will also accept that Jesus was a person who shaped history, who was a good man, who gave us the secret of how to live by the "golden rule." However, there is a "quantum jump" in thinking from the concept of a rational designer of the universe, to an acceptance that a person called Jesus is the Son of God, and that we can have a personal faith in Him.

In circumstances like this, I remind my colleagues that science is based on testing the theory or model by experiment. If it turns out that the model fails in the light of the experimental evidence, then we discard the model and seek a better one. Science proceeds by a rigorous regime of putting theories to the test. There is no reason why the scientific method should not be used in everyday life, and likewise that people should put the gospel to the test, and see if it works for them.

If we were prepared to study the Bible in the same manner that we study our scientific texts, we would discover a convincing description of human nature and behavior, akin to our scientific investigation of the physical world around us, which leads me to conclude that the Bible is indeed the living Word of God.

My testimony is that a faith in a personal Savior has worked for me and for my family and countless numbers of other people. I have based my adult life on the maxim that "I can do all things through him [Christ] who strengthens me" (Phil. 4:13; NRSV). My experience is that a belief in a personal Savior has been the cornerstone of my life.

Gary D. Gordon

Aerospace Engineering

Dr. Gordon is an aerospace consultant. He holds a B.A. from Wesleyan University and an M.A. and Ph.D. in physics from Harvard University. Dr. Gordon worked as an instructor at Harvard before entering private industry as a research scientist in the area of satellite technology. He was a senior engineer in the team that designed the first weather satellite, TIROS. Dr. Gordon is co-author of the reference book Handbook of Communications Satellites *(Wiley, 1989) and the graduate level textbook* Principles of Communications Satellites *(Wiley, 1993).*

Why I Believe in Science

I believe in physics because it works. In 1959 I was on a team building the first weather satellite, TIROS. We had to predict the temperature of the satellite, and the critical temperature of the batteries. If they got too hot or too cold, the satellite would not work. No one at RCA had any experience in predicting satellite temperatures. So I used the Stefan-Boltzmann law to calculate expected temperatures. The satellite was launched on April 1, 1960. The temperatures followed our predictions, TIROS 1 worked, and this first weather satellite transmitted the first photographs of the earth from outer space.

The law of gravity. Physics is based on a few fundamental laws. One of these is the law of gravity. This law is not proved by logic. There is no simple derivation of this law. Isaac Newton proposed this law to explain the motion of the planets. As a matter of fact, when he first thought of it, the motion of the moon did not match the acceleration of objects on earth (such as the fall of an apple). Newton set the law on the shelf because it didn't work. Twenty years later this changed, with a new measurement of the distance from the earth to the moon. Now the law agreed with the experimental data, and he published his theory. Centuries later, I use Newton's law of gravity to calculate satellite orbits, and where the satellites will be in the future. It still works.

I teach courses on satellite orbits, and start by assuming that the law of gravity is true. I can then teach the students how to calculate satellite orbits, and when to fire thrusters to keep the satellites in the desired orbit. If asked, I usually say I believe in the law of gravity. But I have studied the general theory of relativity, and I know the law of gravity does not always yield the right answers. It has limitations. Usually these don't apply, so I continue to believe, and use, the law of gravity. But my belief in this and other laws of science does have limitations.

Observation and experiments. Science took a giant leap forward when Galileo started to observe the planet Jupiter with a telescope, and drop balls to observe the effect of mass. Early in life, Galileo refused to accept any scientific fact based on Aristotle's authority. Galileo repudiated mere appeal to authority, and in its place pioneered the investigative technique of combining mathematical argument with an appeal to observation and experiment. Since then, science has never been the same. Now, most educated individuals have an implicit faith in science. Sometimes incorrectly, they blindly accept whatever any scientist says as an absolute truth! They accept science much as people of old accepted Aristotle's teachings. And yet, many dismiss religion because it can't be proven; and they don't think of looking to see whether it works. It is time for people to follow Galileo, and to accept or reject religion based also on observations.

I believe in science written by authorities I respect. I examine the experimental evidence and observe how it applies to the world. I use the laws of physics in my profession — and they work.

Why I Believe in a Supernatural God

A Christian home. I am a Christian first because I was brought up in a Christian home. I was taught to believe in the supernatural God of the Bible and the principles of the Christian faith, and I saw the results of Christianity as it affected other lives. Like many children brought up in Christian homes, when I grew up I decided, on my own, to be a Christian. This decision did not come on a single day, as it does to many Christians, but progressed as I became an adult.

A medical missionary — Dr. Donald C. Gordon. My observations started with my parents' missionary work. I was eight years old when they started a new hospital in the interior of Brazil in 1937. It was not easy work. I can remember one time when my father was so tired he fell asleep while teaching Sunday school. In 25 years the hospital grew to be a 100-bed hospital with more doctors, a large clinic, and a nursing school.

But taking care of the patients' physical needs was not enough. My father wanted people to know why he had come. From the start, the Evangelical Hospital of Rio Verde was a Christian witness in the community. Every morning there was a ten-minute devotional relayed to speakers in each patient's room (unless they requested their speaker to be turned off). There was Christian literature in the clinic. My father, as well as many of the hospital staff, actively supported the rapidly growing Christian church. A few of the Brazilian doctors who worked with my father shared his vision. Nurses learned a dedication to service, as well as how to dispense medicine, and were welcomed at other hospitals.

Young people were encouraged (and sometimes financed) by my parents to study, and went on to live Christian lives. When I was 14, I tutored a young fellow, Eudoxio, helping him get ready for a pre-seminary school. He became a pastor and ministered to many. His son, Eudoxio Jr., also became a minister, and is now chaplain of the hospital my father started. He and his wife, Lucia, continue the hospital's Christian witness. The effect of my parents' work in Brazil continues to multiply.

Many people are in favor of bringing the benefits of modern

medicine to people who can't afford it. And yet, few doctors start such a hospital — unless they are motivated by Christian convictions. "The Christian era emphasized the hospital as an asylum for travelers and victims of disaster. By the fourth century A.D., Christian church members in the Roman empire had established hospitals for lepers, cripples, the blind, and the sick poor."[4] Fabiola, a dedicated Christian woman, founded the first hospital in the western half of the old Roman Empire. In modern times, thousands of mission hospitals have been started by dedicated Christian doctors, such as Dr. James B. Woods in China. Hospitals in remote areas have been started by non-religious doctors, but these are very few.

I saw the tremendous good accomplished by a dedicated Christian couple — my parents. I also saw the rewards: the joy and satisfaction they received from knowing they served their Lord, and the thanks of thousands of individuals helped by my father's skill and dedication. The town celebrated when my father returned on his 100th birthday. They gave him many tributes, including a special medal from the state legislature.

How can I help my neighbor? The dedicated Christian lives a life of service. Decisions are not based on "what's in it for me?" The Bible teaches love for your neighbor. Who is your neighbor? Whoever is in need. The Bible also promises a reward for a life of service. "For whosoever will save his life shall lose it; and whosoever will lose his life for my sake shall find it" (Matt. 16:25). My observation is that this philosophy often works. Individuals who seek pleasure above all else often end up very unhappy, but individuals who serve others find a reward, a satisfaction, and an ultimate happiness in the life they have lived.

The Bible makes sense to me. God motivates, guides and empowers Christians in many ways. I am impressed by the lives of some dedicated Christians. I see the effect of Christianity. It's the best answer on how I should live. Christianity works.

DOES IT ALL MAKE SENSE?

No, it doesn't all make sense. Some statements in the Bible are easy to understand. Other statements are difficult to understand, and difficult to believe. There are Bible beliefs that don't agree with common sense. Our universe is a wonderful mystery.

It's hard to believe that the universe just happened, without any guiding intelligence. It's also hard to imagine, let alone believe in, a supreme Creator. Neither one makes sense. It would be easier to believe that the universe never happened, but I know that it did!

Some religions teach that you are rewarded for good deeds and punished for bad deeds. Christians pray to be forgiven. Christians do not do good deeds to earn a reward, but because they want to follow God's will. In the end, bad people may be rewarded as much as good people, if they ask for forgiveness. This also may not make sense, and may be hard to understand.

What many religious critics forget is that there are mysteries in science that don't make sense either. In early times it didn't make sense that a lighter object would fall as fast as a heavy object, that the earth was round, or that the earth went around the sun. Newton argued for years that light consisted of waves, not particles. Nowadays we know that it acts both as waves and as particles, even though it doesn't make sense. We usually think of an electron as a very small particle, and yet somehow it goes through two holes at the same time, even though the holes may be an inch apart. In a silicon semiconductor, free electrons may have different energies; some energies are allowed and some are forbidden. Quantum mechanics predicts these energies, but they still don't make sense. Einstein tells us that an individual, travelling near the speed of light, will return to earth younger than his twin brother who stayed behind. That doesn't make sense, and yet I believe it's true.

My References

I study the Bible to see what it says to me. The Bible is a collection of books, written over a period of 2,000 years. Even if I didn't believe in its divine inspiration (which I do), it would merit study as the combined thinking of many individuals over many centuries.

Many times, I find it useful to get other opinions, from a minister, a friend, or a commentary on the Bible. Occasionally I read the Apocrypha, the sayings of Confucius, the Koran, the Book of Mormon, *Science and Health*, and so on. Each of these has some good points, worthy of study and contemplation. However, not all religions are equivalent, as any detailed study will show. Christianity, as presented in the Bible, is unique and, I think, superior in a number of ways. There is forgiveness, there is a personal God who communicates in a more intimate way, there is a freedom not constrained by a rigid, detailed set of rules. Finally, there is Jesus, who came to earth, showed us how to live and was willing to die for us.

In science I have many reference books. Fundamental physics is summarized well in many college textbooks. These summarize in one volume the findings and thoughts of generations of physicists. I use other references for specialized topics. For communications satellites I often refer to two books that I co-authored. They cover, naturally, the topics I think are important and useful. Like the Bible, however, they don't do me much good if they sit on a shelf and collect dust.

MY LIFE AS A CHRISTIAN AND AS A SCIENTIST

As a Christian. The Bible has some general principles and guides to living. These must be interpreted and adapted to our modern age, but not thoughtlessly discarded.

My parents taught me regular church attendance. This enables me to witness to others about my Christian faith, and also renew my spiritual life. Even when on vacation, I look around for a church to attend. I agree with the little boy whose father said, "We can worship God just as well on the beach as in church," to which the boy replied, "But we won't, will we?"

My parents taught me to pray. Prayer is two-way communication, and the receiving is just as important as the transmitting. I pray at regular times, as in church and at meal times, and in special times of need. It's hard to understand prayer on a physical basis. Prayer enables me to focus my thoughts, to reorder my priorities, but it's more than that. It's a conversation with God that is difficult to understand. But if the writers of the Bible were told of someone in Jerusalem picking up a "phone," and talking to someone in Rome, they would find that very hard to understand, and probably wouldn't believe it was possible.

As a scientist. How has being a Christian affected my professional life? One way was my choice of a career. In graduate school there were discussions about pure research versus applied research. Some students believed that pure research was better than applied research. I did my Ph.D. thesis on elementary particle physics (pure research). It's challenging to increase our knowledge, but I wanted something that would benefit humankind in the foreseeable future, at least during my lifetime. Shortly after I got my Ph.D. I was drafted, and the army assigned me to work for two years on biological warfare. This was necessary to prevent other countries from getting ahead of us, but it was not my preferred work. A few years later I chose to work on satellites. One important consideration was that satellites would ultimately benefit many individuals in the Third World.

In my scientific work, I still wanted to help others, both my co-workers and individuals I would never meet. Early in my career I decided I would not worry about getting credit for my work. Sometimes I did not get credit for my work, but other times I got more credit than I deserved. I'm happy with my decision not to be concerned about credit. I co-authored two books on communications satellites. The driving force to do this was to collect the accumulated knowledge of many friends (co-workers) who were retiring, and to help younger workers who are just as smart as we are, but don't have the experience.

I believe in Christianity and in science for similar reasons. In science I listen to authorities I respect, I examine the experimental evidence, and I observe how it applies to the world. I use the laws of physics in my profession and they work. Why do I believe in God? Belief in God is attested to by authorities I respect: the Bible, ministers, my parents, and others. I observe my life and others around me and see the effect of Christianity. In spite of difficult questions, and many mysteries, it's the best answer to how I should live. Christianity works!

Robert W. Hosken

Food Technology

*D*r. Hosken is senior lecturer in the Centre for Advancement of Food Technology and Nutrition at the University of Newcastle, Australia. He holds a B.Sc. in biochemistry and chemistry from the University of Western Australia, an M.Sc. in biochemistry and languages from Monash University, a Ph.D. in biochemistry and an MBA from the University of Newcastle. His specialist teaching and research areas are grain food science and technology and the development of new food products. Dr. Hosken has published around 100 articles in the fields of science and technology.

At the age of 18 years, I found myself asking:

What kind of work should I do?

What is the meaning of life?

Is there a personal God?

Is the Bible any more meaningful than the childish concept of Father Christmas?

Are moral values absolute, or are they relative to my social setting?

Why do snowflakes have such a variety of the fundamental hexagonal shapes, and why do we find these shapes so attractive?

What makes glowworms glow?

Should I care about the pollution, poverty, mistreatment, and sickness in the world?

Why are some things and experiences more beautiful than others?

Why are we limited to live for around three score and ten years?

I now share my answers to some of these questions.

My youth was relatively privileged. I had loving and caring parents, a private school education, and a healthy and happy family life. However, eventually the umbilical cord was broken, and the comforts and values of parents left behind. It was then that I had to rig up a mast, set the rudder, and sail into the future.

I had sort of envisaged that I would be a farmer, like my father, but not having a farm to work on, I sailed into university life, not really knowing which way to go, but having lots of questions about life.

For me, the spiritual dimensions of life began with addressing the most basic of all questions. Is God for real, and if so, how does God have meaning to me? I was, of course, familiar with the Bible; however, I needed something that made these messages more personal and believable. It was in an introductory biochemistry class that I began to find answers to some of my questions about life. I was absolutely enthralled with how the language of chemistry could be used to interpret life processes such as respiration, metabolism, and reproduction. I began to appreciate the concept that these complex processes, so fundamental to all life, could not have evolved by accident but were a masterpiece of intelligent design. It followed that if there was intelligent design, there must be a Designer, whom we call God.

I guess my questions "why this? why that?" provided the fertile soil for my lifelong venture in science. I have heard it said that scientists have the habit of asking questions long after everyone else has stopped.

As a scientist, I now know that the bioluminescence of glow-worms is due to a reaction involving luciferin, a substance called adenosine triphosphate, and an enzyme called luciferase. I have enough scientific evidence to believe in God, and believe in applying Christian values such as fairness and justice to make the world a better place. I appreciate the beauty in nature and the creative arts, and have some insights into the psychology and physiology of my emotive responses. This chapter is designed to share a couple of the insights into how I have come to these conclusions.

Unfortunately, many students have a painful experience learning the basic language of the sciences, and never get to discover the real joy that comes from applying the principles of science: the joy of tossing around ideas, hypothesizing, designing and conducting experiments, then having the time to speculate and interpret the experimental findings.

During my extracurricular activities, I came across the findings of Leonardo Fibonacci da Pisa. The Fibonacci series of numbers provided me with some kind of spiritual link between mathematics, science, and some of the puzzles of life, and also stimulated my search for a greater meaning in life.

Leonardo was born around A.D. 1175 in Pisa, the Italian city with the famous Leaning Tower, and is regarded as the greatest European mathematician of the Middle Ages. This must have been a good time, as another famous Italian — St. Francis of Assisi (Assisi was near Pisa) — also lived around this time. Leonardo Fibonacci made several important contributions to mathematics, including the Fibonacci series of numbers: 1, 1, 2, 3, 5, 8, 13, 21, 34, 55, 89, 144 and so on (add the last two numbers to get the next).

I, like many other scientists and mathematicians before me, was intrigued by the relation between the Fibonacci series and the designs we find in nature. The Fibonacci series has been used to describe how rabbit populations expand and the arrangement of petals on flowers, pineapples, and pine cones. The Fibonacci spiral describes the shape of sea shells. A search of the world-wide web will provide details of these relations.

On many plants, the number of petals is a Fibonacci number: buttercups have 5 petals; lilies and iris have 3; some delphiniums have 8; corn marigolds have 13; some asters have 21; daisies can be found with 34, 55, or even 89 petals. If we look at the arrangement of the tiny florets in the center of a daisy, we will see two distinct sets of spirals, one clockwise, the other counterclockwise (21 and 34). Similar arrangements are found in pine cone scales (5 one way, 8 the other), and pineapples (8 and 13). So we find an incredible level of design in life, and to me this implies a Designer and Creator.

Further, if we take the Fibonacci numbers, and divide each by the number before it, we will find the following series of numbers:

$$1/1 = 1, 2/1 = 2, 3/2 = 1.5, 5/3 = 1.666\ldots$$
$$8/5 = 1.6, 13/8 = 1.625, 21/13 = 1.61538\ldots$$

This provides the golden ratio or the golden number having a value of around 1.61804, and is usually represented by the Greek letter phi. It also provides the related value phi which is simply the decimal part of phi, namely 0.618034.

The curves of the nautilus shell, and the proportions of classic buildings such as the Parthenon in Athens, have their beauty and aesthetic appeal based on the golden ratio, 1:1.618, which is the same as 0.618:1. These ratios are widely used in design for gaining aesthetic appeal.

We can use the golden ratio to develop the Fibonacci rectangles and Fibonacci spiral as shown below.[5]

To obtain the rectangles, we begin drawing squares having dimensions based on the Fibonacci numbers. We begin with a square (1 × 1), then draw another square alongside (1 × 1), then draw along the top another square (2 × 2). We then draw the next square alongside (3 × 3), then the next (5 × 5), then the next (8 × 8), then the next (13 × 13) and so on. We can continue adding squares around the picture, each new square having a side which is as long as the sum of the length of the sides of the last two squares. This set of rectangles, whose sides are two successive Fibonacci numbers in length and which are composed of squares with sides which are Fibonacci numbers, are called

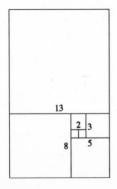
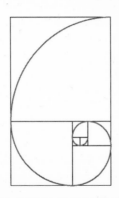

the Fibonacci rectangles. We can then sketch the spiral as shown. These spiral shapes are called equiangular or logarithmic spirals.

We find that when painting, it is aesthetically more pleasing to position objects to one side or "about one-third" of the way across, and to use lines which divide the picture into thirds. This seems to make the picture design more pleasing to the eye and relies again on the idea of the golden section being "ideal."

It was Edouard Lucas (1842–1891) who gave the name "Fibonacci numbers" to the series written about by Leonardo of Pisa. A second series of numbers: 2, 1, 3, 4, 7, 11, 18 . . . were called the Lucas numbers, and these also have great interest.

The concept of intelligent design, and therefore a designer, is found not only in nature but also in the Bible. This provides evidence that God is not only the creator of physical life, but also has a spiritual or moral plan for people. The Bible is a book about prophecy, or foretelling the future, and the way in which the Bible has foretold the events surrounding the life of Christ provides a unique link between God as a creator and the spiritual needs of people.

Let us now have a look at the use of numbers in the Bible.

Why does the Bible consistently use certain numbers? Consider the number 40.

During the Flood it rained 40 days and nights.

Moses was 40 days on the mount.

Nineveh had 40 days to repent.

Christ was 40 days in the desert.

Christ was 40 days on the earth after His resurrection.

The Children of Israel wandered for 40 years in the wilderness.

The writing of the Bible involved hundreds of people spanning thousands of years and several generations, yet the same theme is evident, the number 40 being used to indicate a time length of probation.

As a university lecturer I rather like the idea of sabbatical leave, the concept of having one year to study after six years of work. Sabbatical leave reflects the biblical seventh rest day after six days of creation. Again we find this recurrent theme throughout the Bible and natural world. We, of course, still have a seven-day week. Other examples are seven of all the clean animals went into the ark, and in the Book of Revelation we read about the seven stars, seven churches, seven trumpets and seven last plagues. The number seven is regarded as the perfect number. In nature we find the rainbow has seven colors, and in music we have seven notes before starting a new octave. Is this simply a coincidence, or evidence of a divine plan?

Other numbers that also have biblical themes are 3 (the godhead), 8 (signifies resurrection or new beginning), 10 (signifies ordinal perfection — 10 commandments) and 12 (signifies perfect government — 12 tribes, 12 disciples).

As I studied the many messages written in the Bible, it became apparent that these were not simply meaningless stories, but projections about the future, messages with a deeper purpose and meaning, messages about life and love, and these messages transcend time. Perhaps the greatest of all messages are the prophecies about the birth of Christ, and these begin in the Book of Genesis.

The Book of Genesis is the first book in the Bible and contains the story of Abraham preparing to offer his beloved son Isaac as a sacrifice. As I studied this story, I was struck by the way it points in an uncanny way to the saving power of Jesus revealed thousands of years later in the New Testament. I was struck by the miraculous way this ancient but widely available manuscript can still today speak to us about God's love, just as it has done for generation after generation of people for thousands of years. Surely the author of the Bible must be the same Designer and Creator of all life and human destiny.

Moving on to the New Testament, I found the stories about the life and purpose of Jesus, the greatest miracle of all. I came to recognize that the Bible is not a scientific book, but is far deeper and more subtle than any book that has ever been written.

I have used the discussion above to show that the concept of intelligent design and planning is found in both the natural and spiritual world, and the Designer is God. This God can be part of our everyday life.

Today I have moved on from my student days. However, I have not lost the sweet taste and excitement of discovering the power and blessings of God in daily life.

What are the benefits of following a Christian lifestyle?

Christianity provides a rationale for simply putting our best foot forward in life and running with God. Whether as an athlete competing in the Olympic games, or as a student sitting for an exam, we will be winners, no matter what. The rewards of the winner are:

- peace and contentment about who we are and where we are going in life;
- health, happiness, and wisdom;
- a moral wisdom that provides clear values of what is right and wrong;
- the economic blessings that can flow from above;
- the social benefits of being part of the family of God;
- the privilege of being able to love and give to others;
- an empathy and understanding of rejection and failure; and
- the best retirement policy available.

A.J. MONTY WHITE

PHYSICAL CHEMISTRY

*D*r. White is retired from Cardiff University, U.K. He holds a B.Sc. with honors in chemistry and a Ph.D. in gas kinetics from the University of Wales, Aberystwyth. Before joining the staff at Cardiff University, where he held a number of senior administrative positions, Dr. White specialized in research involving the electrical and optical properties of organic semi-conductors. He is also a guest lecturer at the State Independent Theological University of Basel where he lectures on science and the Bible.

My father was an atheist and my mother was an agnostic. At a very early age I was told that there was no God, that Jesus Christ was not the Son of God, and that the Bible was nothing more than a collection of fairy stories. Although I now believe in God, that Jesus Christ is the Son of God, and that the Bible is the Word of God, I did not arrive at this position overnight, as the following story abundantly shows.

WHY I DID NOT BELIEVE IN GOD

Although as a young boy I attended the local church, this made no impression upon me at all. In fact, attending that church put me off Christianity, for the vicar there had little time for children like me who were from a poor background. He never convinced me that God existed and he never encouraged me to read the Bible. All I remember of attending that church is the purple robes of the vicar and the choir, the smell of the incense and candles, and the prayers for the dead! When I was 11 years old, I passed a public examination which enabled me to attend the local grammar school, and at that time I stopped attending church. Slowly I, like my father, became an atheist.

Although I was an atheist, I used to enjoy arguing with those who considered themselves to be Christians or in any way religious. There were three aspects of the Bible about which I used to argue. The first one was Bible prophecy. I used to argue that what is written in the books of the prophets in the Bible is so general that one can interpret almost anything from their writings. The second line of reasoning concerned Jesus Christ. I could not accept what is written in the New Testament concerning Him — especially His resurrection from the dead. The third aspect of the Bible that I could not accept was the miraculous element. I used to argue if Christianity is such a miraculous religion, as the Bible clearly teaches, why is it that we do not see miracles happening today?

In October 1963 I left home in order to pursue a degree in chemistry at the University College of Wales, Aberystwyth. In order to make friends at university, I attended meetings of the Christian Union and one of the church societies, and at these meetings I met Christians who were different from any others I had met before. It was not that these people believed in God — they knew God. This bothered me and I began discussing with them why I rejected the Bible and why I did not believe in God.

Bible Prophecy Has Been Fulfilled

One of the reasons why I rejected Christianity was because of Bible prophecy. I considered the proclamations of the prophets to be so general that almost anything could be predicted from them. However, it was not long before I was shown that this was not the case. Many prophetic utterances in the Bible were extremely accurate and have already been fulfilled to the letter. One of these concerns the prediction of the destruction of Samaria.

In Micah 1:6 the prophet declares, "Therefore I will make Samaria a heap of rubble, a place for planting vineyards. I will pour her stones into the valley and lay bare her foundations"

(NIV). There are four specific predictions in this one verse of prophecy that was uttered in the latter half of the eighth century B.C. The first is that Samaria's ruins would become a heap of rubble. The second is that the stones used to construct Samaria would be pushed into a valley. The third is that Samaria's foundations would be laid bare. And the fourth is that Samaria would eventually become a place where vineyards would be planted.

Although this destruction of Samaria was predicted by the prophet Micah in c.730 B.C., it was not until A.D. 1265, almost 2,000 years later, that the prophecy began to be fulfilled. No one can argue that the prophet Micah saw this happen and then wrote it down spuriously claiming that he lived decades before the event and so had successfully prophesied Samaria's destruction. Samaria was totally destroyed in A.D. 1265 when Muslims defeated the Crusaders who were defending the city, and it has never been rebuilt. Arabs living in the vicinity cleared much of the ruins in order to use the site for agricultural purposes, and in doing so, they dug up its foundations and dumped them into a valley nearby. Today, grapevines can be seen growing on this ancient site, just as prophesied by Micah over 2,700 years ago.

In view of the many fulfilled Bible prophecies, including the prediction of the destruction of the city of Samaria with such incredible accuracy, I began to think that perhaps Bible prophecy could be trusted.

THE NEW TESTAMENT IS RELIABLE

Another reason why I rejected the God of the Bible was that I could not accept that Jesus Christ was the Son of God and that He rose from the dead. These two factors are linked through the authenticity of the New Testament.

The New Testament writers claim that many of the events in the life of Jesus Christ are the fulfilment of Old Testament prophecy. For example, it is claimed that the fact that Jesus Christ was descended from King David and that He was born of a virgin in Bethlehem is the fulfilment of three specific prophecies. It is also claimed that the fact that Jesus taught in parables, had His words rejected, had an unjust trial and was crucified are the fulfilment of specific Old Testament prophecies. The New

Testament also claims that Jesus Christ is the Son of God and that, after His death, He rose from the dead.

However, I had a problem. Could the New Testament writings be trusted? What if the New Testament had been deliberately written so that the Old Testament prophecies concerning the life of Jesus Christ *appeared* to be fulfilled? How reliable was the New Testament? In other words, how reliable were the documents from which the New Testament had been translated?

In order to answer this question, I turned to a book called *The New Testament Documents: Are They Reliable?* written by the late Professor F.F. Bruce who was Rylands professor of Biblical Criticism and Exegesis at the University of Manchester. In this excellent paperback, he concludes that there is substantial historical evidence for the authenticity of the New Testament writings.[6]

I now had no alternative but to accept that the New Testament documents were reliable and that we can have confidence in the facts they record. Slowly I began to accept that Jesus Christ did exist; that he was who he said he was; and that he did rise from the dead.

GOD ANSWERS PRAYER

Up to the time I went to university, I never experienced miracles happening in people's lives, and this was my third reason for not believing in God. However, I found that as I talked to the Christians I met at university, they could often tell story after story of miraculous happenings not only in their lives, but in the lives of others. These stories could not be dismissed as mere coincidences — they were far too complicated for that.

As an example, the following story shows the lengths to which God will often go in order to reveal himself to someone. I know that this story is true because after my conversion, I met the lady in question.

One day the husband of a childless couple who were devoted to each other died. The woman was heartbroken and used to spend every afternoon at the grave of her husband. One day the pastor of one of the local churches was walking through the cemetery and saw this lonely widow sitting by her husband's grave crying. He tried to comfort her, but to no avail. However, he did manage to get her address and promised to visit her even though she did not seem particularly interested in talking to him.

Soon, it was Easter, and the pastor's church always made a collection at this time for the widows of the church. The pastor told his elders and deacons about the widow he had met at the cemetery and it was decided to give this lady some money from the collection. The treasurer gave the pastor an envelope containing some money for this widow; the pastor put it in his pocket and promptly forgot all about it! A few days later the pastor's wife decided to take his suit to the cleaners. Going through the pockets, she found the envelope containing the money. When her husband came home in the evening, she told him about her find. He was horrified that he had forgotten it so he decided to take it to the widow that very evening. Before doing so, he wrote a message on a Christian greeting card to accompany the money.

When the pastor arrived at the widow's house, it was in darkness for she had gone to bed. So the pastor pushed the envelope containing the greeting card and money through the letter box in the front door and it landed on the doormat in the hall.

The next morning the widow awoke and was very upset for it was the first birthday she had had since her husband died. However, she had prayed to God and asked him to prove to her that he really existed. She had asked God to do for her on her birthday what her husband always did for her — place an envelope with a card and some money inside on the doormat in the hall. As the widow walked down the stairs that morning, she was very surprised to see an envelope on the doormat in the hall. She was even more surprised when she opened it and saw the greeting card and the money! She could hardly believe it, for God had indeed answered her prayer in detail. Needless to say, this widow began to believe in God from the very moment she opened that envelope and saw the card and the money inside. The next Sunday she went to church, repented of her sins and accepted Jesus Christ as her Savior.

BELIEVING IN GOD FOR MYSELF

Within a few months of going to university, I found that all the arguments that I had for not believing in God had evaporated: I was convinced that the writings in the Bible, especially those of the prophets, could be trusted; that Jesus Christ was who He claimed to be and He did rise from the dead; and, finally, that God does perform miracles today. However, my intellectual assent to these truths did not affect my life at all. It was not until February 1964 when I experienced a real conversion as I repented of my sins and knew the joy of being forgiven as I accepted Jesus Christ as my Savior, that I began to experience God in my life.

I firmly believe that the experiential is another reason for believing in God. Since the time of Christ, millions of people from all walks of life have testified of a conversion experience when they have repented of their sins and accepted Jesus Christ as their Savior. Furthermore, such people, myself included, can tell of God's leading and guidance — sometimes through circumstances, other times in a more direct way. Such testimonies cannot, and should not, be dismissed lightly. There is a God. The Bible can be trusted as God's revealed word to humankind. God does answer prayer and does reveal himself to men and women today. I know — I am one of them!

Postscript

Since my own conversion, both my parents have become Christians — my mum a few months after my own conversion in 1964 and my dad in 1997, at the age of 78.

JOHN R. BAUMGARDNER

GEOPHYSICS

Dr. Baumgardner is a staff scientist in the theoretical division at the University of California, Los Alamos National Laboratory. He holds a B.S. in electrical engineering from Texas Tech University, an M.S. in electrical engineering from Princeton University, and an M.S. and Ph.D. in geophysics and space physics from the University of California, Los Angeles. Dr. Baumgardner is the chief developer of the TERRA code, a 3-D finite element program for modeling the earth's mantle and lithosphere. His current research is in the areas of planetary mantle dynamics, global ocean modeling, and the development of efficient hydrodynamic methods for supercomputers.

My own discovery of God's reality occurred unexpectedly while I was in graduate school at the age of 26. Partly for social reasons, partly out of curiosity, I found myself attending a verse-by-verse study of the Gospel of John on Sunday morning at a church near the campus. I had grown up in a largely non-religious home with very little exposure to the Bible, and although I had read brief portions of the Bible on some rare occasions, I generally had found it difficult to relate it to my own frame of reference.

I had some immediate first impressions of this class. One was the depth of insight and understanding displayed by most of the 30 or so participants. I wondered how it was that these students, most of whom were undergraduates, were able to extract such profound meaning from a text that to me was nearly inscrutable. It puzzled me how the message of this ancient document could apparently be so clear to most of the class and yet so obscure to me. Another strong impression of this class related to the participants themselves. I noticed that most of them radiated a disposition of joyful confidence and transparency and acceptance and peace, qualities I found in short supply in my own life if I were really honest. What was the source of this inward confidence and peace? I did not have a ready answer.

As this study progressed into John's gospel, I quickly noticed the main theme of this document was the person of Jesus. I was surprised when it occurred to me that, despite my years of academic intensity, I had never once identified the person of Jesus as a topic essential for me to investigate. This introduction to John's gospel exposed an embarrassing gap. I began to realize in my mental concept of human history a gap I simply could not afford to ignore.

And just what sort of portrait of Jesus did I encounter as the weeks progressed and I found myself a bit more comfortable with the text? I compare it with the response of the temple guards who, when they were sent to arrest Jesus and returned empty-handed and were asked to account for their failure, said, "Never did a man speak the way this man speaks" (John 7:46; NASB). I found His words beyond astonishing, different from those of anyone else in human history. His actions were just as unique. He drew to himself the most rejected and hopeless individuals in the society of His day and granted them wholeness and release. Such words and actions, I noticed, deeply disturbed many who held positions of privilege and power.

Because I deem it so essential to my story, I would like to provide a thumbnail sketch of a few of the highlights I encountered as I participated in this study. John's gospel, much like those of Matthew, Mark, and Luke, is largely a collection of vignettes from Jesus' interaction with individuals, His disciples, and the crowds that followed Him.

Chapter 3, for example, records Jesus' conversation with Nicodemus, a highly respected teacher and member of the elite Jewish council, the Sanhedrin. So as not to be noticed, Nicodemus visits Jesus in the middle of the night and begins the conversation, "We know that You have come from God as a teacher; for no one can do these signs that You do unless God is with him." Jesus immediately cuts to the heart of the matter with Nicodemus and tells him that in his present condition he is incapable of apprehending matters relating to the kingdom of God, matters Nicodemus nonetheless has a desire to understand. Jesus tells him of the imperative of a spiritual birth, a topic about which Nicodemus admits he knows nothing. Although Nicodemus' immediate response is not recorded, later in John's gospel we find him a loyal disciple (John 3:1–16).

In the next chapter we find the account of Jesus' interaction with a woman from, in terms of today's geography, the West Bank town of Nablus, where Jacob's well is located. She is a Samaritan, a group shunned by most Jewish people of her day. Jesus tells her correctly she has had five husbands and the man with whom she is currently living is not her husband. She responds, "Sir, I perceive that You are a prophet," and then volunteers, "I know that Messiah is coming . . . when that One comes, He will declare all things to us." Jesus' simple answer to her is, "I who speak to you am He." She is so excited, she forgets her water pot, rushes back to town, and tells the men about the conversation she just had. Her moral failures fade from her mind because of the acceptance and affirmation Jesus communicates to her. Her report is so compelling, a large crowd comes out to see Jesus for themselves. They are so responsive, Jesus stays and teaches there for two days (John 4:5–42).

In chapter 5 there is the account of a man at the pool of Bethesda in Jerusalem who has been lame for 38 years, to whom Jesus says, "Arise, take up your pallet, and walk," and he does. This upsets the religious Jews who learn of this deed, because it has taken place on the Sabbath. According to their embellishments of the law of Moses, it was a violation both for the man to carry his pallet and for Jesus to have healed him on the Sabbath, because these things were interpreted as work. When they confront him, Jesus answers, "My Father is working until now, and I Myself am working." The text then comments, "For this cause therefore the Jews were seeking all the more to kill Him, because He not only was breaking the Sabbath, but also was calling God His own Father, making Himself equal with God."

Jesus reinforces their concern when he tells them, 'For not even the Father judges anyone, but He has given all judgment to the Son, in order that all may honor the Son, even as they honor the Father. He who does not honor the Son does not honor the Father who sent Him" (John 5:1–23).

The account of Jesus feeding a crowd of some 5,000 men, plus women and children, from five loaves and two fish, is found in chapter 6. This incident occurs on the hillside above the western shore of the Sea of Galilee. This great multitude was following Him, the text indicates, because they were seeing the miraculous healings He was performing on those who were sick. It is noteworthy that Jesus healed in public with multitudes of witnesses present, and He taught in public with many people recording what He said. The day after He feeds the multitude, He discusses the happening with religious Jews in the nearby town of Capernaum. He tells them, "Do not work for the food which perishes, but for the food which endures to eternal life, which the Son of Man shall give you. . . . I am the bread of life; he who comes to Me shall never hunger, and he who believes in Me shall never thirst. . . . For this is the will of My Father, that every one who beholds the Son and believes in Him, may have eternal life; and I Myself will raise him up on the last day (John 6:1–40).

In chapter 7, as Jesus teaches the multitudes in Jerusalem during a Jewish feast, the chief priests and an influential group of religious Jews known as the Pharisees become alarmed enough by what they hear the crowds saying to order Jesus arrested. But the officers sent to arrest Him return empty-handed, marveling at His words. Soon after, as described in chapter 8, the Pharisees engage Jesus directly and challenge His authority, saying, "You are bearing witness of Yourself; Your witness is not true." Jesus appeals not only to His own testimony but also to the testimony of His Father. As the confrontation builds, Jesus declares, "You are from below, I am from above; you are of this world, I am not of this world. I said therefore to you, that you shall die in your sins; for unless you believe that I am He, you shall die in your sins." Further in the confrontation He says, "Which one of you convicts Me of sin? If I speak truth, why do you not believe Me? He who is of God hears the words of God; for this reason you do not hear them, because you are not of God." Still later in this exchange, the Jews say, "You are not yet fifty years old, and have You seen Abraham?" Jesus replies, "Truly, truly, I say to you, before Abraham was born, I am." At this point they picked up stones to stone Him, but He eluded them and left the temple (John 8:12–59).

In chapter 9, Jesus on the Sabbath in Jerusalem heals a man who has been blind from birth. When brought before the Pharisees, this man has the chutzpah to answer them, "Well, here is an amazing thing, that you do not know where He [Jesus] is from, and yet He opened my eyes. . . . Since the beginning of time it has never been heard that any one opened the eyes of a person born blind. If this man were not from God, He could do nothing." In response to this answer, they banish him from the synagogue (John 9:1–34).

In chapter 10 Jesus again interacts with religious Jews in Jerusalem. He tells them, "I am the good shepherd; the good shepherd lays down His life for the sheep." The Jews respond, "How long will You keep us in suspense? If You are the Christ, tell us plainly." Jesus answers, "I told you, and you do not believe. . . . But you do not believe, because you are not of My sheep. My sheep hear My voice, and I know them, and they follow Me; and I give eternal life to them, and they shall never perish; and no one shall snatch them out of My hand. My Father, who has given them to Me, is greater than all; and no one is able to snatch them out of the Father's hand. I and the Father are one."[7] The text says the Jews again took up stones to stone Him. When Jesus inquires for which of His deeds they intend to stone Him, they say, "For a good work we do not stone You, but for blasphemy; and because You, being a man, make Yourself out to be God" (John 10:11–33).

In chapter 11, Jesus is comforting a woman named Martha, who lived in the village of Bethany just east of Jerusalem and whose brother Lazarus had died some four days earlier. Jesus tells her, "Your brother shall rise again." She says to him, "I know that he will rise again in the resurrection on the last day." Jesus then says to her, "I am the resurrection and the life; he who believes in Me shall live even if he dies, and everyone who lives and believes in Me shall never die." Jesus then goes to the tomb, where there is a group of family friends weeping and mourning.

Jesus orders the stone be removed from the mouth of the cave and commands, "Lazarus, come forth." Lazarus stumbles out of the cave, bound hand and foot with linen wrappings and his face wrapped around with a cloth. Jesus instructs them, "Unbind him, and let him go." This incredible event is quickly reported to the Pharisees and chief priests in Jerusalem, who convene a council to discuss the matter. One of those present says, "What are we doing? For this man is performing many signs. If we let Him go on like this, all men will believe in Him, and the Romans will come and take away both our place and our nation." But the high priest, Caiaphas, responds, "You know nothing at all, nor do you take into account that it is expedient for you that one man should die for the people, and that the whole nation should not perish." The text here comments that from that day on they planned together to kill him. His crucifixion at the hands of the Romans occurred a few weeks later, precisely on the Jewish Passover (John 11:23–53).

The study of John's gospel in which I participated covered about a chapter per week. But this pace allowed the astounding implications of these words to penetrate deep into my thinking and being. As the weeks passed it became increasingly clear to me that Jesus had to be the most extraordinary person ever to walk the face of the earth. The simplicity and directness of John's first-person description of Jesus' life served to reinforce the power of the words themselves. What He said and what He did was deeply etched in the objective history of His day and witnessed by thousands of people, even tens of thousands, from a wide variety of backgrounds. It progressively made more and more sense to me why His life had had such a profound impact on the world of that day, and ever since. In addition I became aware that many of the circumstances of Jesus' life matched the written predictions made centuries before by individuals like David and Isaiah and Micah concerning the future Messiah.

It took about three months of this weekly exposure to the text of John's gospel before I finally began to understand that who Jesus really was logically demanded a response on my part. Just as Jesus had invited some uneducated Galilean fishermen like Peter, Andrew, James, and John to give their allegiance to Him and trust Him with their lives, so the same appeal had gone forth to each succeeding generation, to every corner of the earth, and hence to me. Somehow, through means I cannot explain, as I finally grasped the reality of this appeal, I responded in the affirmative. It was in my room on a Wednesday evening in April 1970 that I said, "Yes, Jesus, I want to follow You."

At that point I had no knowledge or expectation my life would change in any significant way. I was engaged in some rather difficult graduate courses in plasma physics at the time. But within days of that transaction I observed some unexpected changes in myself. Almost immediately I became keenly aware just how exploitive and insensitive I was being toward those of the opposite sex. The next weekend I discovered an effect I had never noticed before in relation to alcohol. I could sense almost instantly an impairing of my mind and the blurring of a new exhilaration I had acquired just days before. I also noticed an almost insatiable desire to read the New Testament and began reading it through about once per week. What ensued was like a curtain pulled back on a new dimension of reality I had never known before, a reality I had never even suspected to exist. Things around me suddenly had so much more meaning and significance than I had ever known before. In short, I had a dramatic conversion experience that profoundly altered the course of my life to this very day.

So why do I believe in the supernatural God of the Bible? The simplest and most direct answer is that I have verified through my own experience that Jesus, as revealed in the Bible, is authentic. He is indeed who He claims to be, the Messiah, the Son of God, the second person of the Trinity. Jesus is the centerpiece of my world view, a world view that has comprehensive explanatory power and exhilarating logical consistency. My Ph.D. thesis I therefore dedicated to "Jesus of Nazareth, the Messiah, in whom are all the treasures of wisdom and knowledge" (the latter are Paul's words from chapter 2 of his letter to the Colossians).

Today, just as in the day in which Jesus walked the earth, there is a raging struggle between light and darkness, between good and evil. Jesus has personally called me to play a very specific role in this struggle. This calling gives fullness and purpose and significance to my relationships, my time, my abilities, my work, my thoughts, my passions — yes, my entire being. That this life is only the beginning of an eternal adventure, in which God's wondrous character in its infinite facets shines forth in ever-new ways, is almost too wonderful to contemplate. Yet my awareness of Jesus' authenticity causes me to exult in this certainty. Even more, I exult because "in Jesus" I have found the ultimate treasure.

But I am not alone in this discovery. There are millions through the centuries and across the world today who also have this same awareness of Jesus' authenticity and also exult with the same gratefulness and joy. What a thrill to be part of this heavenly company.

JOHN W. OLLER

LINGUISTICS

*D*r. Oller is professor and head of the Department of Communicative
*Disorders at the University of Louisiana at Lafayette. He holds a B.A.
in Spanish and French from California State University at Fresno and an
M.A. and Ph.D. in general linguistics from the University of Rochester.
After his promotion to associate professor at the University of California,
Los Angeles, he founded the Department of Linguistics at the University
of New Mexico. He is author or co-author of 13 books and more than 200
professional articles. In 1984 he won the Modern Language Association
Mildenberger Medal — an international prize for the best book on foreign
language teaching.*

In 1966, as a doctoral student in linguistics at the University of Rochester, I came across a book by Bertrand Russell
(1872–1970) titled *Why I Am Not a Christian*. Among Russell's
other books that I studied with great interest were *The ABC
of Relativity*, *An Inquiry into Meaning and Truth*, and *Human
Knowledge: Its Scope and Limits*.[8] I wondered if what he had to
say would shake my belief in God. It didn't. Rather, it embarrassed me on Russell's behalf. How could a man of such scholarship as Russell, co-author with Alfred North Whitehead of the
Principia Mathematica,[9] be such an incompetent reader of the
Bible? He commented on texts he barely remembered or simply

did not understand and, in general, showed that genius provides only darkness if it works from a false premise. As Solomon wrote long ago, "There is no wisdom nor understanding nor counsel against the Lord" (Prov. 21:30). The idea that a human being who boasts of his "unyielding despair" as Russell did in *A Free Man's Worship*[10] can be absolutely sure that Almighty God does not exist is absurd. To whom would Russell not yield?

As a literary person Russell was a giant, but as a student of the greatest work of literature ever written in any language, the Bible, he came across as an illiterate ignoramus on a level with a spoiled teenager. He hardly took the trouble to examine the texts he criticized and made no evident effort to find a consistent interpretation. He was not seeking God but rather a place to hide from Him. I remember sitting at my desk at UCLA early in 1970 when I heard of Russell's death. I wondered if he might have done as Whitehead did on his deathbed. Could he have trusted Christ? It occurred to me that he was, regardless of his final moments in this world, no longer an atheist.

Oddly, it was Russell's own touted discovery of a necessary paradox, which some thought at the time was a genuine antinomy, that had rocked the mathematical world like a mental earthquake near the beginning of the 20th century.[11] In fact, Russell's paradox was grounded in an error, but one that would go undetected by himself for the rest of his days. He proposed an ad hoc fix for his problem in what came to be known as the "theory of types" (1910–13), but he would never get to the bottom of the problem he had set out to solve in the *Principia Mathematica*. Nor did he ever appreciate fully the blunder that had led to the paradox in the first place. He had failed to distinguish conventional signs adequately from either the conventions that gave them the power of meaning or from the objects to which they might be used to truthfully refer.

By the time I found Russell's testimony against God, I had been a Christian for the better part of three years, and was beginning to understand the Bible. You might say that I was learning to talk the gospel language. I understood if there was a God of the sort described in the Bible, He would not lie and He would be able to stand the most intense scrutiny. I heard the invitation of Isaiah saying, "Come now, and let us reason together, saith the Lord" (Isa. 1:18), and I knew that either God's Word would have to stand up under examination or else those who believed it must be simpletons. When I started to look at the texts of the Bible as an adult, Jesus and the prophets just didn't come across as babes in the woods.

For quite a few years of my life I had, in fact, subscribed to the theory that all Christians must be benign, childish, gullible fools. After all, didn't they believe in such nonsense (as it seemed to me then) as the Virgin Birth, the Resurrection, the creation of the world in six days? At the time, I had not looked at the Bible very closely so I didn't see any connection between all these seemingly preposterous claims (the so-called miracles) and what I supposed to be the really practical teachings of Jesus, that I should love my neighbor as myself and so on.

About three years prior to entering graduate school on a National Defense Education Act Fellowship, I had met a Christian couple who told me that Jesus had died on my behalf, that He had purchased a forever pardon for my sins, and that if I would receive it, He would guarantee my passage into heaven. At first I did not believe them. I rejected their version of the gospel because the story made God out to be better, kinder, more merciful, and more of everything good than I was able to imagine. I did not believe their understanding of the gospel story could be correct. I didn't believe it was *in* the Bible. Much less was I willing to believe it to be true. The message of such a story was incomprehensible to me.

I figured that if there was a God, He would have to exact a huge punishment from me on account of my overt sins. I couldn't believe that God would be merciful enough and loving enough to forgive me outright. Justice, I supposed, would require that I do something heroic and good to obtain salvation. Consciously, I claimed to be as righteous as most (excepting possibly my next younger sibling), but I figured that God was still more righteous, and so, like Freud and the former President Clinton, I was unwilling to confess my own evil deeds even to my own consciousness. On the outside, and even on the inside, I kept up the pretense of being a hard-working, un-average citizen, a loving son of good (though poor) parents, a reasonably faithful brother to my seven siblings, and a friend to those along the way. My superego, however, was not all there was to me, and after I heard that Jesus had bought me a ticket to heaven, I found myself wondering if it could be true. Would God stoop to rescue me? Why should He care? Wasn't death just becoming a part of the garden?

Of course, I had heard the complaint that Christianity was a bloodthirsty religion indulging in human sacrifice, but up till that time, it was the *only* story I had *ever* heard that was extreme enough to be about what I had already lived through. The terrors I had already known were of sufficient intensity that the shedding of blood seemed reasonable in order to measure up to them. It was clear that no one gets out of this world alive. Surely bloodshed would be required for atonement, if forgiveness were possible at all.

What puzzled me was that this man named Jesus had influenced in an evident way the lives of the 30-something couple that first presented the gospel to me. For some unexplainable reason, they cared for me and I knew it was because of this man, Jesus, who had lived almost 2,000 years before. It was this fact that captured my attention. It recurred again and again to my thoughts over a period of a year and a half or more before I came to a point where I was willing to, as they say, give my life to God. I saw the love those people had in their home, a place I visited often as a Spanish tutor for a few dollars an hour, and I realized that the light, warmth, and love was something missing from my own life. I also came to realize that what they had was because of the man Jesus, who had lived nearly 20 centuries before. Jesus had affected their lives. They showed me in the Bible in many places that salvation was not something I could do for myself but something that God had already accomplished by going to the cross in the person of His own Son. Furthermore, they showed me that Jesus had not only redeemed my life from the grave, but that He himself had assured my entrance into heaven.

Why do I believe the Bible? It's very simple. I have thoroughly examined the things that I can test that Jesus claimed to be true. Loving your neighbor as yourself is a good rule. It works. Also, I discovered that Jesus had practiced what He preached to perfection. He said if your hand offends, cut it off, or if your eye leads you astray, pluck it out. A hard standard for me or you, but He gave up both hands, both eyes, and His entire body to die the death of the cross for you and me. He did not die for those who loved Him but He loved and died for those who were His enemies. He gave himself for the whole world, requiring nothing in return but our willingness to believe the story that we would hear of Him. If He was God, He really knew that only a relatively few of us would believe the story, but He provided a way of salvation to every last human being that ever was born. If He was who He claimed to be, God with us (Immanuel), then He had access to the knowledge of the creation and many other matters that are difficult to measure against our experience. However, if the Word of God is consistent, there can be no reasonable doubt that our experience can be measured against it. As I performed one experimental test after another along that line, I found that the Bible was a good guide in every case and that my experience only made sense in relation to the teachings it contained.

Furthermore, all the things that Jesus said that I was able to test for consistency, comprehensiveness, and simplicity proved to be valid, good, and beautiful. Therefore, why should I not trust Him in matters beyond my ability to test? There are many things in the Scriptures I cannot scientifically assess, but all the ones I have been able to assess check out. God is perfectly consistent in all respects. Further, just as Leibniz noted three centuries ago in his *Discourse on Metaphysics*,[12] God *must be* perfect in all possible ways. Therefore, I find no reason not to trust God in all things. On the contrary, every reason I can find and test compels me by justice, mercy, and love to believe what Jesus said. A sinless man who would die for us must be trustworthy. There is no doubt in my mind any longer that Jesus was who He claimed to be. Had God appeared in history, had He revealed the plan that Jesus spoke of, had He fulfilled all the prophecies of the Old Testament concerning His birth, death, and resurrection, men would have reacted exactly as they did react. First, they would have crucified Him. Then, except for the precious few who were seeking the truth, they would have denied Him. The story rings of truth from top to bottom.

There are countless aspects of God's work in creating this world that remain yet to be understood scientifically, but the evidences that we have from mathematics and the sciences are perfectly consistent with what the Bible teaches us. Moreover, we can strictly prove in the logico-mathematical way (as I claim to have done in recent years[13]) that the determinacy of facts does not reside in the facts per se, but only in true representations of them. This subtle finding, provided it is correct, has an important consequence for physics. It predicts the necessity of the uncertainties associated with the behaviors and properties of subatomic particles (or waves) as demonstrated in findings of quantum mechanics and in the notable uncertainty principle of Heisenberg. It shows that the determined course of events cannot be governed entirely by physical law but rather, if it is determined at all, it must be by the foreknowledge (the representations) coming only from the God who knows every outcome before it appears in human history. Interestingly, all of the modern findings of sign theory (also known as "semiotic theory" or "semeiotic," as Charles Peirce [1839–1914] preferred to call it) are consistent with the necessity that God himself should be consistent, and yet they confute in the most straightforward manner the notion that blind chance could determine anything of consummate order, design, and beauty.

In fact, we can produce a fairly straightforward disproof of the fundamental claims of evolution directly from the exact logic (the mathematicized logic) underlying sign theory. It can be demonstrated that intelligent representation is of a thoroughly different kind from the sort of manifestation found in the material objects of space and time.[14] While the latter are, no doubt, a manifestation of the mind of God as David wrote in the first verse of the Psalm 19, "The heavens declare the glory of God"—inert (inanimate) matter cannot represent itself to be other than it is. It simply is and does whatever it is and does. Yet human intelligence, through the power of language, can represent countless fictional possibilities for which there could *never be* sufficient material in the whole of the present, past, or future universe to manifest even the tiniest percentage. This follows on account of the fact that any part of infinity can be proved to be infinite. Moreover, as Einstein noted,[15] the gulf that separates the world of hard objects from that of propositions is genuine and, as he put it, "logically unbridgeable." Therefore, the arguments put forward on behalf of evolution come up altogether light and empty from the logico-mathematical point of view. The remarkable thing about Darwin's theory was that a pair of principles as dull and unthinking as random mutation and natural selection might actually be supposed to account for our mental life, our language capacity, and all of the other manifestations of intelligence.

Still, the credulous among the world's academics (as noted by astronomer Fred Hoyle[16]) embrace Darwinism. Do they do so on the grounds of science? How would that be possible, since the theory does not fit the facts? For instance, the absence of transitional forms in the fossil record is so well accepted that Gould[17] was able to find countless disciples for his theory of "punctuated equilibrium" in spite of the fact that it is entirely inconsistent with Darwin's gradualism and with sound logic. Gould had no mechanism to propel the huge creative advance that he claimed we can all see in the fossil record from shortly after the Cambrian period.

The theory of evolution lacks logical appeal, but is embraced on account of its false promise of an escape from responsibility to God. As Isaiah might have paraphrased the theory of evolution, "We have made a covenant with death, and with hell are we at agreement; when the overflowing scourge shall pass through, it shall not come unto us: for we have made lies our refuge, and under falsehood have we hid ourselves" (Isa. 28:15). In response, Isaiah continues with the answer of God: "Therefore thus saith the Lord God, Behold, I lay in Zion for a foundation a stone, a tried stone, a precious corner stone, a sure foundation: he that believeth shall not make haste" (Isa. 28:16).

Here is a critical question that evolutionists have not been able to answer, and never will be able to answer unless the God of the Bible turns out to be a liar: How is it possible for inert (inanimate) matter to create the language capacity of human beings? The Scriptures do not teach that in the beginning was the material world, but rather that "In the beginning was the Word" (John 1:1). Failing the demonstration that material objects blindly bumping together can produce the language capacity by accident, it is vastly more sensible to believe in the Logos, the Alpha and Omega, the God who knows the end from the beginning, the Lamb who was slain before the foundation of the world. Is it sensible to bet your soul on the power of inert matter to transform itself by accident into an intelligent being? How different is that from believing that a frog can turn into a prince? For my part, I find the gospel story more compelling.

GRAHAM MADDOX

POLITICAL SCIENCE

Graham Maddox is professor of political science at the University of New England, Australia. He holds a B.A. with honors in Latin from the University of Sydney, an M.A. with first class honors in classics from the University of Sydney and an M.Sc. with distinction in politics from the London School of Economics. Professor Maddox is the author of Religion and the Rise of Democracy[18] *and six other textbooks in the area of politics, as well as more than 50 research papers. He is a Fellow of the Australian Academy of Social Sciences and a life member of the Clare Hall, Cambridge.*

A Christian upbringing and development as a lay preacher have, unusually I think for a political scientist, been reinforced by my professional work in academic politics. It has been a powerful discovery to be convinced, beyond any hint of doubt, that the secular democratic state has been created by our religious traditions or, more accurately, by the movement of the Holy Spirit. One could easily pass that off and say that Christian *values* have been usefully annexed and incorporated into the secular state to produce our beliefs in liberty, equality, fellowship, and justice. But the Christian (and Jewish) connections run much deeper than that.

The famous Jewish political theorist Leo Strauss has a fine illustration of the impact of our God on communal life. It concerns a comparison of the influence of the pagan philosopher Socrates, whom many early Christians were prepared to call a "Christian" out of time, and the prophet of Yahweh, Nathan. Socrates lived through a time when his home community, Athens, fell into the hands of cruel tyrants. He was critical of the actions of the tyrants, and his complaints became known to them. By contrast, Nathan the prophet, learning of the sin of King David, goes to the king and relates the parable of a thief, which inflames the king's outraged sense of justice. With confronting clarity, Nathan points to the face of the king and says, "Thou art the man!" Without in any way denigrating the revered Socrates, I think the difference is the immediacy of the actor under direct instructions from God. Many of God's servants were frightened and unwilling vessels of His truth. Moses, their archetype, and many of the judges and prophets who followed him, feared to take on the work of God until they were directly charged by Him to do so, often being "commissioned" and cleansed by fiery oracles. Once arrested by the Holy Spirit, they had no option but to do that work and to confront the evil that God despised. This sense of direct commission was unknown in the pagan world.

The emergence of our democratic state partakes of this story. One of the first tenets of democracy is that no human government is good enough to rule the people in perpetuity. To take account of this belief, we sanction a political opposition, which surely has its roots in the example of the prophets. For the model of the democratic community itself we have the church congregation established by Jesus Christ to be His physical presence on earth. The body of Christ was commissioned to continue His work, always fearless in the face of countervailing authority, to extend love and justice to "the least of his brethren." In the modern world, democratic communities have indeed been formed by congregations, from the Interregnal English republic of Cromwell to the settler states of New England, directly established by separating congregations.

Those communities were not set up because their founders thought it would be nice, still less because they sought to gain individual profit. The foundational statement of modern democracy, providing a model of Christian charity, comes from the sermon preached by John Winthrop to the pilgrims journeying to Massachusetts on board the *Arbella*: "We must delight in each other, make others' conditions our own, rejoice together, mourn together, labor, and suffer together, always having before our eyes our commissions and community in the work, our community as members of the same body, so shall we keep the unity of the spirit in the bond of peace, the Lord will be our God and delight to dwell among us."[19] It is truly inspiring to come across such statements in the course of one's daily work.

Of course, the secular state cannot impose Christian ideals by force; that in itself would be un-Christian, and our religious tolerance teaches us to be open and respectful to people of other faiths and persuasions. It was for this very reason that *Christians* created and theorized the secular state — not to diminish the influence of religion on public life, as the American courts nowadays seem to think, but to provide freedom of worship secure from the interference of the state.

At the same time, we have numerous examples of devout Christians who have allowed themselves to risk the sullying compromise necessary in the political world while yet retaining an unswerving faith in Christ. "Honor and dishonor, praise and blame, are alike our lot; we are the impostors who speak the truth" (2 Cor. 6:8; REV). We may look to the spiritual fire that inflamed the English reformers such as Wilberforce and Shaftesbury, themselves first and foremost men of God. The great English statesman William Ewart Gladstone lived a spiritual life of extraordinary intensity in constant communion with his God. A similar faith impelled the devoutly Christian American presidents Lincoln and Wilson, who declared that they only took on the risks of the political life because they believed it was their way to do God's will in the world. The point here is not that these people were statesmen *and* Christians, but that they were, like the prophets of old, obedient servants of God's will, drawing constant inspiration from the Bible, and in daily and intense prayerful contact with their God. They were in political life as God's messengers, acting under instruction from the spiritual realm. They were statesmen *because* they were Christians.

This admission of the Christian's "acting under instructions" is sometimes questioned by political philosophers as a sign that they have not embraced the ideal of human liberty. Nothing could be further from the truth. The non-believer will not be satisfied with reference to the Scriptures: "If the Son therefore shall make you free, ye shall be free indeed" (John 8:36). At least since the Reformation, and perhaps from the time of Augustine, Christians have been aware that they live on two planes, or in two worlds, the spiritual and the temporal. Freedom is a human concept, and applies to our conduct in the temporal world. Obedience to God is a spiritual obedience which exists in absolute form in the spiritual world, but which instructs and emboldens our conduct in the temporal world. To be obedient in the spiritual world is to supply a confident and fortified freedom in the temporal world of human affairs. Not to submit to human coercion, but to be imprisoned for the sake of the Master, is a freedom that nullifies the powers-that-be and is not known to non-believers.

Although my work brings me into daily study of the actions of politicians and the systems they create, I do not aspire to be a politician. I am very happy, however, to have my faith confirmed by the faithfulness of those who, knowing that the political life must test their faith, and must unfairly damage their reputation (since others try to succeed through destroying the credibility of those they oppose), yet risk the path of the cross because of the instruction they have to serve others through political action.

For myself, I am daily uplifted by the signs of God's unfailing love: through the reading of Scripture, through prayer with my prayer group and through private prayers, through my own preaching and the preaching of other servants of God, through the unconditional love, though often tested, of my family, through the grandeur of nature and, for me perhaps above all, through the songs of God's faithful servants through the ages: the spiritually inspired music of Bach, Handel, Mozart, Beethoven, faithful Christians all, and all aspiring to glorify the Holy Name of God the Father, and his Son, Jesus Christ, through the Holy Spirit. With them, "I know that my Redeemer liveth."

VIVIENNE WATTS

EDUCATION

*D*r. Watts is senior lecturer in education, Central Queensland University, Australia. She is a Registered Nurse, and holds a B.S. in health science and an M.A. in religion from Andrews University (USA), and a Ph.D. in education from the Queensland University of Technology. Her research interests include the teacher's role in child abuse situations, school bullying, and school violence, and she lectures in the area of behavior management and classroom communication. Dr. Watts is the author of two books, one book chapter, and a number of research articles dealing with these issues.

Change in our world is constant, rapid, and irreversible. It occurs as people observe, question, modify, and reflect upon and evaluate the world around them, so that our current understanding of the world today differs from past understandings. For example, the creation–evolution debate, I believe, has progressed from its previous adversarial position so that presently there is greater consensus that both viewpoints base their trust in the veracity of their assumptions. So, to me, the creation–evolution debate is not a topic of priority in explaining the reasons for my faith. Of far greater significance are the questions: Can we be reasonably certain that God brought this world into being? Could "miracles" have occurred in the past, and more importantly, can we expect that they might occur again in the future?

Finally, if God is the Creator, can we believe that He continues to control our lives, our planet, and our universe? Or are we in control?

This chapter has three sections: why I believe in God, personal experiences that have influenced my belief structure, and the reasons why I choose to be a Christian. The reasons outlined in this chapter describe my current thinking on this topic. Many of the reasons used to justify my faith are not unique. However, the arguments are drawn together in a way that satisfies my personal need for a credible foundation for my faith. My views, as always, are subject to modification as new knowledge and experiences moderate and challenge them over time.

WHY I BELIEVE IN GOD

In this section I outline several basic reasons for my faith in God, most of which are derived from the natural world: design in nature, complexity in nature, the ecological balance of nature, the concept of possibility and impossibility, origin and existence of the life force, and the uniqueness of humanity. This list is not unlike the list of Du Bois Reymond who cited several "insoluble problems": the origin of life, the origin of language, the origin of human reason, the evolutionary adaptiveness of the organism, the origin of natural forces, the nature of matter, the origin and nature of consciousness and sensation, and the problem of free will.[20]

Design in nature. Many people have noted the intricate and often symmetrical features of natural objects such as the eye, the ear, the nautilus, the snowflake, a butterfly's wings, and a budding rose. Actually creating these exquisite objects in their inanimate form would take only a fraction of the skills and sophistication that would be required to place them in a context where they functioned and interacted with other objects and substances in the world. Some of these objects are identical (crystals of a particular chemical substance), some are similar (one ear with another ear), some are related (various varieties of roses), and some are totally different from each other (the unique design of each snowflake). To me, the many levels of structures and types of ingenious designs and functions evidence a superb mind with power to construct them. The designs of these objects are sufficient in themselves to form a basis for my faith in God as the Creator, but there's more.

Complexity. I believe the intricate organization associated with the lives of even the smallest and simplest of forms of organisms provides evidence that a master mind was responsible. In support of this I use three examples: the nature of matter, the glow of a glowworm, and the function of two parts of the body: the ear and the arm.

First, in the natural world, the atom, although invisible to the naked eye, functions like a miniature solar system whose parts move constantly around each other. Whether the smallest atom or the vastness of the billions of galaxies throughout the universe, each "thing" has an organizational structure and interacts with other parts of the whole system. The organization of this complex system, from the minutest to the grandest scale, evidences the existence of an organizer and manager.

Second, I have marveled at the flashing lights of glowworms so that the effect in darkened caves is not unlike twinkling stars. The glowing of the posterior end of the flightless female beetle signals to the flighted male beetle so that he can find his mate in the dark. The glow is from a "cold" source unlike warm light bulbs and phosphorescent watch faces. Laithwaite comments that we understand why, but not how, the glowworm glows.[21] Also unknown is how the female beetle turns her light on and off, although it is well known that a faint flashing light is much easier to see from a distance than a constant light. It is pertinent to the discussion to note that, if the flashing of the glow-worm had fallen outside the visibility range of humans (such as in the infrared range), then we may never have known how the male beetle finds his mate in darkened caves. The complexity of the glow-worm's glow provides but one evidence to me of the level of complexity in the animal realm, and raises questions about the possible existence of realms which are undetectable by our senses and our best measuring technologies.

Third, brain surgeon Ben Carson's description of the complexity of the ear as it functions and interacts with the human nervous system is inspiring, and, to me, it is incomprehensible to believe that this design and function occurred without divine intervention. Imagine for a moment that Dr. Carson had instructed you to raise a hand:

> Let's think about what your brain had to do when I [asked you that] question. First of all the sound waves had to leave my lips, travel through the air into your external auditory meatus, travel down to your tympanic membrane, set up a vibratory force which traveled across the ossicles of your inner ear to the oval round windows, generating a vibratory force in the endolymph, which mechanically distorted the microcilia, converting mechanical energy to electrical energy, which traveled across the cochlear nerve to the cochlear nucleus at the ponto-medullary junction, from there to the superior olivary nucleus . . . ascending bilaterally to the brain stem through the lateral lemniscus to the inferior colliculus and the medial jeniculate nucleus, across the thalmic radiations to the posterior temporal lobes to begin the auditory process, from there to the frontal lobes, coming down the tract of Vicq d'Azur, retrieving the memory from the medial hippocampal structures and the mammillary bodies, back to the frontal lobes to start the motor response at the Betz cell level, coming down the cortico-spinal tract, across the internal capsule into the cerebral peduncle, descending down to the cervico–medullary decussation into the spinal cord gray matter, synapsing, going out to the neuromuscular junction, stimulating the nerve and the muscle so you could raise your hand.[22]

How intricate, and yet this is merely a description of the simple act of raising a hand! As human beings we all engage in far more advanced multiple and complex acts every day, and some people accomplish amazing feats. Think of all the complex maneuvers required to (a) balance while riding a unicycle across a tightrope stretched across Niagara Falls, (b) react quickly while executing the stunt of kissing a cobra on the head without being bitten, (c) play a Liszt piano concerto, (d) play from memory a whole piano concert without looking at a sheet of music, and (e) play a game of tennis in a grand slam event. The complexity of execution required for each of these tasks rises exponentially beyond the simple act of raising one's hand. Ultimately, it is impossible for me to believe that this level of organizational and interactive complexity either occurred spontaneously or developed over long periods of time. To me, such belief would necessitate believing that the theory of spontaneous generation of life (food left under a blanket in a warm dark room spontaneously generating mice) was credible. Besides being personally untenable, such a belief would leave me out of step with the findings of contemporary science.

Ecological balance. In addition to the intricate design of such things as animals, plants, humans, and crystals, and their complexity as they function, a third factor in support of my faith is the ecological balance in which all of these objects are set in their context and interact with each other. One example should suffice to establish my point. The symbiotic relationship between the oropendolas and the cowbirds in Central America fascinates me.[23] The oropendola nests in colonies and each pair of birds builds a nest up to one and one-half meters long, the upper end of which is attached to the tallest trees. The entrance is located at the lower end of the nest and leads through a long constricted neck to the expanded lower part where the main section of the nest is located. The cowbird builds no nest of its own but lays its eggs in the entrance of the oropendola's nest. Cowbird eggs hatch before oropendola eggs, and the cowbird young eat the life-threatening botfly larvae before the oropendolas hatch, thus protecting the lives of the oropendola young. The life on our planet abounds with examples of symbiotic relationships among plants and animals that illustrate the ecological balance in nature that sustains life. So, for me, in addition to the evidence of design and complexity in nature, the evidence of ecological balance and interaction provides a foundation for my belief in a Master Designer.

The notions of possibility and impossibility. So far I have concentrated on evidences of design, complexity, and balance in nature. It might be expected that the next logical step would be to focus on the unalterable and unchanging laws of nature, usually considered popularly to be the laws of classical Newtonian science.

However, I am persuaded that an even greater evidence incorporates the "laws of nature" which change or become limited when extreme conditions are encountered (for example, in quantum or cosmic measures). We are now more aware of, say, the implications of Heisenberg's uncertainty principle and Planck's scale determining the limits of accuracy of measurement in the quantum realm. Many non-Christians have difficulty in accepting that "miracles" are possible, but for me, miracles are simply an unexpected occurrence. That is, their occurrence is contrary to what is expected given the natural laws as they are currently understood. However, I have come to realize that these natural laws are not as unchangeable as I was taught in school and university science. The behavior of matter may change when a new realm is encountered, and certain behavior in one realm becomes the extreme limit of behavior in another realm so that "some classically impossible things become possible and some classically possible things turn out to be impossible."[24] Perhaps our instruments are not calibrated to the same values or range as God's. In any case, my increasing understanding of the impossible gives a new perspective on reality and on the possibility of miracles occurring outside the realm we currently live in, know, and understand.

The origin and existence of life force. One section that is often missing from scientific textbooks is the origin of the life force. The factors that sustain life normally are identified; the anatomy, physiology, and functions of living organisms are present; so is the history of their introduction into the geological record. However, an explanation of how the "spark of life" originated is remarkably absent. Many years ago people believed in the theory of spontaneous generation. Now, one major work associated with how life began is the cloning of Dolly, the sheep. However, the life force imparted in the cloning procedure is still seriously inadequate compared with the sophisticated and interactive way in which life occurs and is reproduced in nature. On the basis of some of the arguments above, the explanation of Genesis that life force originated with God remains the most plausible.

The uniqueness of humanity. Humanity's capacity for thought, reflection, evaluation, creativity, communication using various language genres, consciousness, sensation, and above all love, provides evidence that humanity has reached a level of sophistication impossible to achieve without the intervention of God. The human brain is the most complex thing known in the universe, and human minds are far more powerful than the requirements necessary for survival. The human skill level is not only superior to all other living organisms, even evolutionists admit it is "so far ahead that we have largely now transcended evolution by natural selection."[25] As a conscious human being, I can identify with this experience of consciousness so that my theoretical understanding of consciousness is superseded by the experiential. A poem by Harriet Beecher Stowe (1853) is meaningful to me in this sense:

> Still, still with Thee, when purple morning breaketh
> When the bird waketh and the shadows flee
> Fairer than morning, lovelier than the daylight
> Dawns the sweet consciousness I am with Thee.

Consciousness is something that is not explainable or understandable. Like spiritual awakening it cannot be described, only experienced. For me the question is: Why is spiritual consciousness restricted to humanity?

I believe that it is not so much whether the arguments of creation or evolution are superior, but, on the balance of the evidence available, whether I can believe that God brought this world into being. On the basis of what I have outlined above, I can only answer that I believe He did. Similarly, can events now considered impossible within our understanding of the laws of physics, events that are commonly understood now as "miracles," occur in the future? On the basis of the arguments of possibility and impossibility, I believe that they can. Finally, are we in control of our lives or is God in control of our lives, the earth, and the universe? I believe that the spark of life force originated from God and that He continues to sustain life in all its forms.

This summary, of course, is dependent on my own (and those who have influenced me) finite and incomplete level of knowledge and experience. However, I derive comfort from the fact that my experience is not unique "for our knowledge is always incomplete" (1 Cor. 13; PHILLIPS). As one more knowledgeable than I, Ben Carson, wrote, "I am just a brain surgeon. I can't know everything. Thankfully, I do not have to because I have learned the wisdom of Solomon who wrote, 'Trust in the Lord with all your heart, and do not rely on our own insight; in all your ways acknowledge him' (Prov. 3:5; RSV)."[26]

PERSONAL EXPERIENCES

Not only are our bodies a unique creation based on the arrangements of genes and other hereditary factors, our lives are unique as a result of the many decisions we make. My multidisciplinary background has meant that the contexts in which I have lived and worked have provided a unique blend of experiences. I wish now briefly to illustrate how some of these experiences have provided to me the opportunity to know God and to substantiate my faith in Him.

First, you will have noticed from the foregoing discussion that I am interested in the functioning of the ear. On one occasion I took my eight-year-old daughter to a concert which was held indoors (when it should have been outdoors) and in which agonizingly loud music was played. As a result, I lost part of the hearing in one ear. It was not until my hearing was damaged that I realized how important hearing was to all aspects of my life and communication. There was no agreement among the medical experts as to just what had been damaged. Some said it was the nerves, others the cilia, and yet others that the mechanics of the ear were "unbalanced." Given Ben Carson's complicated description of the functioning of the ear, it is a wonder that my ear withstood an hour of loud music at all. The fantastic, intricate nature and functioning of an ear led me to think about its design and origin.

Second, as a registered nurse working in operating theaters I often saw the pulsating, functioning organs of patients visibly open on the operating table. Their uniqueness and design, and how they came to exist and function in this way, was as fascinating to me as looking into the starry heavens is for others. I remember the first breaths of newborn infants and the last breaths of others as the life force was extinguished in death. I could explain in medical terms why life stopped through "respiratory arrest" or "cardiac arrest," but all the elements for life were still present. The context and the body parts were still there, but the life force had disappeared. It didn't matter how much the medical team applied its procedures or spoke its jargon, nothing could revive life.

Third, when my daughter was four years old, I was diagnosed with a serious and potentially fatal disease. Surgery was arranged immediately for the day after diagnosis, and on the way to the operating theater I asked the nurse, "Please look after me; I have a four-year-old daughter." The nurse confidently and brightly assured me that they would. As I lay in the hospital during my convalescence, missing my family terribly, my thoughts focused on who would do my daughter's hair if I didn't live. This seemingly insignificant "worry" highlighted to me how such a life-threatening experience altered my perception of priorities. What comforted and sustained me at that time were not theories and arguments about the origin of the universe, but simply and confidently knowing that God is the Creator. He is in control, and my family was there with and for me. One of the greatest gifts in this life is that of relationships, and that we have this brief time on earth to share our lives with those we love.

Why Do I Choose to Be a Christian?

I grew up on a dairy farm and, in the resonant dairy shed, I often could hear my parents singing hymns above the hum of the motors as they milked the cows. The words of those hymns, Christian experiences provided by camps, and the Christian example of many people I have known have added to my life a depth of meaning and enriched philosophical thought that forms a frame of reference for my beliefs and values. The associated Christian networks and lifestyle, for me, provide a quality of experience that would be lacking in atheistic contexts.

There are substantial and persuasive evidences to believe in God provided by the design in nature, the complexity of nature, the ecological balance, the realms of possibility and impossibility, the origin of the life force itself, and the uniqueness of humanity. However, the personal experiences I have encountered throughout my life form the primary basis for my trust and confidence in God. Of themselves these experiences are not more important than the intellectual reasonings and evidences, but they support them, are consistent with them, and complement them. A God who has power to create and maintain a universe and to move from one realm to another has power, I believe, to take us with Him to live together eternally. For me, the justifications upon which my faith is based are more credible, more persuasive, and superior to the alternatives. Furthermore, since God has the power to both create and redeem, it is faith in Him that ultimately justifies.

BRIAN SINDEL

AGRICULTURAL SCIENCE

*D*r. Sindel is senior lecturer in weed science, School of Rural Science and Natural Resources, University of New England, Australia. He holds a B.Sc.Agr. with honors, a Dip.Ed. and a Ph.D. in weed science from the University of Sydney. Dr. Sindel specializes in weed ecology, population dynamics and management, and has published six book chapters, 14 journal papers, and 23 conference abstracts.

I have a ritual that on every Monday night I go out into our garden and gaze up at the stars. Monday night is garbage night, you see! On each occasion I marvel at the immensity and majesty of the universe and am overwhelmed with a sense that there is a mighty God who rules it all.

As the writer of the Psalms put it, "The heavens declare the glory of God; the skies proclaim the work of his hands. Day after day they pour forth speech; night after night they display knowledge. There is no speech or language where their voice is not heard. Their voice goes out into all the earth, their words to the ends of the world" (Ps. 19:1–4).

Then when I consider the complexity of the human body, whether it is the intricacy of the eye, the capacity of the immune system, or the sensitivity of the nervous system, I am convinced that we are "fearfully and wonderfully made" (Ps. 139:14).

As an undergraduate I recall a lecture on animal reproduction in which the lecturer made a cynical remark about the so-called "mythical miracle birth," that is, the conception and birth of Jesus. His assumption was that scientists have elucidated the reproductive process and therefore there was no possibility of conception outside these norms. He had not observed miracles in nature and therefore, to his way of thinking, they could not happen.

Was my faith in God incompatible with my academic pursuits in science? Or would my faith be better placed in the explanations of reality provided by biology and genetics, by physics and chemistry? Rather than being compelled by what I saw within the natural world to give up my faith in a supernatural being, I saw an order and design that was so ingenious (from the atom to the ecosystem) that it was, for me, impossible to attribute such existence to chance alone.

In simple terms, science deals with knowledge of material phenomena and therefore, by definition, is limited in its capacity to deal with the supernatural (or, for that matter, the moral) dimension of life. Science is based on observation, experiment, and induction whereby one moves from specific observations to draw general conclusions. If a supernatural God does exist, then His existence can neither be proved nor disproved through scientific methods.

If then this question of God's existence is beyond science, why do I believe? I've already mentioned my intuitive perception of a world with design.

In terms of my personal development, it was my father and mother who first introduced me to the Creator God by taking me to Sunday school and church when I was very young, by reading to me from the Bible, and by encouraging me to read the Bible for myself. I learned that "God so loved the world that he gave his one and only Son, that whoever believes in him shall not perish but have eternal life" (John 3:16). Not only did my parents teach me about God, but their lives provided me with convincing evidence of the reality of His presence and His love for me.

My father recently died from bone cancer. What a comfort it was for Dad and our whole family as he struggled with pain and the anxiety of dying to know that his trust and hope was in the One who had gone before him and had conquered death. I remember, as a young boy, crying in the night over the fear of separation and aloneness that death would eventually bring. But, by God's grace, I discovered, just as my father had done many years earlier, that in the death and resurrection of Jesus, God was extending an offer of love and forgiveness to me that included peace with Him and eternal life.

While my faith as a child was simple — responding to the Jesus who loved me and died to take the punishment for my sins — I came to realize that the One in whom I believed was not only able to deal with the key questions of life and death, but He also gave me direction and meaning for the whole of my earthly existence. A life without hope gave way to a life of purpose — to love and obey God, to care for my neighbors, and to tell them the good news of God's rescue mission for a lost world.

Moreover, Christianity made sense of the world in which I lived — the environment, my personal relationships, my moral failures, conflict, suffering, the existence of good and evil, human dignity and equality, sexuality, and work. All are given perspective in a world created by God but ravaged by the consequences of human sin.

To this point, one could argue that my belief in the supernatural God of the Bible is based on subjective reasoning alone. However, Christian belief also stands up to objective investigation because it is founded on the facts of history. Josh McDowell has compiled hundreds of historical evidences for the Christian faith. For example, the evidence shows that the New Testament portion of the Bible was written relatively soon after the events that are recorded within its pages and that the interval between the dates of original composition and the earliest extant evidence is so small that there can be little doubt that the New Testament has come down to us substantially as it was written. In addition, the large number of New Testament manuscripts (over 20,000), their internal and external accuracy, and the number of eyewitness accounts included therein, all confirm its historicity.[27]

Likewise, the radical turnaround in the lives of the apostles of Jesus following His death and resurrection is solid testimony for the validity of this most important fact of history. Of those

12 men, 11 died martyrs' deaths on the basis that they believed Jesus was raised from the dead and was the Son of God. Some may argue that they were deluded into dying for a lie, but it is difficult to believe that such credible eyewitnesses would die for a lie knowing that it was a lie. They had nothing to gain and everything to lose if such were the case. On the other hand, the alternative explanations for the resurrection — for example, that the disciples stole the body or that Jesus only fainted on the cross — are contrary to all the available evidence.[28] If this miraculous event is true and Jesus Christ is alive today, then He has proven that He is who He said He is and also proven what He can do for the person who trusts in Him.

I have put forward six reasons why I believe in the God of the Bible: my intuitive perception of the ordered world in which we live, God's impact on the lives of my parents as I was growing up, the ability of Christianity to deal with the big issues of life and death and the human condition, the purpose Christianity gives me in life, the sense that it makes of the world, and its historicity and the reliability of its claims.

And yet, I am aware that many people are not prepared to put their faith in the God of the Bible. Why is that? In the end, it is not a matter of evidence for or against Him, "For since the creation of the world, God's invisible qualities — His eternal power and divine nature — have been clearly seen, being understood from what has been made, so that men are without any excuse" (Rom. 1:20). In the end, it is a matter of the will. Am I prepared to take myself off the throne of my life and let Jesus take His rightful place as Lord and God?

When some of the followers of Jesus turned back from following Him, Jesus asked His closest disciples whether they too wanted to leave. Simon Peter answered Him, "Lord, to whom shall we go? You have the words of eternal life" (John 6:68).

Margaret G. Flowers

Biology

Dr. Flowers is professor of biology and chair of the Division of Natural and Mathematical Sciences, Wells College. She holds an A.B. summa cum laude in biological sciences from Mount Holyoke College and a Ph.D. in botany from the University of Texas at Austin. Before joining the faculty at Wells College, Dr. Flowers worked as a research associate in the Department of Plant Pathology at Cornell University.

Why would a scientist — a biologist, of all things — fall prey to belief in things unseen? Talk about bucking the standard of the profession: a 1998 survey entitled "Leading Scientists Still Reject God"[29] revealed that of the "elite" biologists of the National Academy of Sciences of the United States, approximately 95 percent were men or women who did not believe in a personal God! Why would this be?

Popular scientific dogma holds that if something can't be proven scientifically (that is, by observation and experimentation), it really doesn't exist. And since the resurrection of Jesus, the critical point for the Christian faith, doesn't lend itself to such treatment, it is categorized as a myth. Yet despite the lack of belief by my fellow scientists, I am convinced that Jesus is who He claimed to be — the Son of God.

I grew up in a Christian home where belief was a "given"; my coming to a personal faith as a teenager was not of a dramatic nature. At that time, among other things, two observations convinced me of the veracity of the gospel: the miraculously changed lives of the early Christians and the order and complexity that I observed in the natural world. Nearly 40 years later, they remain as powerful arguments for the path I have chosen.

That Jesus is an historical figure is not in dispute, even for scientists. This is something we know not only from the writers of the New Testament canon but also from various Jewish and Roman sources. We also know that shortly after Jesus' death, His followers became suddenly emboldened and began to dramatically increase in numbers. What could cause this? Their claim was that prophecy of the Jewish Scriptures had been fulfilled and that God had raised Jesus from the dead. There was no timidity about this assertion; many held it to be true even at the cost of their lives. Nero's excesses are well documented on this account. Now as someone with a strong logical bent, I asked myself, *Who would be willing to give up his or her life for something known to be untrue?* I wouldn't, and I couldn't think of anyone of my acquaintance who would either!

Peter and Paul are, of course, dramatic biblical examples of the change brought about by an encounter with the risen Christ. Peter, shortly before the crucifixion, was the very picture of cowardice, but less than two months later was boldly proclaiming the Resurrection to an international crowd in Jerusalem. And Paul, arch-persecutor of the Christians, became an outspoken apostle after his experience on the road to Damascus. Why such changes? There is a common thread. In Peter's words, "We all are witnesses" (Acts 2:32; RSV). So when people met Christ, there were changes. Miraculous changes.

Are lives still changed? Emphatically, yes. I think of a young man of my acquaintance who fell into the "bad company" of alcohol and drugs, a lifestyle that nearly cost him his health and life; today he is a vibrant and joyous Christian. Even the coldest observer would have to admit that he has changed from being a drain on society to being a productive citizen. But that characterization can't begin to express the change in the inner life from feelings of despair, loneliness, and rejection to the exaltation of redeemed life. I also think of an unassuming man who was sent to prison for a minor offence and there turned to Christ and found new life, and of the dramatic transformation in the life of a brilliant graduate student whose desperate search for love and meaning in life led her to the risen Lord. Talk to those who unashamedly call themselves Christians. Their testimonies, whether dramatic or not, will have as a common thread a personal encounter with the risen, living Christ.

And God is involved in our lives in other ways as well. Luke, whose accuracy in historical details is well recognized, records the words of Jesus regarding His actions: "The blind receive their sight, the lame walk, lepers are cleansed and the deaf hear, the dead are raised up" (Luke 7:22; RSV). He gave His disciples (and, on a different occasion, 70 others) power and authority to cure diseases (Luke 9:1; 10:1, 9), and promised that anything asked of the Father in Jesus' name would be received (John 14:14). Really? Are these words reliable?

Again the answer is yes! One can read modern medical studies on the efficacy of prayer in the process of healing, and even of spontaneous healings that are medically unexplainable. It is easy to read such studies dispassionately, at arm's length. There is no place for miracles in the modern, scientifically informed world, we are told. Not so! I picture Christian friends and acquaintances who testify to miraculous answers to prayer: a victim of a car accident, a pianist whose severed fingers were reattached and are now functioning normally; an elderly gentleman with restored eyesight in a "medically hopeless" condition; a middle-aged man with a medically documented "unexplainable" remission of cancer. It's just as Jesus promised. God is at work. He answers prayers, sometimes through human agents, sometimes in ways that science cannot begin to explain.

My parents, both Ph.D.-level chemists, were committed but quiet Christians. Long before the "hot topic" in the world of science (at least in academic circles) was the issue of "origins," I vividly remember my mother looking up into the sky one starry night when I was a fairly young child and saying,

"How can someone look at the stars and not believe in God?" That comment was an important witness to me that there was no conflict between faith in Christ and a career studying the natural world.

It also suggested two stark alternatives: to look at the sky and focus on the cold and vast interstellar space, or to concentrate on the millions of bright suns that are organized even from our perspective into recognizable patterns.

Now if I believe that God intervened in human history in the life, death, and resurrection of Jesus, why should it be farfetched to believe that God would intervene in the natural world in countless other ways? As a teacher of biology and geology, I am both amused and appalled at how textbook authors work so hard to eliminate the possibility that God should have any part in the picture. This is particularly true in the teaching of evolution. I wonder why it is so important to imply that there has been a progression (steady or otherwise) through the fossil record, when in fact we lack the missing links critical to the argument. What we do know tells a mighty story of creation; during the "Cambrian explosion," virtually all of the more than 30 known animal phyla suddenly appeared in the fossil record. No links, and no progression. And the record of the plant kingdom shows an equally interesting, but different story. The various divisions (phyla) appeared in a sequence in geologic time, but a sequence that does not progress steadily from simple to complex. Again, the organisms that would link these groups remain missing. The model of evolutionary change that is well documented at the species level doesn't translate to fit the facts of the appearance of phyla in geologic time.

I look at the complex interactions of the lowly lichen, the symbiotic interaction between an alga and a fungus, neither of which can live apart in nature and only with difficulty and special care in the laboratory. How did this complex association come into being? How did the complex life cycles of plants originate? While the basic pattern of alternating haploid and diploid generations is common to most of the plant kingdom, within this framework there are startling differences among the major groups of plants. Some animal phyla have equally complex life histories. It is hard to conjure up step-wise processes that would successfully lead to these patterns. Does this mean that each species and each special interaction was uniquely created? Not necessarily. If God is the Creator and sustainer of the natural world, then He can act also through the materials and the processes of that world. And that we might consider a miracle!

So as a scientist, I look for those miracles in nature. With my eyes (themselves a complex miracle) I observe in a brief moment the emerald green moss on the bank of a nearby lake, and see the bright red roots of the black willow protruding close by into the water. A crayfish crawls among the strands of algae on the underwater rocks as a fish swims lazily by. A tremendous beauty and complexity is found in each organism and in its interactions. Do these observations constitute a scientific proof of a Creator God? No, but I choose to believe. They are pieces of evidence, taken all together, that for me point to only one possible conclusion.

In the final analysis, belief in the supernatural triune God of the Bible is a matter of faith: "The assurance of things hoped for, the conviction of things not seen" (Heb. 11:1; RSV). It is, at this point in time, "see[ing] through a glass, darkly" (1 Cor. 13:12). But is not much of what scientists do also a matter of faith? We believe that by following a certain procedure, a chemical reaction will occur to yield the desired colorless product, or the cell fractionation procedure will yield the desired enzyme. Things unseen. But things whose existence can be shown by what they do. And God is doing things in our world!

PATRICIA NOLLER

PSYCHOLOGY

*D*r. Noller is professor of psychology at the University of Queensland and director of the University of Queensland Family Center. She holds a B.A. with first class honors in psychology and a Ph.D. in psychology, both from the University of Queensland. Dr. Noller has published extensively in the area of marital and family relationships, including ten books and over 80 journal articles and chapters. She has served on the editorial boards of a number of research journals in areas of psychology and was foundation editor of Personal Relationships, Journal of the International Society for the Study of Personal Relationships *(Cambridge University Press). Dr. Noller was elected a Fellow of the Academy of Social Sciences in Australia in 1996 and of the National Council on Family Relations (USA) in 1998.*

There are a number of reasons why I choose to believe in the Christian God of the Bible. These include His work of creation, His provision of redemption in Christ and His working in my life.

I believe in the God of creation, although I am only too aware that many of my scientifically minded colleagues see no place for God in the world. I am somewhat bemused, however, by the fact that these highly intelligent individuals can believe that the variety of landscapes, and of flora and fauna, all came about without a plan or design, and even more incredibly, without a designer. I find it equally difficult to believe that the wonderful machine known as the human body could have come about without design or designer. When I look at the world, I see evidence of God's design all around me, in the beauty, in the order, and in the tremendous variety in so many areas.

I believe in the God of Jesus Christ who sent His Son to die for me so that I might no longer be a slave to sin, but might know His forgiveness and cleansing, and might live my life in the power of the Holy Spirit. I know that many people have great difficulty with the concept that God required Christ's death for the expiation of our sins. What they overlook, however, is something that I overlooked for a long time: although our just and Holy God required a sacrifice, He was the one who provided that sacrifice: "God was in Christ reconciling the world to himself" (2 Cor. 5:19; RSV). I can still remember when this point came home to me. I was about 18 years old and walking home from a basketball game through a large park near my home. As I walked, I was going over the words of the great hymn by John Henry Newman, "Praise to the Holiest in the Height." The verse that really stopped me in my tracks, and increased my understanding of all that God has done for us, declared:

> And that a higher gift than grace
> Should flesh and blood refine
> God's presence and His very self
> And essence all divine.

This point is also made by Paul in the Book of Romans, but made a greater impression on me in the words of this hymn.

I believe in the resurrection of Christ as God's declaration of His power and love, and as the final seal of approval on all that Christ had done through His life and death. I also believe that those who trust in Christ will have eternal life. As the aria from Handel's great oratorio *Messiah* proclaims, "Because He lives, I too shall live." I have great difficulty with those who need to deny anything miraculous in the Bible. It seems to me that this approach leaves us not with a great God who can do anything, but with a too small God, who is totally bound within the rules of His own creation.

Another reason I believe in God is that I have experienced His working in my life in so many ways: as provider, guide, comforter, strengthener, and healer. Although I have experienced God's provision in many ways over the course of my life, the period that stands out is when my husband was in theological college. We had two small children and I was pregnant with our third. We had no regular income as I had stopped teaching at that stage, but week by week God provided for us with gifts of money or food, and even help with housecleaning — all given by people who loved Him. Some of these gifts were totally anonymous, and we do not know to this day who it was God used to provide us with money during that difficult time.

God has also guided me through my life, in many ways. I sometimes stop and think about how differently my life has turned out from what I expected. For example, I never expected to be an academic. When I went back to university just as our youngest child (our fourth) started school, and after 11 years in child care duties, I wasn't even confident that I could get a pass degree. In addition, I certainly wouldn't have been able to afford to study if fees had not been removed that year (1974). I wouldn't have been able to get to the university so easily if we had not, four years earlier, bought a house in the Brisbane suburb of West End, where there was a ferry service to the university. Then, just after my Ph.D. was awarded, one of the lecturers in the department suddenly decided to go back to the USA. Because his teaching was in areas I could also teach, I was able to get a temporary lecturing position. This later became a tenured position, and so my academic career was launched. I am thankful to God for the way He has led me through all these "coincidences."

I have always been aware of the presence of the Holy Spirit, the Comforter, in my life. Life has not always been easy, but I have been conscious of His presence, comforting me when I have had to face difficulties and giving me strength to do what needed to be done in a particular situation. Although no situation stands out, I am always conscious of the comfort that comes from bringing our worries and concerns before God and leaving them in His hands.

I have also known periods of illness in my life, and have been conscious of God's presence with me at those times as healer and friend. For example, I have always recovered very well from surgery, and I see this as a result of the number of people praying for me during those times, enabling God's healing power to be released. I will cite just two examples. From 1985 to 1992, I was seriously troubled from time to time with a tachycardia problem. In 1992 I was able to be part of a research project trialing a new method for dealing with this type of problem using radio waves. I have not had a single serious attack since, and am very thankful for that, as the attacks had previously been quite debilitating and totally unpredictable.

In 1997–98, following thyroid cancer and iodine radiation, I was diagnosed with fibromyalgia. The main symptoms were muscle pain, very low energy, and a painful neuropathy in my hands and feet. This was a very difficult time, and in my search for relief from those symptoms, I saw a number of doctors and other health professionals. While not discounting the help provided by the medical profession, I date the turning point in terms of recovery from the day I knelt in church and was prayed for by the minister and the whole congregation. God's healing power had flowed into my life once again. Thus, I choose to believe in God because it is the only way I can make sense of life. I am here to serve Him, the great Creator God, who sent Jesus Christ to die on the cross and to rise again, and who gives us the Holy Spirit as our Comforter and guide.

Malcolm A. Cutchins

Aerospace Engineering

Professor Cutchins is Professor Emeritus of aerospace engineering at Auburn University. He holds a B.S. in civil engineering and an M.S. and a Ph.D. in engineering mechanics, all from Virginia Polytechnic Institute and State University. Professor Cutchins spent 33 years in aerospace engineering research and teaching at Auburn University, serving as full professor since 1979. He is the author and co-author of numerous technical papers primarily in the area of structural dynamics.

When I returned to graduate school seven years after my B.S. degree in engineering, I was pondering the existence of the supernatural God of the Bible. It was also a time when I began to be exposed to advanced mathematics including complex variables, vector analysis, advanced differential equations, and two quarters of tensors. I had felt particularly drawn to mathematics during the latter part of these seven working years and almost began teaching the subject at the college level parttime at night before the opportunity surfaced to return to graduate school.

I had been exposed to the claims of evolution and really questioned the theory in the absence of any real proof for most if not all of the claims. If the broad claim were true that time and chance resulted in humankind, plants, birds, the earth, and its unique moon, even our entire universe, then that might question the claims of the Bible. But such a claim would also mean that the whole of mathematics just happened by time and chance, too.

Instead, I found the order in the solutions to ordinary and partial differential equations to be beautiful, perhaps best illustrated in the graphical patterns associated with sinks and sources in fluid mechanics. I recall physical demonstrations of these in vivid color in front of a large audience near the beginning of my graduate studies in engineering mechanics, showing streamlines and various properties in brilliant testimony, not to what "just happened," but to what was extremely ordered.

Could all of the transformations in advanced mathematics also have just happened? What great coincidence could have happened, mathematically, for a circle to be able to be mapped using complex variables into an airfoil shape by the Joukowski transformation? There are more than 30 other profound transformations in complex variables, which could hardly have occurred by time and chance. And in tensor analysis, could the tensor transformation laws have come about by time and chance? No, I don't think so. Not only do the tensors of any order transform in perfect harmony, but also properties of tensors such as invariants hold constant in completely different coordinate systems. These "speak" profoundly to purpose, not to an aimless, purposeless, chance-dominated interpretation of our world.

Properties such as gradient, divergence, and curl in vector analysis have numerous applications in science and engineering. Gradient, for example, can be used to derive the equation of a line perpendicular to a surface. No matter how complicated the equation of the surface may be, performing the gradient with the calculus yields that important normal, hardly a result of time and chance.

Orthogonality is a property that shows up in many technical areas. There is no better illustration here than the orthogonal modes of vibration that every physical thing on earth has, from our eyeballs to complicated aircraft, from sloshing fluids to various pendulum motions. A vibrating system not only has order — physically and mathematically — when vibrating at an orthogonal mode, but its motion even in other instances can be modeled with a summation of usually just a few of the individual modes. How could such ordered phenomena have "just happened" without some kind of direction and purpose?

I always had an attraction to flight and have ended up teaching aspects of it for over 30 years. Flight is difficult to achieve, hardly the type of thing that one would expect to develop from chance. Successful flight requires great attention to detail of structure, propulsion, aerodynamic surfaces, structural dynamics, and stability and control. In 2003 we will reach only the 100-year anniversary of flight by humankind. Do we really think we are so smart and so advanced that we cannot reflect upon and give credit to the Intelligent Designer of earliest flight? I believe it to be impossible that the amazing flight of a hummingbird, the silent flight of an owl, or the night feeding of a bat in total darkness could have developed by chance happening. Similarly, both the lens system and the navigation system of the monarch butterfly are far superior to anything that humankind has yet designed. No mechanism has yet been identified that could lead to these types of complexity.

Aeroelasticity is the study of phenomena that involves the interaction of fluid, elastic, and inertia forces. Much of the real world of flight requires solving aeroelastic or aeroservoelastic problems. It pushes our computers just to solve a short time of flight when aeroelastic phenomena are present. Blood flow in our bodies is another example of aeroelastic phenomenon, involving an interaction of the blood fluid, elastic blood vessels, and the inertias involved in the dynamics of the flow. Yet there are aeroelastic failures in the 20th century (like the Tacoma-Narrows bridge in 1940) that are not yet fully explained, even with film of the failure and more than 60 years of analysis. In light of this, it is unscientific to attempt to explain dogmatically the origin of flight, not only once with birds, but differently three more times with insects, flying reptiles (now extinct), and flying mammals (bats), by helpful mutations, gradual changes, and chance and time.

During those four years of gaining a masters and Ph.D. in engineering mechanics while teaching parttime, my third child was born, the first girl. If chance and time were to be gods, what would be the purpose of her life? What would be the purpose of my family that included two fine young boys? Surely there has to be a better answer than the one the completely secular world has to offer.

I also gained an appreciation during those years of advanced study for the dangers of speculation, reinforcing my faith in the supernatural God of the Bible and increasing my resistance to the claims of speculative alternatives. As one example, in the study of materials I was exposed to the phenomenon of creep. Experiments can be performed over certain periods of time and that data can be carefully extended into the region where there is no data (since this is usually a long-term phenomenon), but there are warnings about this process of extrapolation and careful engineering limitations on the length of time to which such predictions can be applied. Now there are no real philosophical world views founded on the creep process; it is strictly a technical phenomenon. But if there are restrictions on a technical process concerning the danger of extrapolation, how much more careful we should be not to swallow extrapolated data in support of a godless world view.

Even in our modern hi-tech world, we have measured very few things over a time period of more than approximately 200 years. In light of the creep description above, extrapolating from these 200-year scientific measurements to extreme periods of millions and billions of years is not science; it's pseudo-science. To illustrate, consider a 100-foot rope to be representative of one billion years. The portion of the length of the rope representative of 200 years is only the width of a piece of paper. (Even for one million years represented by the same 100-foot rope, we have less than 0.25 inch of the rope to represent the 200 years of scientific measurements.) No honest scientist would try to "predict" the shape of the rest of the rope from knowledge of such a short part of it, yet this illustrates the typical method of the adherents to the gods of time and chance in many of the facts they claim and attempt to force on others as being without question.

In contrast to speculative matters as described above, I have found the God of the Bible and His Scriptures to hold good and always appropriate advice for any problem in life: for death of loved ones, for a resource to develop the fortitude required to endure suffering (what better example than Jesus), and for preparing for one's own demise, something that will come to all of us.

On the positive side, this same God can be the inspiration for motivation of all kinds (at 65, I still play full-court basketball at lunchtime two to three days a week, now estimated at well over 10,000 games), for being the best one can be — physically, mentally, and spiritually, for marriage and, after death of a spouse, remarriage.

As we stand on the rim of a great abyss of moral decay and ethical nightmares, there is not a single moral or ethical dilemma to which the Scriptures do not speak. I have found that whatever situation one may encounter in life, Scripture addresses it with great clarity. And if one accepts the promises contained therein, great peace can be the result. I do not believe that can be said of anything else in this world.

DAVID H. STONE

ELECTRICAL ENGINEERING

Dr. Stone is associate professor of electrical and computer engineering, Michigan Technological University. He holds a B.S. and an M.S. in physics from Michigan State University, a Ph.D. in mechanical engineering from Michigan State University and an M.B.A. from the University of Phoenix. Dr. Stone served 20 years in the United States Air Force on a variety of research assignments, including high energy lasers, charged particle beams, high power microwaves, and satellite communication systems, retiring as a lieutenant colonel in 1994. He received the U.S. Air Force Research and Development Award in 1986 for contributions to high power microwave system testing.

The tortuous journey toward my present Christian faith began in a traditional church, detoured into atheism, turned abruptly to a simple faith in the Savior, and finally settled on a solid biblical foundation, recognizing that the Word of God is fully trustworthy, consistent, and perfect, both theologically and scientifically.

As I grew up in my church on the south side of Chicago, I was fully engaged in religious activities, but I felt I had no foundation. In short, I was an eager churchgoer but not a Christian. I trusted that some combination of canned prayers, active service, and avoidance of "big" sins would earn me a berth in heaven. I didn't realize that ALL sins are "big" enough to earn hell — "For whosoever shall keep the whole law, and yet offend in one point, he is guilty of all" (James 2:10).

There were two powerful forces working against my belief system. Although all of my family and my relatives were religious churchgoers, my dad was a skeptic. He took delight in pointing out inconsistencies in church doctrine and in the bloody history of what has often purported to be Christianity — most notably the Inquisition. What I didn't realize was that true Christians were always on the receiving end of persecutions.

The second force was the culture of evolution in which I was immersed. I spent considerable time in the museums in Chicago, which are completely saturated with evolution as a naturalistic explanation for life. Additionally, everything I read and everything I saw on TV that touched the subject of origins was evolutionary. I didn't know that there was also strong scientific evidence that supported creation, since there were very few books on this topic in the 1960s.

As a precocious 13 year old, I brought a flock of questions to one of the senior leaders in my church one Saturday. He couldn't give me an answer for any of my concerns. That unsatisfying meeting confirmed my decision to be an atheist. Who needed God? The Church didn't make sense and everything in the universe could be explained by atheistic evolutionary science — it seemed.

I was a miserable atheist for the next three years. What point is there to life if we are just animals and death means the end of it all? At the depths of my depression, though, God had mercy on me and sent me a friend who was a Christian. He and his family befriended me. I saw the love of Jesus in their lives and I wanted it. So I became a Christian at age 16. The truth of John 6:44 resonates with my soul: "No man can come to me, except the Father which hath sent me draw him: and I will raise him up at the last day." Wow! Did God ever draw me! I praise the Lord for His wonderful patience.

I didn't understand how to reconcile evolution with my new faith, but I began to study the subject over the next few years. Finally I concluded that true science was perfectly consistent with the Bible. I could accept the truth of Genesis — most notably a six-day creation and a literal worldwide flood — without compromise. I did not feel there was a need to invent a hybrid theory of origins such as theistic evolution to try to be accepted by evolutionary atheists. To me, there was no satisfaction down that road, imagining that God somehow used evolution over the course of billions of years to produce His creation. I believed that when God pronounced His creation "good," He meant it!

I thought that evolution would be an awful method of creation for a loving God. Bloody competition, extinction of millions of species of animals and plants — survival of the fittest and destruction of the unfit. That's not the God of the Bible who provides for the birds of the air (Matt. 6:26) and praises those who are kind to animals (Prov. 12:10)!

One particular quote from an evolutionist seemed to powerfully confirm my view. Jacques Monod wrote:

> [Natural] selection is the blindest, and most cruel way of evolving new species, and more and more complex and refined organisms. . . . The struggle for life and elimination of the weakest is a horrible process, against which our whole modern ethics revolts. An ideal society is a non-selective society, one where the weak is protected; which is exactly the reverse of the so-called natural law. I am surprised that a Christian would defend the idea that this is the process which God more or less set up in order to have evolution.[30]

As I studied the literature on origins I was impressed that there were serious weaknesses in the arguments for evolution. These discoveries excited me because my spirit (or the Holy Spirit inside me) seemed to cry out for a simple trust in the Word of God.

I know this is not a book about creation versus evolution, but one of the most important reasons why I believe in the Bible as the Word of God is because I am convinced that there is overwhelming evidence that Darwinian-type evolution is impossible. I would like to explain my position by listing my top ten reasons for believing that science is not an enemy of the Bible and that the evidence for brilliant design speaks against the random processes of mutation and natural selection.

1. The molecules crucial to life are so enormously complex that it would seem *impossible* for them to arise by chance. Example: A single ordinary protein molecule consists of hundreds of amino acids formed into a precise three-dimensional configuration. These molecules are constructed within living cells only with the aid of other macro-molecules such as proteins and nucleic acids. There doesn't seem to be any way for such molecular complexity to arise under non-living circumstances. In my review of the evolutionary literature I have never been able to find any quantitative discussion explaining how such complexity could have arisen under natural, non-living conditions.

2. The simplest conceivable cell — the smallest possible self-replicating organism — is immeasurably more complex than the most sophisticated designs of human science and engineering. Example: There are about 500 different perfectly regulated chemical reactions associated just with metabolism. When confronted with such a wonderfully complex chemical system, it seems that there must be a system *designer,* namely God. We may marvel at the complexity of a construct like the space shuttle, appreciating the work of the thousands of engineers who contributed to its design, manufacture, and operation. It is easy to argue that a single "simple" cell is far more complex than the space shuttle or any other human construct.

3. The two cornerstones of evolutionary theory are mutations and natural selection. As far as I can tell from the evolutionary literature, however, mutations merely destroy genetic information within a given organism. Natural selection also destroys genetic information within a population. I am not aware of any evidence that the opposite occurs — which must happen for evolution to be a viable theory. Furthermore, the reproductive process is wonderfully accurate, avoiding mutations because of their deleterious effects. Example: The DNA replication process for higher organisms includes proofreading to keep error rates at less than one in ten billion. Errors that do occur are almost invariably neutral or harmful and never increase complexity. Even rare "beneficial" mutations involve loss of complexity. I see the replication process and its precision as wonderful testimonies to the genius of the Creator.

4. The genetic differences among species are so substantial

that there isn't enough time for them to occur on the supposed evolutionary timetable. Even if mutation and natural selection could produce new and more complex information, it would take many generations for each change to "take over" a population. Example: Chimpanzees are thought to be our closest genetic relatives. Human and chimpanzee DNA are thought to be only a few percent different. But even a one percent difference amounts to tens of millions of differences in the base sequence of DNA. Human evolution has allegedly occurred over the last several million years. Given a human generation time of perhaps 20 years, only a few thousand significant changes could arise in the population. The numbers don't add up. A few thousand changes cannot account for the millions of differences in the DNA code.

5. The gaps in the fossil record are huge and systematic. Even evolutionists are troubled by these gaps. Fossil gaps are evidence against incremental — mutation and natural selection — evolution. In searching the evolutionary literature, there seems to be no adequate mechanism for creatures to evolve over these chasms. Example: The deepest-lying sedimentary rocks exhibit billions of fully formed, complex invertebrates with no trace of their supposed evolutionary precursors. This "explosion" of fossils remains unexplained by naturalistic mechanisms. But from a creationist perspective I thrill at the immense variety and imagination the Creator used in producing this diversity. Furthermore, gaps in the fossil record are abundant. Gaps occur between invertebrates and vertebrates, especially fish; between fish and amphibians; between amphibians and reptiles; between reptiles and birds and reptiles and mammals; and ultimately between every significant type of creature leading up to human beings.

6. Life exhibits an abundance of irreducibly complex systems. Such systems would seem to have no way of working in any partially formed state. The problem for evolution is to explain how such systems could develop incrementally. The scientific literature seems to be empty of any quantitative model that allows for an evolutionary origin for any irreducibly complex system. Example: The cilium used by some cells for locomotion is a complex, self-contained motor using over 200 different proteins

for structure and operation. As far as I can tell, no one has ever conceived how a cruder version (evolutionary precursor) could possibly function. The Creator, of course, was able to design and build such systems from scratch!

7. The sophistication of living design at the organ and at the organism levels is astounding. A detailed look at specialized organs and optimally designed creatures boggles the mind at the brilliance of the Creator — involving a smaller leap of faith than assuming "design" by random mutation and natural selection. Example: The sonar systems of bats and dolphins are wonderfully sophisticated and exceed the performance of any that man has built.

8. Evolution's advocates support a theory that does not lend itself to the criterion of falsifiability. Genuine scientific theories must be testable! On occasion, some of the evolutionary faithful have proposed a test. But the results are not favorable to the theory. Example: An evolutionist once affirmed that structures like wheels and magnets could not have evolved because they would be useless until fully formed. But these structures have since been discovered in living creatures. The wheel is found in the rotary motor of the bacterium's flagellum and magnets are integral components of the navigation systems of many birds. A creationist is not surprised to find fully developed structures with no hint of incremental development in the fossil record. The most "ancient" bat fossils, for example, exhibit the structures necessary for sonar. In my view, the conclusion is that bats have always had this sophisticated ability from the time they were created.

9. I regularly search the evolutionary literature to find the "best" evidence to support the theory. But the "best" examples seem to be weak. Examples: Bacteria and insects that "evolve" resistance to chemicals often lose genetic information and become less viable in normal environments. Antibiotic resistance that arises from the transfer of bits of DNA among bacteria still does not involve the generation of "new" information, but merely the transfer of existing genetic code. The variations among the beaks of Darwin's finches represent the re-arrangement of existing genetic information through sexual reproduction — just as a husband and wife can have children with noses longer or

shorter than their parents. The literature seems to be empty of any example of an evolved chain of organisms, transitioning from simple to complex.

10. There is considerable evidence that the universe and the earth are far younger than the billions of years required by evolutionary theory. Example: Spiral galaxies would have "wound up" if they had existed for billions of years. They can't be shaped the way they are! A complex "density wave" theory of spiral arm formation was invented to try to explain this, but it is not consistent with detailed observations from the Hubble Space Telescope. Additional puzzles about galactic structure have led astronomers to postulate that unobserved and possibly unobservable "dark matter" will save the day! A simpler explanation would involve a Creator who made the universe fully functional and observable from the first week.

I know books have been written on each one of the points above, but the intent of this "Top Ten" list is to be illustrative rather than exhaustive. I encourage interested readers to survey the creationist literature available through http://www.AnswersInGenesis.org and http://www.icr.org

I praise God that my faith continues to grow stronger. The glorious truth of the Bible seems more vibrant every year. To me, the glories of God's creation speak volumes toward the truth of God's design and handiwork.

As I see my faith, the bottom line is: "The heavens declare the glory of God; and the firmament sheweth His handiwork. Day unto day uttereth speech, and night unto night sheweth knowledge" (Ps. 19:1–2). I believe we serve an awesome God. Wherever I look in nature I see evidence of His brilliance. And wherever I look in the Scriptures, I find truth and encouragement for my soul.

DAVID J. TYLER

MANAGEMENT SCIENCE

*D*r. Tyler is senior lecturer in the Department of Clothing Design and Technology at Manchester Metropolitan University in the UK. He holds a B.Sc. in physics from Southampton University, an M.Sc. in physics from Loughborough University and a Ph.D. in management science from the University of Manchester. Dr. Tyler has authored or co-authored over 50 research papers and abstracts and in 1995 was awarded the Holden Medal by the Textile Institute.

Science has always been a strong ingredient in my own family. I owe my interest in physics to two enthusiastic teachers: one at school and the other at home (my father). My two brothers both developed an affinity for chemistry, and all of us pursued these interests at university level.

During my secondary school years, these scientific interests were supplemented by involvement in various astronomical societies and avidly following the latest discoveries from space probes and telescopic observations. I was familiar with all the major constellations in the Northern Hemisphere, and could locate most of the objects that are accessible using a small telescope.

During these school years, I would have called myself a Christian. I had no formal church links, although I occasionally attended church meetings. However, I did attend a boys' Bible class, which is where I met Christians. I read the Bible and was familiar with much of the Old and New Testaments. However, as I grew older, I found myself becoming more and more skeptical of the miraculous elements of Christianity.

Being a lover of books, I acquired and read numerous volumes that fed my skepticism. There were books that questioned the historicity of the New Testament, and other books that generally presented views at variance with a biblical perspective on life. By the time I commenced university studies, I was conscious of my own skepticism and was no longer willing to be identified as a Christian.

The first year at university is an extraordinary time for young people: new independence, new responsibilities, and many opportunities for meeting people, making friends, and joining clubs. Looking back, I can see the hand of God in the way contact with Christians was continued. One of the Bible class leaders in my home town had a brother in the university town who held "open house" for students every Sunday. Through this link, I was introduced to a number of Christian students and through them to the university Christian Union.

These Christian contacts brought many latent issues to prominence in my mind. Did the miracles of Jesus actually happen? How should a scientifically trained mind approach these questions? I was rapidly coming to a position where skepticism threatened to prevail and where much of Christianity, both theory and practice, appeared vacuous.

Christian Unions, at that time, held week-long missions to students every three years. The appointed time for my university came in my first term (November 1965) and I attended a series of major evening addresses. This was the time when God called me and I put my trust in Jesus Christ. The speaker's theme was Christ, the wisdom of God, based on 1 Corinthians 1:18–31. The particular emphasis was on the way the gospel message came to the Greeks, the philosophers of that generation, who looked for wisdom but who found "Christ crucified" to be foolishness.

The speaker explained why it is that the world's wisdom cannot find God and why it is that God's wisdom in Christ is given such short shrift. It is not that human beings are wiser than

God but that they set themselves up as arbiters of truth and do not recognize their own desperate need. When God sets before them the reality of their condition, they will not be warned. When God sets before them "Christ crucified" as the only way of reconciliation, it is regarded as foolishness. The apostle Paul knew how the Greeks would receive the gospel — but that did not stop him! He was commissioned by Christ to carry the message and Paul's confidence was in Christ who is "the power of God and the wisdom of God" (1 Cor. 1:24; NIV). Paul was confident that "the foolishness of God is wiser than man's wisdom, and the weakness of God is stronger than man's strength" (verse 25). And, of course, the gospel bore fruit among the Greeks as many of them responded to the call of God.

It is impossible to do justice to the effect these thoughts had on me. It was as though the speaker was talking to me personally, putting his finger on the particular issues that were in the forefront of my mind, and giving me an insight into my personal experience of skepticism. That evening was a turning point for me. Faith in Jesus Christ became the start of a personal relationship with Him. The power of God became part of my Christian experience, and prayer was transformed to be an intensely personal meeting with my God and Savior.

While it was an easy thing to share this new-found faith with other Christians, I was apprehensive later that week when I had a lengthy conversation with a humanist philosophy student. This was with a contact I had made earlier that term: then we shared common ground in skepticism of Christianity. After explaining the transformation in my own thinking, I was expecting a frontal assault on my new beliefs. However, it never came! I think the talk of "relationships" was disarming — it had shifted the conversation to a different level. It was an encouragement to me, and a useful lesson: it is not necessary to have worked through all the issues and to have an answer to every question in order to practice the life of faith or to bear witness to Christ.

The InterVarsity Fellowship (IVF, now the Universities and Colleges Christian Fellowship, UCCF) was a great help to me during my student days. I became fully involved in the Christian Union and, during my final year, became the CU Secretary. The science and faith issue within IVF was approached using the concept of complementarity: the scientific explanation of origins (via the process of evolution) and the biblical perspective are both valid ways of understanding God's creation. This was the view I defended during my student days — although I was not happy that it worked with humanity. It did seem to me that an evolutionary explanation of the human race was in tension with the biblical revelation about Adam and Eve.

After taking up employment as a physicist and leaving the pressurized life of a student, I was able more closely to address these issues of science and faith. The first priority, it seemed to me, was to clarify my understanding of Adam and human origins. I set out on a study of the letter to the Romans, particularly the first eight chapters. The crucial section is chapter 5:12–21, where a powerful analogy is made between Adam and Christ:

Adam → One act of sin	→ Condemnation and death of Adam	→Death reigns over all "in Adam"
Christ → One act of righteousness	→ Condemnation and death of Christ	→ Justification and life for all "in Christ"

It appeared to me that Adam had as real an identity as Jesus Christ, and that death, both physical and spiritual, was a consequence of Adam's act of disobedience. The implications for anthropology were profound: any approach to harmonizing evolution and the Bible which involved God breathing His image into a pre-Adamic creature appeared contrived to me. This was partly because of the prevalence of death in the "pre-Adamites," and partly because there are theological reasons for insisting that the whole human race descends from Adam. I also found a total contradiction between the social evolution of humanity presented as science, and the biblical record of Adam's sons being involved in agriculture. (I already knew enough about the pre-Neolithic men to recognize that they were truly human and therefore descendants of Adam.) A consistent

Christian understanding of human origins must reject the conventional evolutionary scenario — of that, there was no doubt in my mind. Complementarity would not work in this case.

Arising from these studies, it seemed quite natural to consider how I could contribute to the development of a Christian understanding of ancient man. Being a physicist, I thought the most useful area for me was that of dating. The conventional chronology was far too long to be satisfactorily harmonized with biblical history, so I inferred that the received scientific time scale must be stretched out by some misreading of the data. Since the most important "clock" for anthropology is radiocarbon (C-14) dating, that was the method I chose to study.

The first paper I produced on the subject argued that there were fundamental contradictions between some of the C-14 dates obtained from archaeological samples and equivalent C-14 dates obtained from dendrochronologically dated wood.[31] There must be unrecognized errors in either the assigned archaeological dates, or the tree-ring dates, or both. I sent the manuscript to an archaeological journal that had previously carried quite a few interesting radiocarbon papers. The referees' response was to say that my manuscript was not sufficiently novel to warrant publication. I was disappointed, as I had not seen the argument presented elsewhere in this focused way, but I interpreted the feedback as an implicit acceptance of the validity of my argument, which was, in a way, an encouragement. A creationist journal subsequently published the paper and, some time after that, another with my approach to developing a non-equilibrium model of radiocarbon variations, with C-14 time "stretched out" prior to about 1000 B.C.[32] I followed this up with a study of Neolithic Man, particularly the British Neolithic, suggesting that these communities are best understood as descendants of the migrants from Babel (Gen. 11:8–9).[33]

Returning to my studies in Romans, I had reached the conclusion that complementarity was a seriously misleading way of harmonizing "science and faith" issues related to mankind. This fired me up to look at the much bigger issues of earth history and the origin of species. My next serious biblical study was Genesis 1–11. It took a long time and required much reading around the subject. Genesis 1 raised some of the most challenging questions for me to address. I was not attracted at all to the idea that the chapter is poetry or parable or proclamation or drama. I found that the "gap theory" and the "day age theory" raised more problems than they solved. The "literary framework theory" seemed much more substantial. I acknowledge my debt to Edward Young's monograph *Studies in Genesis One*[34] which helped to establish in my own mind that this passage is not an ahistorical conveyor of truth, but is intended to be trustworthy history, accurately recording those matters of which it speaks. Although the length of the days is not stated, we are not free to say that they can mean anything! The "day" is a period of time which may legitimately be called a day.

Having established in my mind that Genesis is intended to be a history of beginnings, my break with the complementarity approach was complete. The creative acts of God recorded in Genesis 1 are intended to teach us the miraculous origin of the heavens and the earth. Whatever we might speculate about possible natural means for bringing the cosmos into the form we know it today, Genesis informs us that that is not how God did it. When the Scriptures say "For he spoke, and it came to be" (Ps. 33:9; NIV), we are intended to understand an immediate, miraculous response to God's creative Word, not a process that we can understand scientifically.

The next major transformation in my thinking, based on this study of Genesis, related to the Flood (chapters 6–8). During my student days, the Flood was not considered a particularly important aspect of apologetics, and the consensus was that it referred to an inundation of the Mesopotamian region. As I considered the issues, I found numerous biblical and scientific reasons for rejecting this thesis. At the time, the most important related to anthropology: for theological reasons, the Flood had to be co-extensive with humanity. The only human survivors were those in the ark. (There is an eschatological dimension to this: the day is coming when a greater destruction will come, when the only humans who escape God's judgment will be those in Christ.) I knew, from my studies of early humanity, that no Mesopotamian flood would suffice, because mankind was already to be found in Europe, Africa, and America.

The only option, it seemed to me, was to say that the Flood was not only anthropologically universal, but also geographically universal. This, of course, brought me into conflict with historical geology, which knows nothing of such a global flood. Although I have not lost my interest in radiometric dating methods, I have felt the need to develop my understanding of earth science. The issues are so far-reaching that every effort must be made to develop a community of informed Christians with competence in geology.

Reading the writings of flood geologists (during the 1970s and subsequently) left me with mixed feelings. On the one hand, I was encouraged to find Christians addressing the issues and grappling with field data — sometimes convincingly. On the other hand, several concepts were given prominence that I could not relate to my experiences of field geology. The most notable were: rejection of the geological column, the claim that biostratigraphy involves inherently circular reasoning, and the rejection of large-scale overthrusting. This perception that "all is not well" in flood geology circles has made me an enthusiastic advocate of simultaneously considering alternative interpretations of data and for the extensive testing of hypotheses.

Since about the year 1980, I have sought to give priority to the earth sciences in my personal contribution to apologetics. It has been an interesting experience! I have enjoyed meeting lots of people, being a member of three geological societies, studying a variety of courses, and experiencing the delights of fieldwork. As well as traveling extensively in the UK, I have been on study visits to the USA, Cyprus, Iceland, Spain, Sweden, and Germany. This has been a learning experience and a privilege. The general conclusion I have come to is that most of the "problems" stem from ignorance. The more expertise we develop relating to particular localities, the more natural it is to infer an environment of catastrophism, and then to seek integration within a more comprehensive flood model.

When asked, "What geological evidences are there for a global flood?" I point people to these five factors that I find significant in my own thinking.

1. *The lithological successions accompanying the fossil successions.* Not only do I think that the fossil successions are real,

but I find it very significant that there is an associated pattern of lithologies. The proposed explanations for this within conventional geology are very weak, but not within a geology involving a global flood.

2. *The changing character of the major divisions of the geologic record: Archaean, Proterozoic, Palaeozoic, Mesozoic, Tertiary, and Quaternary.* Briefly, these go from global, mega-scale patterns of deposition in the lower divisions, moving to small-scale, localized patterns of deposition in the upper divisions. I associate this with a general decline in the intensity of erosional and depositional forces associated with global catastrophism, and find these trends anomalous within conventional geology.

3. *The near-global discontinuity associated with the Cambrian unconformity.* This is not the base of the Flood, as some have suggested, but it does indicate a global pattern of erosion (preceded and followed by global patterns of deposition).

4. *The failure of conventional geology to do justice to field evidences.* This is the fruit of fieldwork: the suggested depositional environments do not, in my opinion, stand up to critical scrutiny. (Some of my own field studies have been published: the Jurassic rocks of the Yorkshire Coast,[35] and a depositional model for the Chalk.)[36]

5. *The benefits for field interpretation for adopting a rock cycle that is dynamic and tectonically driven.* I have long thought that an alternative to Hutton's rock cycle is needed — simply to provide an alternative approach to field data. My published contribution to this (a tectonically controlled rock cycle) was the fruit of testing ideas in the field.[37]

I have always tried to avoid the concept of a "proof site" or a "specific creation evidence" because this is not how most students encounter the data. Geology is experienced in the field, and it is there that flood geologists must provide the intellectual resources to grapple meaningfully with direct observations of rocks, fossils, and minerals. I have greatly benefited by talking with other Christians about the issues, but there is even more value in discussing the geology at outcrop.

Contemporary with these field geology interests are the issues: "Why has conventional geology got it so wrong?" and "Where and when did geology go wrong?" I am convinced that there are satisfying answers to these questions, but there is a need for Christians to rethink their philosophy of science. For too long, we have accepted a situation where science is autonomous: the Baconian approach. Most Christians in science seem to think that they are continuing a noble Christian tradition by continuing to give adherence to Baconian principles. There is a myth that science is value-free, and that it provides a level playing field for scientists from all sorts of cultural and religious backgrounds. I think this position is fundamentally flawed. Contemporary "science" has adopted naturalism as its rule for playing on the field, and is quick to dismiss non-naturalists as advocates of anti-science. By contrast, my vision is to see a Christian intellectual community, holding to the integration of all knowledge in Christ. Science cannot be autonomous: like everything else, science finds its true role when it is subject to Christ's lordship and is receptive to His Word.

The cultural issues that are of vital importance when rethinking science are relevant also to every other aspect of life. We all have cultural and sociological values that we imbibe from our parents, peers, and society. Some of these values will be Christian and will be helpful to us. Other values will derive from other sources and are likely to be unhealthy. My own experience is that the process of discovering and changing my personal culture and values is lengthy — actually lifelong. One of the lessons I learned early in my Christian life is that the new birth (regeneration) is an *act* of God's free grace, whereas conversion is a *process* led by God's Spirit within us, ever transforming us into the likeness of Christ.

I also learned early that conversion affects my *mind* as well as my *heart*. Jesus said that we are to love God with all our heart, soul, *mind*, and strength (Mark 12:30). Paul wrote about being transformed by the renewing of our *minds* (Rom. 12:2). Jesus commissioned His followers to go into all the world, making disciples — and a disciple is one who learns from his master and submits to his discipline. So, insofar as conversion is a lifelong experience, the renewing of our minds is also a lifelong experience. This has been my experience. Many of the beliefs and practices I acquired when I was first converted have had to change as I have come to see their social and cultural roots.

My approach to science is merely one major example of these changes.

Sometimes, changes in me have not been well received by other Christians. At other times, changes open new opportunities for fellowship. But whether a change is painful or positive in relation to fellow Christians, change is always exhilarating and liberating before God. Jesus said that the truth would make us free, and experiencing that freedom is something that I can testify to in my own step-by-step conversion.

Why am I a Christian? I first came to Christ when God opened my eyes to see Jesus Christ as the way, the truth, and the life. I then realized that God had revealed himself in history in an objective way, in the person of Jesus Christ and in the Scriptures. Since then, the Lord has led me through many experiences of change, and has taught me more about myself, more about others, and more about life. I include in these experiences the partnership of marriage, the blessings and challenges of parenthood, the varied demands of different jobs, and the physical and emotional changes of growing older.

My reasons for being a Christian today include all of my earlier reasons but they are now much enhanced. I've grown in the knowledge of myself and of the environment in which I live. I know a lot more about the evils of sin and about God's grace and wisdom. My confession today is nevertheless very similar to when I first believed: the Lord Jesus Christ is my Savior and Lord; He is the power and wisdom of God and the Light of the World.

DANNY R. FAULKNER

ASTRONOMY

Dr. Faulkner is professor of astronomy and physics at the University of South Carolina, Lancaster. He holds a B.S. in mathematics from Bob Jones University, an M.S. in physics from Clemson University, and an M.A. and Ph.D. both in astronomy from Indiana University. Dr. Faulkner's primary research interest is stellar astronomy and, in particular, binary stars. He has published 38 technical papers in the area of astronomy research.

I was born into a Christian family. In fact, for most of the years during which I grew up, my father was the pastor of a small church. I became a Christian at the age of six when I understood that I was a sinner and needed salvation through repentance and faith in the death and resurrection of Jesus Christ.

In my early teen years I came under the influence of some Christian writers who believed most of what modern science claims about the origin and history of the world. Seeing that science contradicted the traditional view of Genesis, these writers tended to re-interpret Genesis in light of what science says. As a result, my opinions began to move in this direction as well. However, in high school I encountered the writings of scientists who took the Bible very seriously. They took the opposite approach of interpreting science in light of the Bible. I very quickly saw the wisdom of this. I believe we should submit all areas of human endeavor to biblical scrutiny, not the other way around.

Perhaps one reason why I found this change of thinking so easy was that I was not yet immersed in general science as I am today. I suspect that many of the authors in this book were keenly interested in sciences of all types from an early age. Except for astronomy, I was not. I am often asked how and when I became interested in astronomy. I can honestly say that I cannot remember a time that I was not fascinated with the heavens. Before the age of four I can remember sitting on the front stoop of our house on warm evenings and looking up at the stars. I had many questions that my older friends (every bit of nine or ten years old!) were able to answer. I attended several different schools while in grade school. At each school I usually managed to read all of the books on astronomy in the library. I doubt that any of the libraries had more than two or three books on astronomy.

It was not until my second year of high school that I learned two things. The first was that one could actually make a living doing astronomy, and the second was that I was capable of doing this. It was also at this time that I became committed to biblical authority in all things. I made a decision to dedicate my life to become an astronomer to demonstrate God's creation to others.

So why do I believe in biblical creation? First, because this is what the Bible teaches. The Genesis account of creation gives us some detail of the manner in which God made our world and us. Creation is a foundational doctrine in that the first few chapters not only tell us how we came to be, but also lay the basis for other important facts, such as our accountability to our Creator, our sinful nature, and our need for salvation.

The second reason that I believe biblical creation is that I believe that it is a reasonable inference from science. Astronomy is singled out in Psalm 19 as something that should stir a realization within us that there is a Creator. This sentiment is echoed in the first chapter of Romans. I think that one of the things that attracted me to astronomy is the tremendous beauty and fantastic sizes of things that we see in the sky.

Modern instruments such as telescopes have enabled us to appreciate this even more. It is difficult for me to contemplate the universe without the conclusion that there must be a God. In my lifetime the space program has flourished. Space probes have unleashed a flood of images and data unimagined in early times. All of this amplifies the fact that the heavens do declare God's glory.

The space program has resulted in many missions to the planets that have shown us how unique the earth is. There are many factors about the earth that make it suitable for life. For instance, while water is relatively common in the universe, the earth is the only place that we are certain liquid water, which is essential for life, exists. Distance from the sun is critical, for we can see worlds that are too close (Venus) and worlds that are too far away (Mars). However, distance is not enough, because the moon, while the same distance from the sun as the earth, is hostile to life. A suitable planet must be of the correct size and composition as well.

A moon of the correct size is also important, because our moon stabilizes the axial tilt of the earth. If our moon were too small it could not do this, but if it were too large it would cause many other problems such as damaging daily tides. The earth has one of the largest moons for its size in the solar system. None of the other planets near the earth's size even has a moon of any appreciable size. Our moon also is the only major satellite of the solar system that orbits in the orbital plane of the host planet. This is important in the stabilization mentioned. Perhaps the purpose of the other planets in the solar system is to demonstrate how special the earth is.

In recent years many planets orbiting other stars have been found. The impetus for the search for these planets has been to show that planetary systems, including planets like the earth, are common. What is often lost in the excitement of these discoveries is that none of these planets is earth-like. Furthermore, they are foreign to everything we know about planets. Their sizes and orbits defy explanation. Just as the planets in our solar system demonstrated the uniqueness of the earth, perhaps these extra-solar planets may reveal the uniqueness of our solar system.

It is unlikely that there are many, if any, other earth-like planets in the universe. Even if there were many other planets suitable for life, that does not mean that life is common. I know enough of other sciences to understand that the possibility of the development of life through natural means is so remote as to be virtually impossible. Therefore, it is reasonable to conclude that life had an unnatural origin, that is, it was created. And that is why I believe in the supernatural God of the Bible.

MICHAEL J. LAWRENCE

INFORMATION SYSTEMS

Professor Lawrence is Emeritus Professor of Information Systems, School of Information Systems, Faculty of Commerce and Economics, University of New South Wales, Australia. He holds a B.E. with first class honors and a B.Sc. from the University of Sydney, and an M.S. in engineering and a Ph.D.in engineering (operations research), both from the University of California at Berkeley. Professor Lawrence is currently a director of the International Institute of Forecasters, which is the leading academic and professional body concerned with practice and research in forecasting. He also serves as associate editor for the International Journal of Forecasting, Managerial and Decision Economics, and Omega. Professor Lawrence has held visiting professor positions at Lancaster University, London Business School, and City University, London.

I have been a Christian since my youth and cannot remember a time when I did not claim to be a follower of Jesus Christ. I am not sure how I first came to accept this position, but I can think of many influences, both rough and smooth, which have played a vital part in my development.

I had a fairly difficult time at school, partly owing, I believe, to my Christian faith and my unwillingness to be pressured into taking part in actions I disagreed with. Although at the time the bullying I put up with was not pleasant, in retrospect I think it had the effect of toughening me morally and spiritually. (God does have a way of bringing blessings out of hardship.) Getting out of school and into Sydney University was like a breath of fresh air. Engineers seemed a civilized bunch in comparison to schoolboys, and there were many other Christians and the Evangelical Union for encouragement and support.

Another significant factor for me was starting a fellowship at our local church with my late brother James and a number of friends. This played an important role in my social and spiritual development. Over 30 of us would gather after church each Sunday evening to discuss aspects of our faith and our attempts to live it out. These were deeply formative times for me, which continued when I traveled to the University of California, Berkeley, to further my studies. They were happy years which led on to the blessings of marriage, a job, and children.

However, the path of faith has not always been without temptation to waver. I have many times been deeply challenged by some great event or wave of doubt which has forced me to re-evaluate my commitment and challenged me to rethink the purpose and end of human existence and whether all I have believed is fantasy or truth. Just as the Jews frequently recounted God's decisive role in their history, so at these times I have reminded myself of His hand in my life and in the history of the world — the historical certainty of the life, death, and resurrection of Jesus and the dynamic presence over many years in my life of the Holy Spirit.

One such event and demonstration of God's decisive role was associated with my coming to work for the University of New South Wales. When I completed my Ph.D. I decided to work in industry, not teach in a university. After eight years of quite rapid promotion, I was in a relatively senior position when suddenly my services were terminated. My first work crisis! After some months of unemployment with not much success in job applications, I decided to give academia a try. Working at the university has exceeded my expectations in every way — deep intellectual satisfaction, wonderful colleagues, and the freedom, unknown since my student days, to pursue ideas. How could I have been so seduced by money? It took a hard knock to wake me up and give me the courage to take a 50 percent pay cut. I have never regretted the change. The Lord does bless us richly even if it takes powerful prompting at times.

To be Christian impacts everything in life, not the least how one teaches and researches at university. A university is concerned with knowledge and truth. Since Jesus is the starting point of all truth, if we want to understand anything, we need to start with what we know of Him, the One through whom all the universe was created. The theories we adopt, and the way we understand the world, need to reflect the truth we have in Him. Some may feel this goes too far and smacks of "head-in-the-sand fundamentalism." I submit that the way any person reacts to a set of facts reflects his or her beliefs. For example, in my field of information systems, one person may see a highly efficient computer system (where efficient = many people replaced) and say, "Fantastic!" Another will be concerned about the de-skilling, the lost jobs, and whether the system does provide a sufficient quality of working life. Sadly, many Christians have for too long been afraid to stand up for the truth they have in Jesus and act on this knowledge. In my view, Christian faith has been increasingly relegated to the private life of the believer while many other "faiths" like right-wing free market capitalism or left-wing socialism, have been accepted as public truth. These "faiths" are each founded on a set of statements of faith and values which cannot be "proven" in any objective way.

Working in the area of information technology, I see my Christian faith impacting the attitude I adopt to the technology and its application. Computers inspire admiration, even worship, and have much in common with the carved gods of old. One sees examples of worship in rave reviews of new computer or software developments which promise a new heaven. Many people look to technology for a kind of salvation and meaning. The Internet is touted as putting humankind on the verge of a new age. But the growing signs in our world of chaos and fragmentation suggest that the technology is, in subtle ways, exacerbating the communication and relational problems at the heart of so much human suffering. I believe that technology can only distract us for a short while from our deep crisis of loss of hope — a loss which can be remedied only by the gospel.

EDWARD J. ANDERSON

APPLIED MATHEMATICS

*D*r. Anderson is professor of operations management at the Australian Graduate School of Management, University of New South Wales, Australia. He holds an M.A. with first class honors in mathematics from Trinity Hall, Cambridge, and a Ph.D. in control and management systems from the Department of Engineering at the University of Cambridge. Dr. Anderson taught at the University of Cambridge at both graduate and undergraduate levels in operations management and operations research from 1979 to 1995. He is a referee for many academic journals and has published two books and 52 papers in journals and refereed proceedings in the areas of applied mathematics and management.

I sometimes hear someone describing the occasion when he or she first decided to follow Christ. For me it is not so easy to recall a single day and say "that was the day I first believed." I was brought up as a Christian and I have gone to church regularly throughout my life. However, there was a time, while I was studying for my Ph.D. at Cambridge, which I look back on now as the period when my eyes were really opened.

Even before this I was convinced that Jesus was who He claimed to be, the Son of God. I believed that He had been raised from the dead. When I stood in church to recite the old words of the Apostles' Creed, I did so with a wholehearted belief.

But it was during this period, when I was 23 years old, that I began to trust in Jesus as my Savior in a much more personal way: someone who loves me and someone who can deal with my problems and failings. This was also the time when I began to be excited about the great truths of the gospel. And now, 23 years later, I still turn to Jesus in prayer, quite sure that He can be trusted, and I still get excited by what seems to me the astonishing way that God deals with the world.

As I look back, I can see I had an easy time at the small grammar school I went to in the UK. I managed to get top grades in mathematics, physics, and chemistry at A-level and was delighted to get a place to study mathematics at Cambridge. Cambridge was a very different world to the one I had grown up in. I remember arriving at college and being amazed at the way every student I met seemed incredibly accomplished and clever. I thoroughly enjoyed myself at Cambridge and I became firmly convinced that when it came to thinking things out, whether it was a complex problem of mathematical analysis or some question of free will versus determinism, then I was as intellectually well equipped as anyone.

At the time I thought of my faith as a bit like a construction. It was something that I had worked on over the years, fitting pieces together till I had ended up with a complete building. This building was a world view that enabled me to give some kind of answer to the difficult questions of life. These were the questions outside the range of scientific inquiry, like "What is the meaning of 'right' and 'wrong'?" But this faith was *my* construction. Others might be happy enough to take their faith ready-packaged from a Christian minister or leader, but I was not.

But then a new vicar arrived at the church I had started to attend. It was decided to start a weekly Bible study. This consisted of 15 to 20 people meeting for an hour or so, led by a theology student. We began by studying the first few chapters of Paul's letter to the Romans and I was greatly impressed by the way these studies were led. For the first time in my life I met someone with whom I could identify, and whose whole aim was to understand what the Bible was saying because he believed this was the truth.

In a sense, all my previous experience of reading the Bible or listening to sermons fell short of taking the Bible seriously.

The Bible might be a valuable source book — Jewish religious thought down the ages. It might be a book full of quotations that provided suitable material to hang a sermon on — "My text for today. . . ." But extraordinary as it now seems, I had not come across anyone who struck me as being driven by a desire to really understand what the Bible meant, in its own terms. (I must have met and listened to many such people before, but for some reason I did not notice at the time.)

Several things about these Bible studies were eye-opening. First, I found out the extent of my ignorance. I did not really understand even the meaning of the words in the Bible. Whatever I had previously understood by "righteousness," for example, was clearly not what Paul meant by the word when I came to look hard at his letter to the Romans. And even when I understood the words, I was a long way from understanding the message.

Second, I discovered that when you look hard at the Bible it does not disintegrate under close inspection. The Bible is a much more impressive book than I had given it credit for. As I studied it, I found it to be quite different from the book I thought I knew. I found the Bible to be far more subtle and sophisticated than I had thought, far more coherent and comprehensive than I had assumed. Up to then I had felt, somewhere at the back of my mind, that if I studied the Bible carefully I would end up disappointed. It was a huge relief to find I did not have to set aside my critical faculties when I came to read the Bible.

Third, in studying the Bible I found that its message, and the view of the world it contains, were much more satisfying than the faith I had constructed on my own account. Some of the pieces were the same, of course, but the beliefs I had before were a very stunted version of the real thing.

For many people a belief in the God of the Bible is like belief in Santa Claus — something that might be nice for the children, but we adults know better. There are others who, instead of pitying my gullibility, are a little envious. "I wish I could have your beliefs" is one of the most common remarks made to Christians. I think that people who say this view religious belief as a personal matter, perhaps like choosing the kind of clothing one wears. Though this may not be admitted, the implication is that beliefs are quite unconnected with any kind of reality. But for me, Christianity is nothing if it is not about the real world we all live in.

The training in science I received at school makes me look at the world with analytical and dissecting eyes, and this has an influence when I read about what Jesus did. I know that when water is turned into wine something must happen at the level of the physical molecules in the water. This is not an illusionist with a trick involving mirrors, so that it would all seem obvious if we just knew the secret. It can only be something truly extraordinary: God himself choosing to work powerfully in the world He created.

What is biblical Christianity? I could summarize it by saying that God, who made the world, planned from the beginning to deal with the rebellion of us, the people He made. The punishment that we deserved was instead inflicted on God's own Son, Jesus: He was executed as a criminal. And then God raised Jesus to life. This is certainly a surprising set of beliefs if presented to someone who has no knowledge of Christianity. In many ways Christianity goes counter to the views that seem to be most natural for people (for example, most people would assume that we need to be good to attain God's favor). But I do not think that the fundamentals of biblical Christianity are somehow harder to believe than any other religious system.

And if Christianity is true — if it is real rather than some postmodernist fable — then nothing else in the Bible seems so remarkable. Is it easy to believe that Jesus was the Son of God and yet His birth was quite ordinary? Is it easy to believe that Jesus was the Son of God and yet He did nothing for the desperately ill people in His society? Is it easy to believe that Jesus was the Son of God and yet His bones lie buried somewhere in Israel? Once I accept that Jesus is who He claims to be, then miracles are not hard to believe.

NOLA PASSMORE

PSYCHOLOGY

*D*r. *Passmore is a lecturer in psychology at the University of Southern Queensland (USQ), Australia. She holds a B.A. with honors and a Ph.D., both in psychology, from the University of Queensland. Dr. Passmore is a registered psychologist and taught psychology part-time at the University of Queensland and the Kelvin Grove College of Advanced Education before joining the faculty of USQ in 1989.*

In my years as an undergraduate student, I didn't give much thought to how my faith related to my studies. I was a Christian and believed in the God of the Bible and what He had done for me, but it didn't occur to me that the Bible actually had relevance for me in my future work as a psychologist. That all changed one day when a student came to see me about some problems she was having with her psychology units. I was doing my doctorate at that stage and was working as a part-time tutor in the psychology department. Her "problem" was that she was a Christian and found that some of the things she was learning in psychology conflicted with her faith. Someone had told her I would be able to help her. After all, I was a Christian tutor. Surely I had worked through the same issues. I am embarrassed to say I had not, and her dilemmas were something of a revelation to me.

Ever since then, I have been on a journey as a Christian in my profession, and God has shown me more and more that He is the only solution to the deepest human needs. By this, I do not mean to imply that there are no useful concepts or techniques in psychology. If I thought that, I would not have stayed in the profession for the last 20 years. Indeed, many people are helped significantly through psychological interventions. However, I believe that psychology can never totally meet a person's deepest needs. The heart cry of the human race is for meaning and purpose, a sense of belonging when human relationships fail to satisfy, a need to know we are unconditionally loved in spite of our circumstances, a need to know that we are not an accident of chance but people of design, a need to know that we have a future and a hope even when everything around us seems to be falling apart. I can teach you behavioral techniques to help you develop better social skills, I can teach you strategies to manage your stress, I can affirm you and tell you that you are a person of worth, I can challenge you to think rationally and negate your self-defeating thoughts. But I cannot satisfy the deep longings and needs of the heart that only God can fulfil. Until we realize this, psychology runs the risk of being nothing more than a band-aid that "patches us up," while ignoring the causes that make our wounds erupt.

To be fair, there are many psychologists who do dig below the surface and try to address the root causes of people's problems. However, if this is done purely from a humanist perspective, with no room for the God who created our very souls, then I believe we will continue to miss the mark.

Let me give some personal examples to illustrate why I hold so strongly to this belief.

For the last few years, I have been conducting research on issues facing adult adoptees, an interest sparked by my own experiences as an adopted person. While I realize that great care is needed when investigating anything of personal significance, I felt God leading me in this direction both for my own individual growth and for the help I could be to others. During a leave of absence from my lecturing job in 1995, I did a course called "Introduction to Biblical Counselling" with the international Christian organization Youth With A Mission. Since I had a Ph.D. in psychology and knew a lot about counseling theory, I was expecting that much of the course would be "old hat" to me. I soon became acutely aware that while I had a lot of head knowledge about the human condition, I had little heart knowledge that I could apply to my own life.

There was an emphasis on working through our own issues during the first few weeks of the program, while actual counseling techniques were taught in the latter half of the course. I vividly remember one day when we were encouraged to think about some homework exercises prior to the following day's lecture. With my pen poised, I opened my workbook and read the first question: "Who am I?" I would usually have rattled off dozens of things, yet I sat there and stared at the page for at least 15 minutes without writing a thing. What was happening to me? Why was this question affecting me like this? I'd certainly answered similar questions before. The difference was that I really felt God was putting His finger on a deeper issue.

It's hard for those who are not adopted to understand why identity issues are so critical for an adopted person. I grew up in a wonderful family that I would not trade for anything, yet who was I really? Who did I look like? Where did my gifts and abilities come from? What was my heritage? Why was I given up for adoption?

Not long after I finished that course, I began to search for my birth parents. Although I discovered that my birth mother had died about ten years previously, I was able to make contact with some of her family and subsequently went to England to meet them. They received me warmly and it was a wonderful time of learning something of my human heritage. Many of my questions were answered, though I had to come to terms with the fact that many other questions would never be answered in this life. As I continued to grapple with these issues, God clearly showed me that I was more than a product of biological and environmental determinants — the classic nature–nurture debate in psychology. He began to show me more and more of who I was in Him and who I could become. I am not an accident or mistake, but was designed by a loving Father who knew me intimately before I was even born. My true heritage is not of this world, but lies in my relationship with Him.

Psalm 139 has always been one of my favorites, but when I saw the translation of it in the Amplified Bible a few years ago, it became even more special to me. The Amplified Bible is a translation that brings out more of the original meaning of the words from the Hebrew and Greek texts. Verse 15 especially touched me:

> My frame was not hidden from You when I was being formed in secret [and] intricately *and* curiously wrought [as if embroidered with various colors] in the depths of the earth. . . .

Those words "embroidered in various colors" conjured up for me an image of God sitting in heaven deciding every intricate detail of what I would be like. I could almost see Him saying to himself, "I think I'll make this one with brown hair and blue eyes." The words "formed in secret" also took on special meaning for me. When I was born in 1961, it was generally considered a shameful thing to bear children outside of wedlock, and adoption was typically veiled in secrecy. My biological mother had kept my birth a secret from her family and friends, yet it was no secret to God. Verse 16 of Psalm 139 goes on:

> Your eyes saw my unformed substance, and in Your book all the days [of my life] were written before ever they took shape, when as yet there was none of them.

I hold nothing against my birth mother and never have. I'm sure she made the decision she thought best at the time. Sometimes I have been asked whether I wish I wasn't adopted, but an affirmative answer would mean I wouldn't have had the wonderful family and friends I have known throughout my life. How could I wish to change that? Indeed, I probably wouldn't have met my husband if my life had taken a different course. But I do know that God cared enough about that little newborn baby to place me with parents who would nurture me and ensure that I grew up to know Him. As it says in Psalm 71:6 (AMP), "Upon You have I leaned and relied from birth; You are He Who took me from my mother's womb and You have been my benefactor from that day. My praise is continually of You." I literally identify with that verse because of my adoption experience, but I believe it is true for everyone, even for those whose lives have been sad or difficult. Indeed, the Lord is close to the broken-hearted and comforts us in every distress. He created each of us to have an intimate relationship with Him. If we invite Christ into our lives, we have the promise that He will never leave us, no matter what our circumstances. He loves us so much more than we could ever imagine.

Earlier, I mentioned that I had been researching issues facing adult adoptees. This is still very much a work in progress, involving surveys of more than 200 adult adoptees. As I have read comments written by these adopted persons, I am convinced more than ever that we will never truly be free to be who we were created to be unless we seek our identity in Christ.

Many of the adoptees in our sample have had good experiences, but there are also many whose lives have been filled with sadness and despair. One man explained in very colorful language how his adoption experience had ruined his life. A middle-aged man candidly wrote that there were tears in his eyes even now as he recalled how he had found his birth mother, only to have her refuse further contact with him. Rejection is at the very heart of these problems. It's no use for someone to simply tell these people that they are worthwhile or lovable. At the core of their being they know that they *have* been rejected by the most significant person in their early experience. Only a relationship with Jesus Christ can heal those wounds. He too was rejected by His earthly family for a time, yet He knew who He was and willingly gave His life so we could know our Heavenly Father.

Although my research has focused on adoptees, I have also had contact with some birth mothers as a result of the project. I am still just learning about the myriad of issues that confront them, and I certainly do not wish to gloss over their pain. While some may have relinquished their children for other reasons, I believe most birth mothers thought they were doing the best thing at the time. Some may have wanted their children to have the advantages they knew they could not give them. Some may have been afraid of the ostracism they knew they would receive from a society that placed such a stigma on "illegitimate" children. Others were pressured, either directly or indirectly, to place their babies for adoption. Many have regretted their decisions, and in some cases have mourned that decision for the rest of their lives. They do not need platitudes. They do not need counselors and friends to tell them they did the right thing. They need someone to validate their feelings, to agree with them that they have made a mistake, and to encourage them to reach out for the forgiveness and peace of heart and mind that is always there for those who seek the Lord.

I experienced this firsthand when I was on a Christian counseling project some years ago. Our team had been running counseling seminars through churches and Youth With A Mission bases, and those who attended had the opportunity to also sign up for counseling sessions if they wished.

One of the team leaders and I were counseling a woman who seemed to have a variety of issues, one of the main ones being that she was divorced and her ex-husband had custody of their teenage children. She obviously loved her children, but it surprised me that she seemed to have a fairly fatalistic view of the situation and had not attempted to gain custody. Of course, we did not know her husband or the circumstances that had led to the divorce, but something just didn't sit right. Then in the middle of a whole jumble of different bits of information, she mentioned that she had given up a baby for adoption when she was 17. The comment was so casual. I can't remember the rest of the conversation, but it was almost as if she had said something like, "I ate toast this morning, I gave a baby up for adoption when I was 17, I'm going to the beach tomorrow." This was at a time when I had only just started to work through my own adoption issues and before I had read any material on the topic.

After several more minutes had passed, and with God's prompting, I finally asked her if she thought she was a bad mother because she had given up a child for adoption. She just looked at me and burst into tears. Some may say it was just intuition or a logical deduction, but in that moment I knew the Holy Spirit had given me a key that could help her. The fact that she had been "randomly" allocated to the counseling pair that included an adoptee was surely part of God's provision for her. Even if she had not told anyone about her feelings, God knew her pain. He was there when her child was conceived, He was there when she struggled with her decision to relinquish her baby, and He was here with her now wanting her to be healed.

We shared with her about God's forgiveness, and prayed with her as she wept on our shoulders. I'm not sure what happened to her after that, but I do know that God really touched her in that moment when she knew she had been forgiven. Such a moment is beyond the rational and part of the supernatural. It was not the product of a technique or a program, but of the living God working directly in the life of one of His children.

On the same counseling project, the women in our team were asked to lead a women's meeting at one of the local churches. We prayed together and felt God had given us direction regarding what He wanted us to do. One person would give some teaching, others would share brief testimonies of what God had done in their lives, and my part was to sing a song I had written called "Wounded Bird." I was not supposed to say anything, as the others would have already given the teaching and testimonies that provided the background for the song. As I moved to the microphone, however, I felt God prompting me to share the story behind it.

The inspiration for "Wounded Bird" had come from a photo I had seen in a *National Geographic* magazine some months before. The photo showed a beautiful little bird lying in a snowy field with mountains in the background. I was thinking what a lovely photo it was, and then I read the caption: "A wounded bird in the snow. It will probably die." I felt sad when I read that, but I remembered some teaching we had had on the wounded spirit and how God wants to release us from those wounds and bring healing. I told this story, still not knowing why God had prompted me to do so, and then I sang.

At the end of the meeting, a middle-aged woman came over to me and shared how much the song had meant to her. She had just returned from a memorial service for her 19-year-old son who had died in the snow several years before during a peacetime military exercise. None of the lyrics in the song refers to snow. If I had just sung it, she may well have liked it and perhaps even been moved by it. But it was the story of the wounded bird in the snow that really touched her as she thought of the parallels with her own dear son, left in the snow to die all those years ago.

God cared enough about that one woman to prompt me to tell a story that would minister to her. That woman's son had died while serving his country, but she received a personal touch from the God who gave His own beloved Son to die for our sins. If we believe in Him, we will not perish like a wounded bird in the snow, but will have everlasting life.

I am convinced that God is relevant for every human problem and that He intervenes directly in the lives of those who seek Him. He has surely given people the ability to reason, to explore the world He has created, to attain knowledge, and to ascertain truth. But any human philosophy or teaching that is incompatible with His eternal wisdom will surely fail. I am an academic, but I am first and foremost a child of the Most High God from whom all things come. I do not always "get it right." I struggle and have my down days from time to time. I often fall short of the mark God has set for me. And yet I know His grace is always sufficient for me and that He holds me in the palm of His hand.

He has embroidered me with His eternal colors and, with His help, I intend to live the life for which I was designed — a life of close fellowship with Him and a life that seeks to make Him known to a hurting world.

OLIVER ST. CLAIR HEADLEY

CHEMISTRY

The Honorable Dr. Headley is professor and former head of the Department of Chemistry, University of the West Indies (UWI), Cave Hill, Barbados. He holds a B.Sc. with honors in chemistry from the University of the West Indies, Mona, Jamaica, and a Ph.D. in inorganic chemistry from University College, London. He is currently director of the Center for Resource Management and Environmental Studies, UWI, Cave Hill, Barbados, serves as chairman of the National Commission on Sustainable Development and leads the Prime Minister's Millennial Project in Solar Energy. He has been awarded a number of prizes for his research, including the Guinness Award for Scientific Achievement in 1982 and the Pioneer Award from the World Renewable Energy Network in 1996. He was made a Companion of Honor of Barbados in 1996.

People have asked me how a senior scientist such as myself is a Bible-believing Christian. I hope that this essay will give some insight as to why I believe.

Many Christians like to look at the teachings of the Bible as components of a foundation for faith in God and His plan for our salvation from the consequences of sin. Foundations are constructed in a manner to ensure that the building does not move from its place on the earth. However, let us look at biblical teachings in a different manner. I suggest that the teachings of the Bible constitute the structural integrity of the Christian faith, which has to move with the times in a world where cultures are changing and knowledge is increasing rapidly.

When you take an airplane and fly to New York, as the plane takes off, where are its foundations? All the people on the plane are praying — there are no atheists on an aircraft at takeoff — that it flies to New York safely and it remains intact for the whole journey. We in physics and engineering say that we want it to retain its structural integrity. This is the key to the survival of a moving entity. Loss of structural integrity is usually disastrous in moving systems, and the Christian faith is a moving system in this fast-paced world.

Let us examine two cases. During an earthquake in Japan, the foundations of a 16-story building were destroyed, and lacking a good connection to the earth, it fell over on its face. But the structure of the building was sound — it had not lost its structural integrity — so they merely built a new foundation and jacked the building back onto it. Quite a different result happened with a similar building in Venezuela. Here the shaking left the foundations intact, but the vibration of the earthquake was near the natural frequency of the building and it behaved like a concertina. Floors telescoped and squashed the people living in the building. The foundations survived, but the building had lost its structural integrity, with disastrous results for its occupants. Now you understand why I am concerned about the structural integrity of the Christian faith.

Some Christians are trying to keep the Christian faith popular in the modern world and are willing to remove the Bible's more unpopular doctrines. By doing this they are compromising the structural integrity of the Christian faith. In fact, I believe they are doing what John the revelator forbids in Revelation 22: 18–9. They have forgotten that the Bible's doctrines form a self-consistent set and that John said that God would subtract from the Book of Life the name of anyone who subtracted anything from the set.

Some Christians want to be like the world, so people are saying, for example, that committing fornication or adultery is not so bad if the couple love each other. Even if some people argue that the original seventh commandment is in the Old Testament and may be a bit old-fashioned, Revelation, the last book of the Bible, is totally against all forms of sexual misconduct. In its 22 chapters, it condemns sexual impropriety about 20 times. This sin is clearly very bad news for anyone wanting to go to heaven — for example, Revelation 22:15 reads: "For without are dogs, and sorcerers, and whoremongers, and murderers, and idolaters, and whosoever loveth and maketh a lie." Another sin which the Lord particularly abhors is love of money. First Timothy 6:10 spells it out: "For the love of money is a root of all kinds of evil."

I believe these sins, sexual impurity and love of money, are two of the devil's best traps. They are as bad for serious Christians as mercury is for aircraft. Mercury and its compounds are *completely* banned from planes. This is because it removes the protective oxide film on aluminium alloys and exposes the metal to attack by atmospheric oxygen. I have shown my students what happens by taking an old aluminium saucepan and putting mercuric chloride into it. After less than a week, it turns into a pile of white powder — total loss of structural integrity.

Paul is also very explicit about what is bad for access to heaven. In Galatians 5:19–21, he lists the works of the flesh, which include such things as "adultery, fornication, uncleanness, lasciviousness, idolatry, witchcraft, hatred." He finishes by saying, "They which do such things shall not inherit the kingdom of God."

On the other hand, faith seems to be the principle that unifies the moral and physical laws of God. The faithful righteous are in harmony with *all* of God's laws, and He permits them to do things with His physical laws that an unrepentant sinner cannot aspire to. In other words, God's faithful are empowered to perform miracles. In Matthew 17:20, Jesus makes reference to the devout having enough faith to move mountains; this was when He chided His disciples for not being able to perform a miracle and cure the young man who was demon-possessed. Most people consider this to be allegorical, but I suspect it is the absolute truth. He means it when He says, "and nothing shall be impossible unto you." Verse 21 clinches it: "Howbeit this kind goeth not out but by prayer and fasting." The disciple has to be devout and morally pure. Look at Daniel and his three companions (Hananiah, Mishael, and Azariah, to give them their original names). These young men in Babylon were lion-proof and fire-proof.

One of the consequences of the success of modern science is that it has put a lot of emphasis on logic and mathematics. Unfortunately, mathematical logic and faith seem to be incompatible; mathematical logic dominates the physical parts of the universe, but the non-physical parts are the dominion of faith, love, confidence, trust, and similar entities which do not obey the rules of mathematical logic. Perhaps this is why some scientists, and physical scientists in particular, have trouble with these concepts; they cannot be made subject to rigorous mathematical proofs. However, non-physical entities such as confidence are essential for the survival of many of our social institutions; everyone knows what happens to a bank or a marriage when confidence disappears — it collapses, illustrating that mathematics and physics are not the sole criteria for stability.

As I look at the famines, the wars and fighting, the environmental degradation, and the deterioration of moral values in Western civilization, I suspect that the Lord is about to shut down this experiment of having humans looking after this beautiful planet. The signs that Jesus gave in Matthew chapter 24 are there: the same conditions that prevailed before Noah's flood. I believe we have to make sure we are ready to meet our Creator in the judgment, and that is why I choose to be a Bible-believing Christian.

JEREMY WALTER

MECHANICAL ENGINEERING

*D*r. *Walter is head of the Engineering Analysis and Design Department within the Energy Science and Power Systems Division at the Applied Research Laboratory (ARL) of Pennsylvania State University. He holds a B.S. in mechanical engineering with highest distinction, an M.S. in mechanical engineering and a Ph.D. in mechanical engineering, all from Pennsylvania State University. He was a 1975 recipient of a prestigious National Science Foundation Fellowship, funding graduate study at the institution of his choice. At ARL, Dr. Walter has been the leader of a number of undersea propulsion development projects for the U.S. Navy. His research involves multidisciplinary development and testing of advanced air-independent engines and thermal power systems for various autonomous undersea vehicles.*

In today's industrialized nations, believing in one supernatural God is often considered outdated and unenlightened. A strange paradox exists when scientific academia claims to accept only the natural and observable, while the popular media produces entertainment programming focusing on angels, unsolved mysteries, the occult, and other unnatural but sensational phenomena. It seems that anything supernatural that entertains, is sufficiently fantastic or is from another galaxy *but does not make moral demands* is politically acceptable, popular, and somehow more believable then the concept of a Creator God.

As a person trained in the scientific disciplines, I know the struggle of reconciling the things taught in schools with the concepts of the God of the Bible. But the more I have learned about the true facts of science, the teachings of the Bible, and what we know about history, the more convinced I am that there must be a God who supernaturally creates and sustains the life, order, and beauty of our world. In addition, the experiences of life have persuaded me that the Bible is God's inspired revelation of truth.

I believe each person must work out his or her convictions about what is true. But beware: if no absolute standard of truth exists, then we are left to invent for ourselves whatever concept of truth suits our fancy. For a time, I may like *my* freedom from God's rules, but I may not like *yours*!

In this essay I will explore some of the reasoning that underlies my own convictions of what is true — namely, that the God of the Bible is who He claims to be. For me, faith in what I cannot see is not contradictory to the things I do see, but combines objective evidence, the testimony recorded in the Scriptures, the testimony of other people, and my own experiences.

Objective Evidence (Does God Exist?)

As a young man, the inventions, machines, and accomplishments of humankind fascinated me. It seemed that science could accomplish nearly anything and I wanted to be a part of that endeavor. My older brothers tinkered with and built things ranging from electronics to canoes, giving me firsthand insight into how things can be made to work. I have natural abilities in mathematics and science that allowed me to pursue a career that applies physical laws to building advanced power systems. In designing components and systems, I have come to appreciate the predictability and dependability of the natural laws that govern our universe. The properties and behavior of matter in fact seem to be absolute in many respects, and we normally expect no intervention or suspension of natural laws. For example, the prediction of planet, moon, and spacecraft trajectories is only possible because of the dependability of natural laws. The moon is never seen suddenly flying across the night sky, even on Halloween!

However, as unchangeable as natural laws may seem, the development and application of these laws is based on the fundamental principle of cause and effect, which demands that any complex and intelligent effect have a cause that is of equal or greater complexity and intelligence. The more we learn about the complexity and interdependence of all living things, the more amazing the grand design seems to be. To suppose that random nuclear and chemical reactions produced the first complex organic compounds, followed somehow by the "forces of nature" selecting the most likely candidate molecules for the first living system, followed again by another mysterious starting of the first functioning life form, followed once more by the chance development of the amazing interdependence between flora, fauna, and earth systems . . . defies logic, mathematical probability, the laws of thermodynamics, and common sense. The case remains the same regardless of how much time and energy is available.

The only reasonable conclusion is that an infinite cause transcends the greatest aspects of the universe. The big bang will not do; the cause must be living and intelligent — it must be God! The unchangeable character of natural law tells us that God is no longer creating material systems, and that His character is also unchangeable.

Miracles are miracles because of the dependability of natural law. If gravity only sometimes worked, then a floating axe head or a man walking on water would not qualify as a miracle. If dead bodies often returned to life, then Jesus calling Lazarus from the grave would not be a miracle. If intelligent information were spontaneously generated, then prophecies that foretell the future or explain the distant past would not require supernatural inspiration. However, the existence of a Creator God makes the concept of miraculous intervention believable and even reasonable when He desires to reveal himself or accomplish His will.

Many people don't realize that the facts of science actually support the concept of a supernatural God. Assumptions and presuppositions that exclude the possibility of God are often underlying the popular conclusions about origins, and we are led to label as fact things that are actually tenets of a scientifically cloaked belief system. Consider that life has never been observed to arise from non-living matter, meaningful information only comes from an intelligent source, and the immaterial realities of consciousness, emotional feelings, and relationships extend the domain of reality past the mere material. Value and purpose imply intent on the part of a Creator. Feeble attempts of evolutionary materialism to find cause and utility fail when considering the beauty of a rose, the loyalty of a dog, and the tenderness of a mother. To me, these objective realities that surround us truly cry out for the existence of an infinite and loving God.

THE TESTIMONY OF SCRIPTURE (HAS GOD SPOKEN?)

Once convinced of at least the possibility of God's existence, the next level of awareness is found in God's revelation of himself. The collective writings of the Old and New Testaments in the Bible have the unique characteristic of being able to describe the distant past and foretell the future, a domain of knowledge inaccessible to mortal human beings. The early chapters of Genesis tell us things from the past that require someone who was there to reveal them to us. Earth history as revealed in Genesis steps through the original creation, the fall of the human race, the judgment of a great flood, the dispersal into language groups at the Tower of Babel, and the work of God in calling out a people for himself in order to provide restoration and salvation to humankind. This information provides a solid framework to answer life's three most important questions: Where did I come from? Why am I here? And where am I going?

Prophecy in the Old Testament reveals a characteristic impossible if written only by mortals. The messianic prophecies predict the birth of Christ with great precision with regard to place, mode (birth to a virgin), time in history, and family lineage. In addition, the Messiah's ability to heal the blind and the lame, the price of His betrayal, the kind of death He would suffer, and His burial in a rich man's tomb were all written about hundreds of years before they happened. These predictions were so precise that many doubted that the writings could have been written when they claimed to be until the discovery of the Dead Sea Scrolls. Now, only a person's personal desire to remain in control of his or her own life (or wilful ignorance) can resist the evidence that the Bible is true. The small number of minor textual discrepancies proves the rule that the Bible is trustworthy.

Perhaps even more important than the facts of history are the Bible's guidelines for life. By reading the Scriptures, I know the cause of suffering and death in the world. Rebellion against the Creator and His design resulted in a necessary separation from His infinite sustaining power, and the principle of decay was introduced. In order to avoid ruining my life, I need to recognize the rebellious nature in my own heart and seek to allow God to reshape me in a manner that conforms to His original design (confession and repentance!). I also learn that even though God would be justified in judging the world because of our rebellion, He chose to work to reconcile us to himself, at great cost. The irony is that I sometimes think serving God will cause *me* to give up too much! The opposite has proven to be true. God has blessed me with a wonderful family, faithful and loyal friends, important work to do, and an eternal hope for the future. My awareness of the source of all these things and my responsibilities toward them is built on my faith and obedience to the Scriptures. No other religious writings measure up to the standards of the Bible.

THE TESTIMONY OF OTHERS (IS ANYONE LISTENING?)

During the formative early years of life, close personal relationships have tremendous influence on our development. In my case, I was exposed from an early age to family and church members whose lives were conformed to the truths of the Bible. Numerous individuals gave testimony of amazing transformations in lifestyle, emotional stability, moral courage, joy, and hope.

Perhaps the most powerful of these testimonies to me has been the courageous and joyful facing of the aging process among devoted Christians who reach old age, such as my wife's parents and my own. Solomon warned as he closed the Book of Ecclesiastes that we should "remember also your Creator in the days of your youth, before the evil days come and the years draw near when you will say, 'I have no delight in them' " (Eccles. 12:1; NASB). This admonition applies as much to preparing for old age as it does to making our youth productive, and I am thankful for the privilege of having observed good examples of applying this truth.

Regardless of your profession, status in society, or wealth, you cannot escape the aging process or the specter of your exit from this life. The comfort of a peaceful relationship to God, loving family members, and realistic hope of life after death are rooted in belief in God and the truths of the Scriptures.

Although subjective, the supernatural nature of this comfort has become undeniable to me. It is impossible for me to think that a supernatural God is not involved, or that these things are merely psychological wishful thinking. Perhaps the apparent conversion of an individual at an evangelistic meeting could occasionally be the result of psychological manipulation and not truly the result of supernatural work of the Holy Spirit. But the perseverance and courage I have seen in numerous people approaching the end of life requires more. The knowledge and wisdom obtained by a life lived for God produce a maturity in spiritual things that is undeniable when life gets tough at the end. Many of us who claim the name of Christ fail to faithfully build that maturity, to our own hurt. But to those who do, it is truly a stronghold.

Although only one example among many, my father's final years were a particularly moving example to me. The Bible and theological books that he was reading during that time all contain personal notes of comfort and joyful anticipation of entering into God's kingdom. To him, his age and health were not denied, but faced realistically and usually courageously. What a marvelous testimony of God's work within the heart of a man! Not that my father was extraordinary; he was not. He just yielded to a God who desired to comfort him in spirit and truth.

Many others have endured great physical suffering, the untimely loss of a child or spouse, persecution, imprisonment, loss of property, or other trial with great courage. Some I have met in person, and some through the printed page, such as Job of the Bible. Underlying the endurance of all these saints is the solid foundation that Jesus spoke of at the end of the Sermon on the Mount: "Every one who hears these words of mine, and acts upon them, may be compared to the wise man, who built his house upon the rock. And the rain descended, and the floods came, and the winds blew, and burst against that house; and yet it did not fall, for it had been founded upon the rock"

(Matt. 7:44–25). Individual Christians may fail by stepping off the rock onto the shifting sands of our time, but the rock is still there and available!

MY OWN EXPERIENCE (TO WHOM AM I LISTENING?)

Our current age might be called the "experience" generation. Years ago, I saw "Been there; done that" painted on the boom of a navy ship's crane. It reminded me of listening to men in the workplace, where the conversations often followed the "my experience is better than your experience" line. In the American vernacular, I don't want to go there. The experiences we have, however great or mundane, can be accurately evaluated only when interpreted in light of God's revealed truth. What I intend to communicate here is that the trials of life can build an inner confidence in the foundation laid in the previous sections. The order of priority is critical for the foundation to be firm. Hebrews 11:6 states that "without faith it is impossible to please him, for he who comes to God must believe that He is, and that He is a rewarder of those who seek Him." We must first have confidence that God exists, and then listen to what He says with positive expectations.

In January of 1994, I was teaching through the Book of Genesis in our church adult Sunday school when our fourth child was born. As a class, we had learned that God created a perfect world, but humanity's rebellion had resulted in the Creator and sustainer allowing decay and death into His universe, as written in Genesis 3. The concepts of redemption and reconciliation are also introduced in the Book of Genesis. For believers, the Bible clearly teaches in Romans 8 that our bodies will be redeemed at the time of our glorification. But until then, the gradual loss of genetic information from generation to generation will decrease our adaptability, and increase the likelihood of errors as the systems of life degrade. Josiah was born that January with one extra chromosome, and all that theory took the form of my son who has very real Down's syndrome. As I was writing this paragraph, a six-year-old Josiah walked up smiling, hugged me, and said, "Good night, Daddy." He still has Down's syndrome, but Daddy has changed! God has used Josiah's genetic condition, combined with his older sister's diabetes, to teach in my heart what I had known in my mind: that physical or mental deficiencies do not remove the image of God from a man or woman. Josiah has a nearly infinite capacity to encourage and make others smile, and is as human as I am. I thank God that Josiah is in our family, and for the lessons I have learned.

However, I do not desire for Josiah to have Down's syndrome eternally, and neither does God. I know that from the Bible. The analogue for God as the Heavenly Father is also taught in the Bible. God loves us regardless of our faults (spiritual Down's syndrome, as it were), but He has no desire for the faults to be permanent. He has promised that one day all those who receive Him will be changed and will put on immortality (perfection restored!). That expectation of a miraculous hope for the future is made believable by the foundation of truth that undergirds my experience. Subjective experience alone is as changeable as the shifting sands of a seashore, but the Word of God can make all the experiences of life an opportunity to learn and grow.

Have I proven God exists? No. Do I believe there is reasonable evidence that a supernatural, prayer-answering God exists? Absolutely! Those who refuse to submit to God's standard of truth will receive or invent an alternative standard of truth and thereby be deceived to believe falsehood. Much postmodern "truth" is not truth at all!

I recently read a quote from the great British preacher C.H. Spurgeon: "Nothing is easier than doubting. A poorly educated person with mediocre abilities can raise more doubts than can be resolved by the cleverest men of science from all over the world."[38]

King David wrote, "The fool has said in his heart 'there is no God' " (Ps. 14:1). My advice is: don't be a fool!

FAITH

AND

EXPERIENCE

CHERYL E. PRAEGER

MATHEMATICS

*D*r. Praeger is professor of mathematics, University of Western Australia. She holds a B.Sc. with first class honors in mathematics from the
University of Queensland, an M.Sc. in mathematics from the University of
Queensland, an M.Sc. and D.Phil. both in mathematics from the University
of Oxford, and a D.Sc. from the University of Western Australia. Dr. Praeger
is joint editor-in-chief of the Journal of Algebraic Combinations and is currently a member of the editorial boards of seven other professional journals
in the area of mathematics. She has served as a member of the Prime
Minister's Science and Engineering Council and the Women in Science,
Engineering and Technology Advisory Committee to the Federal Minister
for Science. Dr. Praeger has published more than 180 research papers in
international mathematics journals and is a Fellow of the Australian Mathematical Society and the Australian Academy of Science. She was made a
Member of the Order of Australia in 1999.

On looking back on my life it seems to me that I have always believed in God. My childhood was spent in several country towns in Australia, as my father, who worked in a bank, was
transferred every few years. My parents attended a Protestant
church and their Christian commitment extended further than
weekly attendance at church services. For example, I remember
rather regularly listening to missionaries reporting on their expe-

riences, most usually in Africa. When my two younger brothers and I got tired we would go to sleep on blankets on the floor while the meetings continued.

I was a painfully shy child who found it difficult to speak with adults. I remember surprising myself by making a public decision to be a Christian at the age of 11 by responding to an invitation to walk to the front of the hall at an evangelistic meeting. Following that occasion I read many parts of the Bible. I wished for knowledge, and I read through the Books of Psalms and Proverbs. I found there much about wisdom, but no "permission" to ask God for knowledge. I began to pray for wisdom, thinking at the time that this was second best to knowledge. It took many years before I understood that wisdom is by far the more important.

My process of becoming a mathematician happened in stages. In my extended family I was the first of my generation to study at university. The only other member of my family to have had a university education before me was my father's eldest brother, an industrial chemist, who lived a thousand miles away. My studying at university was viewed with misgivings by one of my aunts. A major concern for her was whether I would remain a Christian in such an environment.

Life has brought a number of challenges to my religious faith, each requiring an active response. One such challenge occurred while I was a research student in England. It illustrates the major reason why I am a Christian: a personal experience of God's love and presence in my life.

Among my Christian friends there was debate about the role of the "gifts of the Spirit" for contemporary Christians. These gifts all related to a heightened awareness of God's presence in our lives. The Bible describes in particular two such gifts present in the early Christian church, sometimes called "baptism of the Spirit" and "speaking in tongues," and the issue we debated was whether these gifts were intended only for Christians in the first century or for Christians in every age. I found these discussions unsettling and personally challenging.

At the time I was making bi-monthly visits with a group from a London church to a "borstal," a prison for young men.

Through these visits and through letters I had regular contact with an inmate named Allan. At our first meeting, Allan told me of his frustration at being confined by prison walls which he could easily imagine scaling. The temptation to escape proved irresistible, and some months later Allan absconded briefly while on gardening duty outside the prison grounds. He was caught, but then followed an incident in which he broke into the matron's quarters. The punishment for this was a period of solitary confinement, something he found so intolerable that he slit his wrists, but not too badly.

At that point I was invited by the prison governor to make a special visit to the prison to see Allan. He was frustrated and angry, but not suicidal. At the next group visit to the prison, I was greatly concerned about him. By this stage in the debate about gifts of the Spirit, I was willing to accept whatever gifts God intended for me. I prayed in the local village church with one of the women in the church group and experienced something I find difficult to explain. I felt completely surrounded and filled by God's love. Several hours later in the prison, at Allan's request, I was able to speak easily about God's love for him with a clarity and understanding I had not known I possessed. I believe that this understanding was given to me that afternoon in the church so I could help Allan.

A major philosophical issue for me as a research mathematician is whether the mathematician's role is that of creator or discoverer. My belief is that all mathematical discoveries are just that: discoveries of part of the abstract mathematical reality that is integral to our universe. Sometimes new mathematical understanding is hard won after months of painstaking work with the results gradually unfolding. On other occasions, after equally many months of hard work on a problem, an unexpected flash of insight will bring the solution.

For me, the most significant example of the latter occurred in 1977, after I had been working for six years on a fundamental problem in my area of group theory. At the beginning of 1977 I decided to allow myself one more year of struggle with the problem before admitting defeat. After six months of immersing myself in the details of the mathematical structure I had made some progress with proving certain necessary preliminary results. However, the core strategy of the proof still eluded me. One night the inductive proof became clear in complete detail. I woke myself up sufficiently to write down some ideas at several stages during the night. In the morning I was able to piece together the full proof strategy, although writing out all the details took several weeks. I felt that this major theorem was a gift from God, a special insight into His mathematical universe.

In all my dealings with colleagues at my university and in the wider academic community I try to be in tune with God's Spirit within me in what I say and what I write. I feel thankful to God for the gifts I have been given and freely share these gifts with others.

JAY L. WILE

NUCLEAR CHEMISTRY

Dr. Wile, who is currently a private education consultant, served as assistant professor of chemistry, Ball State University. He holds a B.S. in chemistry magna cum laude and a Ph.D. in nuclear chemistry from the University of Rochester. Dr. Wile, who also served as assistant professor of chemistry at Indiana University, Bloomington, has published 25 research articles in the areas of nuclear physics and nuclear chemistry.

As I was growing up in Indiana, I went to public school. From the time I was in second grade, my teachers noticed that I had an aptitude for mathematics and science. As a result, they pointed me in that direction. I was given extra research projects to do, extra mathematics concepts to learn, and many, many extra books to read.

One lesson that seemed to repeat over and over again was that scientists do not believe in God. As I look back, I'm not exactly sure how this message was imparted to me, but it was, nevertheless, strongly imparted. Perhaps part of it was the fact that none of my schoolwork ever had anything to do with religion. Perhaps part of it was the fact that while my atheistic teachers were allowed to share their beliefs with me and were able to encourage me to believe likewise, my Christian teachers were not allowed to do so, because of the ever-present "separation of church and state" that has taken on such a nasty tone in the United States. Whatever the reason, the only religion I learned from my early scientific role models was atheism.

My parents were strong Christians and tried to encourage me to believe likewise. They forced me to go to church, but I had been so brainwashed by my early education that I simply shut my mind to any religion other than atheism. In the end, I figured that Christianity was good enough for those who didn't know any better, but for a scientist such as myself, religious nonsense was simply inexcusable.

When I finally reached high school, I was a full-fledged atheist. I was so proud and confident of my position that I actually led an atheist discussion group which met once a week after school. We read all of the great atheistic philosophers, from Russell to Nietzsche, and spent the rest of our time bashing religious people. One day, however, a friend of mine asked me to accompany her to a debate that was being sponsored by a Christian group called Campus Life. The debate was on the existence of God. I was very reluctant to go at first, but in the end, I decided that I might learn a few arguments from the atheist debater. I also had another motive, which I will discuss later. In the end, then, I went to the debate with her.

My first surprise was to find that both debaters were scientists. The atheist was a professor of biology while the Christian was a professor of physics, and both of them taught at very prestigious universities. I was, quite simply, in shock that a professor of physics could actually believe in Christianity. My education had made it clear that real scientists were all atheists! What was this professor of physics doing up there defending something as unscientific as Christianity?

I honestly don't remember many of the details concerning the debate. I can't even tell you who, in my mind, won. I only remember one exchange between the two sides. The atheist said that it was the scientist's job to try and reach a naturalistic explanation for the world around him. Everything that we can see, smell, hear, or touch had to be explained in terms of natural causes. Any reference to a supernatural being, in the end, was simply a cop-out: an admission of ignorance. The Christian, on the other hand, said that a scientist's job was to look at all of the facts in an unbiased way and draw the most logical conclusion based on those facts. He then looked out into the audience and said that he challenged anyone out there who claimed to be a rational person to investigate all of the facts. He was confident that anyone who looked at all of the facts would, in the end, believe in Christianity.

I never spoke to either of the debaters. I can't even remember their names. But I did take the professor of physics' challenge. All of my life, up to that point, I had only looked at the facts on one side of the issue: the atheist's side. In response to his challenge, I began to look at the facts on the other side of the issue as well. I read the works of Christians such as Josh McDowell, Henry Morris, Peter Stoner, and F.F. Bruce. I also studied other world religions, including Islam, Buddhism, and Hinduism. At the same time, I continued to read the works of atheists such as Steven Gould, Carl Sagan, and Peter Atkins. In short, I gathered up as many facts as possible on both sides of the issue.

In the end, the data were very clear. Although I had been taught all of my life that the only scientifically sound belief was atheism, I found that the science presented in the works of Morris pointed unmistakably towards the existence of God. Furthermore, the data in the works of McDowell, Stoner, and Bruce showed me that this God is clearly the God of the Old and New Testaments. The works of atheists and other religions had no solid arguments compared to these. I was truly amazed! The data really demonstrated to me that the most rational belief system was that of Christianity.

That's not quite the end of the story, however. Although my rational mind was clearly convinced, my emotions were still in control. After all, I had grown up a proud atheist. I had led atheist discussion groups. I had made fun of those "stupid" Christians! There was no way I could just admit I was wrong.

The Almighty, however, had a plan. Remember the "friend" who took me to the debate? Well, she was really more than a friend, at least in my eyes. I was head-over-heels in love with her. There was only one problem — she was not in love with me! Typical of young men that age, I decided that the whole reason she didn't love me was that she did not know me well enough. Thus, I decided to spend as much time as I could with her. That way, she would get to know me, and then she couldn't help but fall in love with me!

Well, she never did fall in love with me, but I did get to know her better. As I got to know her better, I found out something terrible. Her father beat her on a regular basis. When she finally confided in me about this, I was outraged. I felt helpless. She made me promise I would not go to the authorities. She made me promise not to confront her father. What was I to do?

One night, after a particularly bad beating, she called me and I took her over to my house for the evening. I was horrified by the bruises I saw. I honestly thought that the brute who had the audacity to call himself her "father" might have actually broken some bones. My rage grew and grew until I *had* to do something. Suddenly, everything became crystal clear. The solution was obvious.

I went to my dad's closet and got his gun. I knew where he hid the bullets. I began to load the clip. It was all so simple. I would go over to my friend's house and simply rid her of her problem once and for all. As I loaded the clip, a peace came over me. At first I thought it was due to the fact that soon, the brute responsible for destroying my love's life would be dead. However, as I continued to load the clip, a phrase started running through my mind: "Test me in this, says the Lord God Almighty." It came from a book that I had read a few days earlier. The book was a scholarly study of Judaism, and the author used that phrase while discussing the practice of giving money to the temple. The author was quoting the Old Testament (Mal. 3:10), and when I read that passage, I read it as a dispassionate scientist. Now, however, the passage seemed to be talking directly to me. It seemed to be saying to me that the Lord wanted me to test Him with the problem I was having.

Up to this point, I had only *studied* about God and Christianity. I had already come to the conclusion that Christianity was, by far, the most rational of all belief systems. However, I could not bring myself to allow that rational concept to become something real in my life. That night, I had the opportunity to do just that. I was suddenly struck with how stupid I was being. Here I was, this proud intellectual, honestly thinking I could just walk up to someone, shoot him, and that would fix everything!

I got down on my knees and prayed, probably the most honest prayer I have ever prayed. I said, "God, I know in my mind that You are real. I just don't know it in my heart. I will test You in this. Show me how powerless I am, and show me how powerful You are. Fix this problem, please." I then proceeded to empty the gun clip, return the bullets to their hiding place, and replace the gun in my dad's closet. Somehow, I had the assurance that everything would be okay.

The next day, my friend called in tears. I thought she had been beaten again. When she finally calmed down enough to talk to me, however, I found out that her tears were tears of joy! She told me that just a few hours before her father had apologized to her. It was the first time he had ever apologized for beating her. Then she told me why he had apologized.

It seems that after he had beaten her the previous night, he went out for a drive. He said that he drove for a long time, eventually finding himself on a lonely country road. He saw a tent surrounded by cars in a field alongside the road, and something told him to go inside. He did, and he found himself in an old-fashioned, Bible-thumping revival meeting. He said that he stayed for a moment, curious to see what had brought so many people out to this lonely area.

Soon the preacher got on stage. He told the audience that he had planned his whole sermon out, but that the Lord was telling him to talk about something else that night. He said the Lord told him to talk about child abuse and how it was one of the greatest evils in modern America. My friend's father realized that the message was intended for *him*. My friend told me that her father had just told her the story, and he said that he had promised God he would never beat her again. As far as I know, he kept his promise.

That was enough. All of my investigations had already led me to think that Christianity was the most rational belief system available, but God himself demonstrated that He is real. Had I not been convinced of the rationality of the Christian faith, I would have never prayed the prayer I prayed that night. However, until I prayed that prayer, I could not take what was in my head and place it in my heart. God asked me to put Him to the test, and I did. I still do so to this day, and He has never disappointed me.

JOSEPH MASTROPAOLO

AEROSPACE PHYSIOLOGY

Professor Mastropaolo is Emeritus Professor of Biomechanics and Exercise Physiology, California State University, Long Beach. He holds a B.S. from Brooklyn College, an M.S. from the University of Illinois and a Ph.D. in Exercise Science from the University of Iowa. He has published 20 research articles, 12 abstracts, three book chapters, a monograph and two textbooks. Professor Mastropaolo was awarded the Royal Aeronautical Society's Medal for Exercise Physiology for winning the Kremer Cross Channel Man Powered Flight Challenge in June 1979.

My earliest memory is of looking at a crucifix while experiencing excruciating pain. I was two years old and prone on my parents' bed, looking above the headboard as a physician eventually dug out of my buttock, after many tries, a broken hypodermic needle. That memory never faded and seemed to form a backdrop, a possibility, in my search for the meaning of life. As my mother told me many years later, I was close to death.

My first day at school was on Valentine's Day. I remember standing in awe at the classroom door, staring at the red hearts and mounting paper on everyone's busy desk as the new smell of white paste seemed to welcome me in. I had never been in a four-story building before or a classroom, and the cutting and pasting struck a fearful note because they might well be beyond my ability. So much was brand new in this place where so many different sorts of people lived so close together.

Every summer our family left the sweltering city and went to live in a simpler country house amidst unpaved roads, trees, fields, wildflowers, butterflies, birds, and brooks. I milked the cow and learned to make butter. The horse was the mightiest animal I'd ever seen or touched or fed. Yet it was the chickens that seemed strangest of all. They scratched the ground most of the day and laid eggs that could hatch to miniatures of themselves, tiny wings and all. I can remember being supine on a blueberry hill chewing a sweet stalk of redtop hay while watching the clouds make their animal shapes against a sunny blue sky. This was a time of taking inventory. The frogs were very different from the newts, and neither of them swam like the crayfish or the baby fish in the shallows of the creek. Plants were alive in a different pattern from animals, and the animals in water, in the air, and on land were each uniquely designed. And there seemed no end to the variety and the harmony within and among them. I wondered whether it was possible to understand what it all meant.

My parents were not churchgoers but they insisted that I go and stay for Sunday school. The gist there was that God created everything according to a plan wise beyond complete understanding. That made sense. He was the origin of life. To find the meaning of life, one needed to study to understand, then harmonize with, God's wisdom. It worked well because the more I studied, the more I admired the harmony of God's handiwork.

The jolt came in high school with my first class in biology, a favorite subject. There, staring back at me from my textbook, were the monkeys, apes, and cavemen that "evolved" in stages to modern humans. The story was that there was no plan, no wisdom, no handiwork. The implication was that the God story was only a story and the real truth was what science had discovered, the same science of automobiles, of skyscrapers, of aeroplanes, of enormous ships.

I could see science making inanimate things with huge girders, but I could not see science make any living thing. My friends became atheists, but I held out as an agnostic. I was not sure and wished to study the matter. There was no rush.

My friends studied hard, found good jobs, bought clothes of the latest fashion, then bought cars. Those things put one in the right social circles where the attractive people played, and that was happiness. So I did likewise and kept expecting an inner feeling of peace and joy just around the next corner. At the ripe old age of 16, I was a freshman in college smoking a cigarette or the right blend of aromatic tobacco in the right kind of joe-college pipe while sporting my varsity team sweater. Girls I did not know smiled and said, "Hi." I had arrived. I had it all. My friends confirmed it. Yet I felt miserable.

World War II was on and I went into the army. There was no one I knew and my new buddies came from parts of the country only vaguely familiar from geography class. Discipline required training in uniform with a variety of weapons to kill efficiently the opposition in the enemy's army. Excellence with weapons and physical fitness seemed the foundation for survival, the new meaning of life. Proof that you would be an asset in battle, not a liability, was paramount.

Then, smaller things were added. Smoking a cigar was considered manly, so I took to smoking cigars. After giving it a fair trial, I thought it was as stupid as the pipe and cigarette. There was no benefit, no pleasure that I could tell, aside from the manly aura. The other manly activity was drinking whiskey. Whoever put away the most whiskey with the least loss of faculties, or partially digested food, was considered toughest. Early unconsciousness was considered a frailty, and the challenge was to engage in drinking contests with the tough drill sergeants. My arrival was heralded by drinking one of the toughest sergeants to the point of dry heaves while helping him back to the barracks. Once again, I had arrived. Once again, I thought the ritual stupid. And once again, I felt that there must be a greater dimension to life.

After army days, a return to college seemed the most logical thing to do. With a bachelor's degree one could earn more money, have a larger wardrobe, a better car, and a greater chance for happiness. After achieving those things, the happiness did not appear. A master's degree was touted as the place where it would happen. Well, it didn't, so I tried a doctorate, then a post-doctoral research fellowship and obtained better jobs than I had ever imagined. The material benefits were so remarkable that they hatched something new: they became a burden. Striving beyond that point seemed as senseless as the insult to the body of smoking or the insult to the brain of drinking. What was supposed to bring happiness was actually diminishing life.

From elementary school through to graduation from college, we were told about the missing link. It was the ape-man peering at us from the biology book. It was the term of derision used on the playground for any mesomorphic bully. It was what convinced my friends to become atheists and convinced me to become an agnostic. The most famous ape-man was the "Piltdown Man," *Eoanthropus dawsoni*, the dawn man discovered by Dawson. Five books were written on this crude forgery constructed by fitting the jaw of an orangutan to the skull of a man.

The orangutan's teeth were abraded artificially to resemble human flat wear, and chemical analysis revealed the skull and jaw had been stained the same brown color using chromium and acid iron sulfate, with neither chromium nor sulfate occurring in the locality of the dig. It was so transparent a fraud that it had to be guarded from skeptics for 40 years in the British Natural History Museum. For 40 years, the world was led to believe that the missing link between apes and man had been found.

Another ape-man, the "Nebraska Man," *Hesperopithecus harold cookii*, this time associated with the American Museum of Natural History, was concocted from a single tooth from a wild pig. The ape-men were frauds, but they converted hundreds of my classmates to amoral atheism as if they were true. We blindly believed our teachers and textbooks and had our lives ruined with great efficiency nonetheless.

Still in the high school and university biology textbooks, another mainstay of evolution is the "biogenetic law," by the confessed forger Ernst Haeckel. His forged embryo data made it appear that human embryological development repeated evolutionary history. This has been known for more than 130 years. It rivals the ape-men at ruining lives, and biology textbook writers are so morally incompetent they refuse to expunge Haeckel even when they see his work documented in the journal *Science* as "one of the most famous fakes in biology."

I believe that the statement "life arose in the ancient seas" is as probable as blue fairies like the one that animated Pinocchio. In my opinion, witch doctors are more scientific than the evolutionists who write the biology textbooks, and it may even be that witch doctors do humanity less harm overall.

From my earliest memory, my public school biology education must be the greatest betrayal of my life. I feel ever so strongly that every lie and betrayal of my life, or anyone known to me, cannot begin to compare with the lies, betrayals, and ruined lives caused by the teachings of my public school evolutionist biology teachers.

I have also performed experiments outside the field of biology. The memory of one that won't go away concerned a single one dollar bill. At a coffee and doughnuts gathering, I was collecting the money for the doughnuts. A lady arrived with two small children. "Three doughnuts," she requested. I said, "Seventy-five cents." She opened her purse and exclaimed that she had forgotten her wallet. Without thinking (for there are times when deliberations hinder) I took out a dollar bill and handed it to her. She handed it back and I gave her 25 cents change. A few minutes later she handed me the remaining 25 cents back for two soft drinks for the children and I gave her five cents change. The puzzle, or perhaps mystery, is why on earth anything as trivial as that would be at all memorable? Why should that have given me the feeling of joy which the spending of hundreds of thousands of dollars never gave? Why should that have the power to dissolve the many betrayals and lies that no amount of rationalization could? Why?

The answer can't be found in any textbook. It is in the completely different kind of book that can't tell lies, the book I was tricked from studying a long time ago. The One who said it would happen, the way it would happen, I saw for the first time when I was two years old, close to death. He is the truth and the way. He saves lives compassionately and abundantly. He now has my allegiance every minute of every day. He is now, and forever shall be, my commander in chief. He is the origin and the meaning of life.

SUSANNE KOLARE

MEDICAL RESEARCH

*D*r. Kolare is lecturing in cell biology and histology, Department of Neuroscience in the Faculty of Medicine at the Karolinska Institute in Sweden. She holds a D.D.S. from the Faculty of Odontology and a Ph.D. in immunobiology from the Faculty of Medicine at the Karolinska Institute. Dr. Kolare has served as course director in the Department of Humanities, Informatics and Social Sciences within the Faculty of Medicine and has published 22 research papers and abstracts.

It seems to me like I have always been going to school, either as a student or as a teacher. If I count the years I have spent in academic institutions, they add up to 20. During the first 11 years I was the normal, nice, caring Swedish person, intellectually good, wanting good for others and working for the benefit of others. I was walking the path in life which others had walked before me, having them as my guiding light and wanting to contribute to society with the talents I had. At the same time I was really searching for the truth, both in science and in my private life; the truth about myself, what kind of personality I had, and the truth about life.

Ten years ago, as a post-doctoral fellow with new, exciting, ongoing research and a private dental practice, I had, materialistically speaking, everything I could wish for. I had many friends.

I felt emotionally happy as long as I could give to others. But deep inside I was empty. I was crying for a love that only God could give to me — but at that time I did not understand it. I prayed to God at bedtime for comfort, as my grandmother had taught me, but I did not fully realize to *whom* I was praying.

On January 3, 1991, I was walking along in downtown Stockholm. I was going to get a haircut and while waiting for it I had glanced through a horoscope and read the weekly message for Pisces. That message is still in my mind: "You will meet a religious person who will greatly influence your life." Following the haircut, I lit a cigarette and started to walk home. About ten minutes later I was stopped by two very polite, nicely dressed ladies who wondered if I would like to come to a Bible study discussion group. They were almost surprised when I answered, "Yes, I would like to." The invitation was for a meeting a couple of days ahead, but since I worked as a dentist two afternoons per week, that particular night was already booked. I told them I would come the following Thursday. During the next week three of my patients needed appointments because of acute problems and the only free time I had was Thursday night. I remember the battle inside me — I had promised to go to the Bible study but felt I could not since my patients were my sole responsibility. On Wednesday night I called Harriet, one of the ladies I had met, to tell her I could not come, but there was no answer on her phone. Thursday came and to my surprise all three patients called and cancelled their appointments. I could finally go to the Bible study.

This was my first real conscious encounter with God — a powerful, loving God who could rearrange my everyday life and even cancel appointments to meet the needs of my heart; a caring personal God who wanted so much to reach me that He would use my habit of reading horoscopes. When I arrived at the Bible study, the atmosphere was very warm and it totally felt like coming home.

From that point I started to fully understand that God was reaching out for me. As Jesus said, "No one can come to me unless the Father has enabled him" (John 6:65; NIV), and I was baptized into the body of Christ seven weeks later. Thanks to the prayers of others I was also able to stop smoking 10 days before my baptism, breaking a habit I had had for more than 20 years.

Since I was baptized as an adult in the middle of my career, with a more than full agenda, my whole life needed to be rearranged to give room for new friends and for quiet times with God. God started to change me slowly but steadily. I temporarily needed to leave close relationships to friends and family since they did not bring me closer to God. I left my dental practice and finally my position at the dental school. It was then (about four years ago), when I was totally alone and undistracted by my working life, that I started to be lifted up by God's love and to be secure in the fact that His good power was in control of my life (see Mark 10:29–30). My academic life is now slowly returning to me, and in an excellent way. I am now lecturing in cell biology and histology to a variety of students and I have also been directing a course in humanistic medicine. There is a huge difference in the quality of my life. I have learned to be persistent in trusting God and to never quit. And I have learned instead to wait for the actions of God to appear and to always strive for excellence.

WERNER GITT

INFORMATION SCIENCE

Dr. Gitt is a director and professor at the German Federal Institute of Physics and Technology, Germany, and serves as the head of the Department of Information Technology. He holds a diploma in engineering from the Technical University of Hannover and a doctorate in engineering summa cum laude, together with Borchers Medal, from the Technical University of Aachen. Dr. Gitt has published more than 50 research papers covering the fields of information science, numerical mathematics, and control engineering.

The purpose of the following recounting from my personal experience is to show how the Lord found me through Jesus Christ, and how He has worked in my life ever since.

CHILDHOOD AND ADOLESCENCE

I was born on February 22, 1937, on my parents' farm in Raineck/Ebenrode, East Prussia (this was the easternmost province of pre-World War II Germany). Until our flight as refugees, I had a happy and untroubled childhood in this peaceful rural environment.

In October 1944, when I was seven and had just started my second year at school, the Russian army was advancing relentlessly westwards. We fled with our horse and carriage from Raineck to Peterswalde (southern East Prussia). The news of the

153

imminent Russian invasion of that region reached us in January 1945, far too late. The curt official announcement was bound to cause panic: "Save yourselves, those who can." Since I was ill with a high fever, they just carried my bed from the living room and loaded me onto the refugee wagon.

Once more, a trek by horse and carriage commenced in haste, but we were soon stopped by the Russians. My brother Fritz, then 15 years old, was abducted. He never returned. My mother was deported to the Ukraine not long afterwards, and died soon after. The fellow captive in whose arms she died returned to Germany (Schwerin) several years later, and told us that my mother's last words were, "What will become of my little Werner now?"

Two of my aunts, my cousin Rena, my grandfather, and I were expelled by the Poles in November 1945. My grandfather died of exposure after a night without shelter, even before the ten-day trip from Osterode/East Prussia got under way. This forced departure from our homeland was under appalling conditions, in cattle-train wagons without any provisions. After a stopover, we reached our involuntary destination, the town of Wyk on the North Sea island of Fohr.

My father was a prisoner-of-war in France and knew nothing of his family's fate. Unlike his fellow prisoners, he could not make use of the monthly distribution of sheets of writing paper to write to his family; virtually all our relatives had fled East Prussia, and he did not know their new whereabouts. One night at camp, he dreamt about a distant relative who had lived in the Rhineland before the war. In this dream they talked for the first time in years. As they parted, the relative said, "Hermann, do come and visit me." My father answered in his dream, "But where do you live? I don't know your address." The relative replied, "Bochum, Dorstener Street 134a." My father woke up, lit a candle in the middle of the night, and wrote down the address revealed to him in the dream. He told this strange dream to his friends in the dormitory. They laughed at him when he took it so seriously as to say that he would write the following day. But the reply he received confirmed this address to be absolutely correct, and through this distant uncle my father was able to contact my Aunt Lina in Wyk.

The news of my father's survival filled me with joy. I could scarcely believe that I was no longer an orphan but had a father again. My father returned from French captivity in 1947, and found me to be the sole survivor of his missing family.

His search for work led us to a farm in Niedersachsen (Lower Saxony). What stands out in my mind about that time is that some boys from the village invited me to a children's hour. I could not imagine what a children's hour might be and thought they would tell fairy tales. So I went along and experienced the first of many hours spent in the only room of the community nursing sister who worked in that village. With great charisma, Sister Erna told us Bible stories every Sunday morning. She prayed and sang lots of joyful songs of faith. Before the first hour had passed, I knew that this had nothing to do with fairy tales. Touched in a very personal way by the message, I began to attend these meetings regularly.

My father remarried the following year and I soon moved in with his new wife in the nearby village of Jeetzel, while my father worked on the land several villages farther on. My stepmother became very fond of me. She had to work hard as a seamstress for the local farmers, struggling to make do with the little she could earn in addition to free board. She was a religious person, but she never tried to persuade me to convert to her particular religion during this susceptible age, and I still think highly of her for that. I continued to go to the children's hour regularly, come rain or shine. The faithful ministry of Sister Erna sowed the seed of God's Word, which would later germinate in my heart.

When my father found a job in industry in Westphalia in 1950, we moved to Hohenlimburg. Unfortunately, I was not to find such faith-encouraging fellowship — in fact, quite the opposite. The religious instruction in school had such a liberal, Bible-critical orientation that it caused me to look back on the children's hour and think, *A pity that those Bible stories which Sister Erna told us are not true after all.* But the smoldering wick, the yearning for truth, was never completely extinguished. The occasional church attendance was no help in my search for God, either. The sermons were usually very non-committal and did not call people to a change of heart.

I finished my degree in Hannover, and after doing my Ph.D. in Aachen, I started as head of what is now information technology at the Federal Institute of Physics and Technology in Brunswick (Braunschweig) in October 1971. My situation then can be summed up as follows: I had been successful professionally. I had passed the degree examination in two specialized fields effortlessly with credit, and my doctorate with distinction; I also received the Borchers Medal from the University of Aachen. I was immediately offered a leading position as a scientist. In 1966 I got married. We had two children and were a happy family. We were well off all around, without any family problems; we were all healthy and had no money worries. One might have thought we had no need for God in our lives. I stress this because I often hear testimonies of people who only opened up to the gospel because of a particular personal problem. This was not so in my case, since God's ways with the individual are as diverse as there are people on this earth.

In the autumn of 1972 my wife and I attended two series of evangelistic meetings in Brunswick that were somewhat different from each other. A small Christian group was responsible for one set of meetings, at the secondary school in our neighborhood. They handed out a Bible and a red pen to every visitor, an insightful approach which meant that core Bible passages were carefully worked through with the audience and simultaneously underlined in color. On completion of this unusual but very effective week of preaching, we could keep the Bibles. Thus, my wife and I both had our own identical Bible and when reading, we often came across the passages marked in red, a reminder of the teaching we had received.

The other campaign took place shortly afterwards. Every day approximately 2,000 people came to the City Hall in Brunswick. The center point of each day was the preaching — thematically structured messages which each unequivocally pointed to the need for a decision. The call to faith, the invitation to commit one's life to Jesus Christ, issued forth clearly each night. One night Canadian evangelist Leo Janz spoke on Luke 17:33–36.

He called for the decision which God has placed in our hands: to be saved or lost, heaven or hell, a life with God or one without. My wife and I followed the invitation to come forward, in order to seal the decision in a prayer.

Subsequently, I spent a lot of time in intensive study of the Bible. I was astonished at the number and variety of the themes it contained. I found in it answers to many questions that were of burning interest to me. Who was the actual author of the Bible? How did this world come about, and how will it end? Who am I? What is the deeper meaning of life? What will happen after death? The more I read the Bible, the more it became clear to me — this is God speaking to me and answering all my questions. I came to the important realization that the Bible is God's Word in its entirety and carries the absolute seal of truth. This proved to be a stable foundation, rock solid in all situations of life and thought. Not only did I regain the simple trust in God's Word which I had known in the children's meetings, but I was so convinced of it that I was now ready to pass this on to others. At first I did this by leading Bible studies within the church fellowship which we had in the meantime found, as well as giving some talks now and then.

In this way I came to know Jesus as the Christ, the Son of God, the Savior who rescued me from my lost state. He, who had been from eternity, came from God the Father, became man and saved us in accordance with a plan which no intellect could have thought up. It became very significant to me that God, through this same Jesus, created the entire universe, including this earth and all life on it. I repeatedly read that in the New Testament: "Through him [the Word, that is, Jesus] all things were made; without him nothing was made that has been made" (John 1:3; NIV). Not only were all things made through Him but also for Him, as the goal and purpose of creation (Col. 1:16).

For me, this is one of the most sublime of thoughts: the Creator and the man on the cross are one and the same! What caused this Lord of lords and King of all kings to go to the cross for me? John 3:16 gives me the answer, though my mind cannot plumb its depths. It is His infinite love which did everything for me so that I would not be eternally lost.

One set of issues in the Bible always fascinated me, and that was the link between the Scriptures and scientific questions. Was the Bible only reliable in matters of faith, or could it also be trusted in areas of rational inquiry?

It was a very special experience for me to realize that the Bible gives us fundamental information which enables us to do well-founded science. It became clear why all atheistic systems of thought led to error. The Bible became for me an indispensable yardstick for evaluating and judging philosophical systems. I now saw well-known statements by poets, thinkers, and scientists in an entirely new light. The Bible was now also an important yardstick by which I could evaluate the many religious systems.

From the vantage point of my own discipline, information science, I was aware that information was not a material substance or quantity but, rather, a mental one. Information arises only from a creative thought process, that is, through the application of intelligence and knowledge, never in chance systems of matter and energy. In this world, the highest information density is found in the cells of living things. The logical consequence of this became ever clearer for me — this information, too, requires an intelligent source to explain its origin. This fitted very well with the biblical account in Genesis.

It was not long after my conversion to Jesus Christ that I began to be invited to give talks here and there about the relationship of science and faith. I did this very willingly, because I had in the interim already read much and thought extensively on the subject. Eventually this led to the writing of books. If someone had told me in my younger years that I would one day be the writer of books, I would have found that inconceivable. In my school days I would rather have taken ten math tests than write one essay. But my scientific work changed that. Because of my research in the realm of information, I was able to formulate a number of scientific laws about information. This "Natural Law Information Theory" was presented at numerous universities, both in Germany and in many other parts of the world, as well as at scientific conferences.

After such lectures, I was often asked if the content was available in written form. This led to me writing books in addition to the lectures.

In the course of time, I took up various areas of inquiry which kept coming up after lectures, and which seemed important to me. I have developed these thoughts progressively through a series of paperback books. The fact that what the Bible says can always be trusted is expounded in depth in *So steht's geschrieben [It is written]*. The book *Questions I Have Always Wanted to Ask* has had a particularly wide distribution, having reached half a million copies in its 16th printing in Germany, as well as appearing in 15 other languages.

The paperback *If Animals Could Talk* takes a light-hearted and conversational, though scientifically based, approach to creation issues. The many ingenious design features of the animal kingdom are not only able to elicit amazement but can also lead to faith.

The common question as to whether the many religions offer alternative paths to salvation, apart from the gospel, is extensively analyzed from the standpoint of the Bible in the book *What About the Other Religions?*

As I am told again and again, there is a high reader demand for books that relate scientific facts to the message of the Bible. I would say that this has now become the main focus of my writing. The paperbacks *Stars and Their Purpose — Signposts in Space?*, *In the Beginning Was Information*, and the colorful illustrated hardcover *The Wonder of Man* all fall into this category. These works deal with scientific material on the basis of complete trust in the Bible, and call for faith in Jesus Christ with clear evangelistic passages.

As a result of a telephone call from a stranger in 1990, a completely different field of work opened up to me. This person explained that he was born, and had studied, in the Soviet Union. Dr. Harry Tröster is German, but speaks and writes excellent Russian. He said, "I've read some of your books. Could you see us traveling together to the former Soviet Union and holding similar lectures there? I would translate your talks into Russian." After thinking it over for a time, I agreed. Since that time, we have given many lectures in Russia, Kazakhstan, Kirghizia, and

Lithuania. Because several of the books have been published in Russian, for each tour large numbers of these, as well as Bibles and children's books, have been trucked to our destinations in advance.

Looking back, I am astonished at how a scientist could become an author of Christian books and a lecturer on biblical topics without having wanted or anticipated this in the slightest. When I try to explain God's leading of my life, an expression of the theologian Heinrich Kemner takes on a personal significance for me: "We do not push, we are pushed." That's how God does it — He puts us in particular situations. When a door opens, one should walk through it, because only that which God has prepared rests under His blessing.

DARLENE E. McCOWN

NURSING

*D*r. McCown is professor and director of health services, Roberts Wesleyan College, Rochester, New York. She holds a B.S. cum laude in nursing from Seattle Pacific University, a B.S.N. and an M.N. in nursing from the University of Washington, Seattle, and a Ph.D. in human development and family studies from Oregon State University. Over a nursing education career which has spanned more than 30 years, Dr. McCown has held academic positions at a number of universities, including Virginia Commonwealth University, Seattle Pacific University, Oregon Health Sciences University School of Nursing, and the University of Rochester, where for several years she served as associate dean of academic affairs in the School of Nursing. Dr. McCown is the author or co-author of 27 research articles and book chapters and is listed in Who's Who in American Nursing.

During the summer polio epidemic of 1951 my closest cousin was stricken with paralytic polio, the dreaded disease. After a year in the children's hospital, forever paralyzed in both legs, she came back home. She often visited my family and stayed overnight with us. On one of those visits, she told me she had asked Jesus to forgive her sins and to live in her heart. At that moment, as an eight-year-old child, I closed my eyes and prayed for Jesus to come into my heart, too. For more than 50 years, that experience has been nourished and reinforced by God's loving and sustaining presence in my life.

LIFE EXPERIENCES

God gifted my life with wise and loving parents and extended family. I can never remember sensing any attitude of disapproval from my parents. They encouraged and assisted me to develop in all areas of life — social, artistic, physical, intellectual, and spiritual. In my early teens, I spent part of my summers on a small island in British Columbia living with my grandmother and cousins and helping at a Christian mission home base camp. During those summer experiences, I lived with men and women whose lives were devoted to God's call to help others and show God's love. I saw Christianity give hope and change the lives of the people the missionaries served.

Also as a young person, my parents gave me the freedom to make choices and to follow my dreams. They approved of my choice of a husband and loved and accepted him into the family as a son. His life and personal and professional dedication to God have been a blessing to me over our almost 40 years of marriage.

One of my life dreams was to go to college and become a professional nurse — the first in the family. While in high school at age 17, I got a job working as a nurse's aide in a nursing home. In my second week of work, one of my elderly patients died after a long illness. I was awed by the peace and simplicity of her death and by the stark reality of the passage from life to death. It was a spiritual moment for me when I witnessed the departing of the life spirit of my patient and recognized that the essence of her life had departed and only her physical body remained. Because of that first positive experience with death and my belief in God and heaven, I have never been uncomfortable with death. My career has focused on the area of grief, loss, and death. I have worked with many families facing the loss of a loved one. Again and again, I have seen the power and mercy of God to give love, strength, and comfort to families when a member is ill and dying.

I have witnessed the healing touch of God in answer to prayer and faith. I recall one young teen with meningitis who had been in a coma and on a respirator for several months. Her prognosis was poor and there were clear indications of brain death. Her family was African American and unsophisticated about the medical system, but they refused to accept the medical staff's recommendation to turn off the respirator and end her life. They believed that God would heal their daughter. The parents and their church prayed for her healing day after day. To the amazement of the medical staff, after months in a coma the girl aroused and within days was renewed to her previous self. To God went the glory.

A few years ago, I developed ophthalmicus herpeticus, otherwise known as "shingles," in my left eye. It was misdiagnosed for several weeks and resulted in a chronic herpetic eye condition with significant vision loss and eye problems. After five years of care, my ophthalmologist decided I needed some surgery on the cornea and scheduled the procedure. The morning of the surgery I asked my husband to pray for my eye. He did. He prayed that I would not be anxious and that the surgery would heal well and I would not have any pain. He did not pray for the eye to be healed. When he finished his prayer, I continued with my head bowed in prayer and asked the Lord to heal my eye so I did not have to have surgery. I went to the doctor, who prepared me for the surgery and then said he wanted to examine the eye carefully before the procedure. After the exam, he looked at me and said that it was much better and he had no rationale for performing the surgery. He sent me home, without the surgery, rejoicing and thanking God for healing power.

PROFESSIONAL EXPERIENCES

Throughout my professional life there has been an easy and natural integration of faith and practice. My professional study of human anatomy and physiology continually affirms the presence of a master planner, a God, with unlimited ability to create and sustain.

As with many, God also revealed majestic power to me through the birth of a child. The birth of Jesus brought kings, shepherds, and wise men to their knees just as it still brings awe and faith to new parents today. The miracle of the birth speaks of God as the creator of life. The amazing and brilliant precision of the creation of life is affirmed through the uniting of the egg and sperm, the inner physiological nurturing by the placenta, uterus and umbilical system, and the process of birth. I continually marvel at the genetic likeness and mirror image of children and their parents. The Bible reminds us on a daily basis that we too are made in the image of God the Father.

One of the basic skills of nursing involves the use of massage as a modality for relaxation and pain relief. In 1975 Delores Krieger published an article reporting her research that showed the laying on of hands with the intent to heal raised hemoglobin levels.[39] This article encouraged me to search the Scripture for biblical accounts of healing by Jesus and the apostles. I compared the biblical accounts of healing with the scientific and theoretical basis reported by nurse theorists. Though not from the same philosophical base, the biblical and scientific accounts were compatible and my faith in healing and laying on of hands for therapeutic purposes was stimulated. I began to practice therapeutic touch with my pediatric patients and family members.

Later, I began to teach the art and faith of healing practices to my students at the university where I taught. Before long I was invited to give lectures and workshops on therapeutic touch.

During my teaching on the topic, I always approached the subject from a Christian perspective and shared with the students my own belief that the healing was from God and that I asked the Holy Spirit of the Living God to work and heal the person. The practice of therapeutic touch is now an accepted professional modality and part of nursing practice in most institutions. The experiences of healing touch profoundly reinforced my faith in the God of the universe and the power to heal.

In my years of working as a nurse practitioner, I have been thankful for the presence of God in guiding my intellectual ability to think clearly and to give insight into the physical and mental problems and health of my clients. God brings amazing memory and detail to mind when forming a diagnosis and facing decisions that are life-giving for my clients. I recall an event where I received a late midnight call from a patient I had never seen. After some vague, questionable symptoms were reported briefly and only partially to me, I intuitively decided to direct the person to the emergency room. That person was diagnosed with toxic shock syndrome and was severely at risk and in need of immediate care.

God has directed my professional career path over the years. I have studied nursing and been part of the faculty at the best colleges and universities the profession of nursing has to offer (University of Washington, Oregon Health Sciences Center, Oregon State University, University of Rochester). God has put me where He wants me to work, faithfully providing a place for me to share my professional skills of teaching and nursing practice. One time early in my career, I wanted to start teaching but did nothing to look for a teaching position until October, after the college term had started. I merely phoned the university with a nursing program in my city and inquired about their need for a pediatric nursing professor. Due to a plane accident, there was an urgent immediate need for a pediatric faculty and the next week I was teaching there. On my first day, one of the students waited after class and told me that a group of Christian students in the class had been praying for a Christian faculty member. God answers prayer. Another time my husband's career change, much to my despair, forced me to resign my tenured position and seek a new job. With deep sadness, I prepared my resume and sent it off to several institutions with nursing programs in the state where my husband had accepted a new position. I mailed the resume on Monday and by Friday at five I had a job offer from a prestigious university. Within three weeks, I had been offered faculty positions at three institutions. I chose to accept a position at a private Christian college and experienced the happiest years of teaching in my career. God provides.

SPIRITUAL JOURNEY

Following the completion of my doctoral work in human development and families studies, I experienced the typical feelings of post-doctoral letdown. During that time I had the opportunity to attend a faith development workshop given by James Fowler. Fowler was involved in studying the stages of faith.[40] He approached the study from a cognitive, life cycle, developmental perspective. He spoke my theoretical, developmental language of Piaget, Erikson, Kohlberg, and Maslow. Fowler's work mapped out the stages of faith based on hundreds of interviews and empirical data and research.

The workshop involved the participants in an analysis of their own faith journeys. It opened my mind to the influences of my faith and my professional path that I had taken to know God. For me, this experience integrated my own faith and professional training and education knowledge at a higher level and gave deeper insight into my relationship with God. I welcomed the challenge of a higher level of faith.

My faith continues to be central to my life. Trusting God in obedience and serving others in Christian love has been the goal of my life. I share a part of my life story so that others may know the power and peace of God the Father, Son, and Holy Spirit. Amen.

BRIAN M. SPICER

NUCLEAR PHYSICS

*P*rofessor Spicer is Emeritus Professor of Physics at the University of Melbourne, Australia. He holds B.Sc., M.Sc., Ph.D. and D.Sc. degrees in physics from the University of Melbourne, where he was appointed to a personal chair in physics. He specialized in nuclear physics research and published 123 papers over the course of his career. He is a Fellow of the Institute of Physics (London), the American Physical Society, and an Honorary Fellow of the Australian Institute of Physics. Professor Spicer was appointed by the prime minister of Australia to the Ionising Radiation Advisory Council and in 1993 was appointed Honorary Fellow of the Australian Institute on Nuclear Science and Engineering for "distinguished and dedicated service to the institute."

My scientific work has had to do mainly with the properties and structure of atomic nuclei. These, of course, cannot be seen with the naked eye, or even with the most powerful microscope. Therefore, one must try to account for data obtained by postulating models (or mind pictures) of what the atom or nucleus "looks like" or acts like. These models are then used to make predictions of how a particular nucleus will act under certain conditions. After the discovery of the electron late in the 19th century, for example, J.J. Thomson likened the atom to a plum pudding, with the positively charged "pudding" dotted with negatively charged electrons much in the manner of plums in a pudding (though arranged in an orderly manner). Then came an experiment in which alpha-particles (helium nuclei) were "fired at" gold foils, and observations were made of the collisions, which were expected to be "billiard-ball like." It was shown that Thomson's model was sadly astray, and this led Lord Rutherford to replace it with the "solar system" model of atomic structure.

Scientific knowledge is *public knowledge* in the sense that an experiment performed in, say, London under the same conditions as the same experiment in Melbourne will be expected to lead to the same result. Repeated a second time in some other location, it will be expected to give the same result again. This is the property of what we know as public knowledge.

In contrast, there is another type of knowledge which I shall label *personal knowledge*. It is not public knowledge; it results from the interaction of two personalities. In this case the observer, if you will, is part of the system which is being observed. It is in this area that I place my faith in God and, as a consequence, my belief in the Scriptures.

I was brought up in what would be labeled a Christian home; both my parents were "believers." Though I did not (in my view) go through a "wild time" in my youth, and though I went through the motions out of obedience to my parents' wishes, I was not a believer in the way that I understand that term today. That all changed one Sunday evening when two young women testified to their faith in Jesus Christ in a worship service, and, near to midnight that night, I felt an overwhelming need to embrace that same faith. This I did, and it has not been lost to this day.

In the years since that decision, innumerable experiences have added to my personal knowledge of the God I worship and seek to serve. I can outline only a few here.

First, my studies. After sharing a prize at the end of my M.Sc., my professor encouraged me to seek a scholarship which would take me to England to work for a doctorate under Lord Rutherford himself and his colleagues. I duly entered for the scholarship but was bitterly disappointed when he informed me that three scholarships had been awarded that year and I had been placed fourth. Some weeks after that disappointment, a colleague and friend asked what today seems to be a logical question: "If you can't go to England, why not try to go to the United States?" We sat down together and selected three U.S. universities, and I wrote to them asking about the possibility of doing some research there towards a doctorate. One did not even reply; one said, "Come, but we have no funds with which to support you"; the third said, "Come, and the best we can offer you is $2,700 per year." This was duly and gratefully accepted, though my wife and I had no real idea how far the offered stipend would go.

There were no trans-Pacific flights in those days, so to get to the University of Illinois, we had to sail to London, then to New York, then travel by train from New York to Champaign-Urbana. We left Melbourne without any idea how we would pay our fare back at the end of whatever period we stayed for. I had applied for a Fulbright scholarship, and we were well on our way before word was received that this application had been successful. A three-week wait in England before we could get a berth on a ship for New York further depleted our minimal reserves. Then when we were halfway across the Atlantic we were informed there was a dock strike in New York. How would we negotiate that?

We were worried for nothing. When the ship berthed in New York, a lady was unexpectedly there to meet us. She had been a neighbor of my wife's parents until a few years before, when she moved to New York. I have no doubt we had my in-laws to thank for her presence there; but to us she was literally a "God-send." She persuaded a taxi to come through the picket line to pick up our baggage (how, I don't know) and then took us out for dinner before putting us on the appropriate train. When we arrived in Champaign, we were met by a minister who had been contacted prior to our departure from Melbourne; he had arranged for a couple to house us until we could find our own lodgings. In all the time we lived in Urbana, the stipend offered and paid by the university covered our requirements (though only just!).

Two very profitable years were spent at the University of Illinois, and looking back from the perspective of a career concluded,

I say without any hesitation or doubt that that career was built on the solid base laid down in those two years in Illinois. I don't know that I would have had such a good grounding in England. You may say that "the chips fell in my favor" or something like that. I don't buy the "chance explanation"! I believe with all my heart that the whole sequence of events that took place was a result of the guidance of God.

Another example from my non-professional life. One of the customs that became fully developed in my later life was that of reading Scripture every day. My wife and I use a study guide, but in 1985 I chose to read the Old Testament through serially as well, rather irregularly in that no fixed portion was read each day. On September 24, 1985, the day on which I was to enter the hospital for bypass surgery, I had reached Isaiah 41. As I read that chapter, the following passage literally "jumped out at me," and a strong inner voice said to me, "These are my words for you today." That passage (verses 9 and 10) read:

> I [God] said, "You are my servant. I have chosen you and have not rejected you. So do not fear, for I am with you; do not be dismayed, for I am your God. I will strengthen you and help you; I will uphold you with my righteous right hand" (NIV).

In these verses the God of Israel was speaking to Israel, but that morning He was also definitely speaking to me. As I read and re-read those lines, the fear of the surgery to come left me. And what I consider to be a series of remarkable things then happened to me.

First, while in the hospital I received no fewer than six cards which quoted that verse of Scripture to me. Also, two of the youngsters in our church colored a text for me — Isaiah 41: 13, whose content is a repeat of verse 10 quoted above. I was surely meant to take it seriously!

Second, the male nurse who "prepared" me for the surgery was an Old Boy of Carey Baptist Grammar School, which I had attended as a youngster.

Third, the sister who sat with me for some of my 36 hours in intensive care after the surgery (those for which I was conscious!) was the niece of a physics department colleague of mine.

Fourth, the physiotherapist who helped me get my lungs working properly again was the lady with whom our "physio" daughter took her first job.

Fifth, I have a brother-in-law surgeon who "popped" his head around the door each day to see how I was doing. I didn't even know he worked at that hospital.

Sixth, when I was moved into an open ward, I was placed in a bed next to one occupied by a man who soon made himself known to me as a "Christian brother" —a fellow believer in the Lord Jesus Christ. At that stage of recuperation, we were expected to walk — and walk, and walk — and David Leed and I shared many wonderful moments reflecting on the goodness of God in bringing us through this particular surgery.

While some would regard these six coincidences as just that — coincidences — I prefer to regard them as evidence that the Lord God gave them to me simply to assure me He was keeping the promise which was given me from Scripture that He would be with me.

The final "incident" concerns the neurosurgery that my wife had only a month ago. The first remarkable feature of this is the way the need for it was discovered. My wife, Pat, has a hearing problem, and had decided to have her hearing tested before making a request for a new hearing aid. The result of this test was odd, and the audiologist sent her to another, more qualified audiologist, who obtained the same sort of result. He suspected something other than that the hearing mechanism was amiss and authorized an MRI scan. This showed the presence of an unwanted "object" above and forward of the right ear.

Again, we thanked God for a brother-in-law with whom we could discuss matters and who advised us of a surgeon with whom to seek a consultation. We obtained an appointment with that surgeon. About then we both commented independently on the great peace which each of us felt about this whole matter. There was no apprehension at all regarding the possibility of forthcoming surgery, just a great peace about the situation, and we firmly believe that this was a gift from God. The fact that this "object" was on the right temporal lobe was also good news for a right-handed person like Pat, for it meant that the surgery would be concerned with the "quietest" section of the brain.

The surgery took place without a hitch: Pat was discharged from the hospital seven days later and is making a very good recovery even as I write. Through all of this, we have both been greatly encouraged by the kindness and prayers of our Christian friends, and have no doubt that Pat's recovery will be complete. Again, in this situation, we both felt that all the events that took place occurred because God guided.

In all of the above events, and in our daily living, we are conscious of the hand of God upon our lives. There has been too much happen for us to simply put down to "chance" all that has occurred — and only a small part of that has been described above!

EDWARD A. BOUDREAUX

THEORETICAL CHEMISTRY

Professor Boudreaux is Professor Emeritus of Chemistry at the University of New Orleans, Louisiana. He holds a B.S. in chemistry from Loyola University, and an M.S. and a Ph.D., both in chemistry, from Tulane University. Professor Boudreaux has spent 29 years in graduate education and research in the area of theoretical and inorganic chemistry and chemical physics, and is the author or co-author of four technical books in the area of physical/inorganic chemistry, as well as numerous scientific papers in peer reviewed journals and textbooks.

I was born in New Orleans, Louisiana, on October 30, 1933. This was during the time of the great American Depression, but, of course, I was totally unaware of its effects on me and my family at that time. My brother and I were the only siblings of a father having French/Acadian heritage (at that time referred to in a derogatory way as "Cajun"), and a mother whose parents originated from Paris, France (she always referred to herself as pure Parisian French). Because my mother's family was of "pure" French stock and my father's ancestors were from immigrant stock originally settled in Nova Scotia, my brother and I were not allowed to learn or speak French. Thus, we became an English-speaking family, because had we spoken French it would have been a further embarrassment to my father, who was distancing himself from his "Cajun" heritage.

Ours was a practicing religious family within a mainline Christian denomination. But, in all honesty, I must say that although I learned the dynamics of practicing religious ritualism, I never learned what true Christianity was all about.

My pre-graduate education involved attending a parochial Christian grammar school, a Christian high school (secondary) and a Christian undergraduate college. During this time I experienced intense exposure to doctrinal theology, particularly during the tenure of my high school and undergraduate college education. However, there was little involvement with the Bible (insofar as it being the documentation of the Word of God) or even with the explicit doctrines of Jesus Christ. In fact, the denominational church to which I belonged even taught that all Old Testament books were only myths or stories having no real foundation. Their position was that special creation/evolution was acceptable as long as all was attributed to God.

As a youth, during my adolescent and early teen years, I was intensely interested in the wildlife indigenous to the confines of my city dwelling. While most of my friends were devoted to playing ball and various mundane games and related activities, I was involved in collecting butterflies, insects, small reptiles, birds, fish, plants, and so on. There was a close friend living with our family, Mr. Emile Hern (German/Swiss), who had quite a diversified educational background and was knowledgeable about many things. This person played a significant role in fostering my interests in nature, science, history, foreign cultures, and much more. It was no surprise that I became amazed at the design and complexity in nature and at the complexity of life itself. A paramount question that frequently entered my mind was that evolution had to be a most amazing process if all things had developed systematically from a common origin. Yet, there was still the issue in the back of my mind that God was the Creator, because my religion demanded that I believe this. Furthermore, from early childhood to adulthood, my life was influenced with aspects of Christianity as I had been taught or indoctrinated. However, it must be said in retrospect that although I was a practicing religious person, I was not truly a Christian.

The years of my college education were quite diversified, but the courses of study were primarily focused on the physical sciences and mathematics. Oddly enough, in spite of my prior interests as a naturalist, I never took a formal course in biology or life sciences. My major was chemistry with a minor in physics, and I obtained my B.S. degree in chemistry in 1956.

My high school sweetheart, Carolyn, and I were married in February 1955, but we had already agreed that I should attempt to complete graduate school. So I entered the graduate chemistry program at Tulane University, New Orleans. My area of concentration was inorganic chemistry, but I gravitated more toward physical chemistry and chemical physics. Quantum theory of structure and chemical bonding and magnetic properties of matter were my specialities.

I share all of this to emphasize that my professional training immersed me in an environment that was essentially agnostic, at least insofar as it encouraged the growth of whatever rudiments of Christianity I had experienced during my formative years (theistic evolution). But I was becoming more exposed to atheistic beliefs and opinions. Although my family and I were still actively practicing our religion, the way I was living my life was far from holy.

In 1959 I obtained my M.S. degree, and I was awarded a Ph.D. degree in 1962. During the course of this time all four of our children were born. Needless to say, it was imperative that throughout my graduate education I earn sufficient income to meet our family needs. I was fortunate to have a teaching fellowship and two research fellowships providing income. But there was additional stress in our lives, stemming from illnesses afflicting my wife and two of our children. I must say that without the invaluable assistance of my mother-in-law and others in our families, it is doubtful we would have survived this time of trial. In retrospect, it is obvious that our survival of this period in our marriage was nothing less than miraculous. But it was not until some years later that I finally realized the "invisible hand of God" had guided us through this troubled time.

In August 1962 I was appointed to the faculty of the Department of Chemistry, Louisiana State University in New Orleans (now named University of New Orleans). The major portion of my professional activities was committed to undergraduate and graduate teaching, plus basic research. Of course, there were those numerous committees on which all faculty members, including myself, were expected to serve as well. Throughout the span of some 13 years this was the manner in which most of my time was consumed. I did not make enough effort to devote adequate quality time to my wife and family; consequently, I was becoming more vulnerable to being led astray from my marriage commitment.

In 1974 my promiscuous behavior caused me, my wife, and our children to succumb to a most devastating tragedy. I was legally separated from them, and my wife had every intention of divorcing me. I can't find the words to describe exactly how painful this was. I know that my wife was totally devastated, but I'll never know just how truly painful the trauma was to her, not to mention my children. But as far as I was concerned, all I can say is that the realization of losing the most treasured gifts in my life, my family, was beyond my strength to bear.

It was within the first two or three months of our separation that my oldest child (a son soon to be 46 years old) encouraged me to attend a prayer meeting taking place at a newly formed church. I was totally unaware of what transpired at such meetings so naturally I was not inclined to get involved. But my son (thank God) was persistent and convinced me that this would be most beneficial in helping me with my distress.

To please him, more than anything else, I attended the meeting. It was an exceedingly strange environment to me. There was the most jubilant singing of religious songs, hands raised in worship to God, audible prayers of praise, thanksgiving, intercession, and petitions. I met people who, surprisingly to me, were genuinely pleased to see me and welcomed me with open arms without condemnation.

I was strongly encouraged to attend additional meetings, which at first I was hesitant to do, but I found myself being drawn (as it were) to return. From that point on I participated on a regular basis. I found myself being genuinely drawn closer to God and He was drawing closer to me. It was through the influence of these meetings, the many prayers of friends, and much prayer on my own — plus the consulting and encouragement of these loving prayer group leaders — that I finally came to truly know who Jesus Christ really was and what great sacrifices He had made for me.

I came to understand that His hideous death on a cross and glorious resurrection into heaven with God the Father paid for the sins of all people for all time, and that eternal life with Him in heaven was available to all who believed in Him and accepted Him into their hearts. The Bible came alive to me. It was now understandable that this was truly the Word of God and not just some ancient book of stories and myths. I hungered and thirsted for this Word and for all that this glorious, loving God had to offer. I now knew what it was to be a true Christian; it was not a religion but a way of life centered in Jesus Christ.

Just as fairy tales end happily ever after, I can joyfully say that the love and mercy of the Lord restored our marriage exactly one year from the time of the separation. Our lives are now better than they ever were; not that it has been a bed of roses, but we now know what it means to have God in charge of our lives during both times that are good and times of trouble. My wife and I, along with most of our children, are now actively involved in a true Christian church.

In closing, it can truly be said that the reason I became a Christian was that God put me in a position wherein I had to make a choice: *life or death*! There is no life without life in Christ, and any alternative is nothing but certain death.

ROBERT G.V. BAKER

ENVIRONMENTAL RESEARCH

Dr. Baker is senior lecturer in the School of Human and Environmental Studies, University of New England (UNE), Australia. He holds a B.Sc. with honors in geography and a Dip.Ed. from the University of Sydney and an M.S. and a Ph.D. in applied geography from the University of New South Wales. Dr. Baker serves as vice-chair of the International Geographical Union's Commission on Modeling Geographical Systems. He is on the editorial board of three international journals and has published about 30 research papers. He received the UNE Vice-Chancellor's Award for Excellence in Research in 2000.

I am a Christian and a scientist. I love the truth and I consider I have an open mind. My path to God came through the recognition that there is symmetry in nature, intrinsically beautiful, far beyond the capabilities of chance.

As a scientist I look toward a theory of everything, but so far it has eluded the great minds. In this theory, however, we would be reduced to mere specks of matter as human beings, not important and part of random events in the evolution of life on one solitary planet in the complex universe. Yet, does God play dice with the universe? The Christian view is where everyone is unique and special to God, and human beings have a particular place in God's plan in a special world. In this plan there are not only the physical dimensions of space-time, but a spiritual dimension that each one of us possesses as well as a nose or a smile. A fundamental construct from this dimension is love: evolution has no hope of explaining how human love appeared through physical constructs from the primeval swamp. Love is from God, and as we are created in the image of God, I believe love is meant to underpin our whole human experience.

My moment of truth as a Christian came in 1992, lying on a gurney in a queue outside the operating room. All the other patients in the queue were old or smokers, but I was part of the 5 percent of young non-smokers who suffered from this cancer. The previous week I had been diagnosed with a Grade 2 bladder carcinoma. If it had spread beyond the bladder wall it was inoperable, but if it was contained then there was every chance of long-term remission. I love statistics, but when you could become a statistic in a 67 percent survival rate after five years for bladder cancer, it becomes very personal.

No one knows the experience of cancer unless they have suffered it. Similarly, no one knows the truth about Christianity until they have experienced the Holy Spirit. Christianity deals with the ultimate truth of who we are and our relationship with God. Statistics dismiss less than the 95 percent confidence limit as not significant and a function of chance, but I am significant to God. Science argues that in the universe I am nothing, but to God I am everything (as the parable of the lost sheep suggests). To say that Jesus was there with me through this ordeal is rubbish to a scientist. But science has no answers for a young man waiting to see in what part of the statistics he will appear in five years' time. All I could hear as I waited were the nurses discussing excitedly where they were going to spend their holidays that summer. Yet I was in a very different world on my trolley, a very personal world, where the God whom my colleagues dismiss as an illusion was with me in the Spirit of His Son, Jesus Christ. His words, "Surely I am with you always, to the very end of the age" (Matt. 28:20; NIV) gave me an inner peace to face my nightmare. The God who allows suffering was with me intimately within my suffering.

My cancer was not the totality of my nightmare. I had become ill in 1990, two months after submitting my Ph.D. and six weeks after marrying my wife, Sue. I was head of department at Fort Street High School, overstressed, and I caught a viral infection like others on the staff at that time. A common enough event, but three months later I was worsening, suffering lethargy and headaches. Physical activity put me into bed for the day. Exhaustive tests by my hematologist brother, Ross, showed that I had abnormal liver function.

Over the next 12 months the test results continued to deteriorate. I had acquired chronic active hepatitis as part of a post-viral syndrome: I had a 33 percent chance of getting liver cancer and a 33 percent chance of getting cirrhosis of the liver. Ross said I had about ten years before "problems" would set in. My liver was being slowly strangled by my immune system, which treated my liver cells as the enemy.

In desperation, I went on a treatment of prednisone in April 1992. It was the last hope of cure. The effect was to make my suffering significantly worse. Prednisone had the highest death rate of a prescribed drug in Australia. It would suppress the immune system that was attacking my liver and had a 50 percent chance of success. But it came at a high cost. I now could not eat without feeling terribly ill. I could not walk 100 meters without sitting down. My adrenal glands had stopped functioning with the prednisone substitute. I could no longer perform effectively as a teacher. To their great credit, my colleagues at Fort Street covered for me at every opportunity. I would break out in cold sweats in class. The students also knew I was suffering and did their work quietly and with sympathy.

My liver function results did not improve initially with prednisone, so I finally went to the hospital for a liver biopsy. To the great delight of my doctors and brother, for the first time the results came back showing an improvement in my abnormal liver function enzymes. This continued over the next round of samples and, to my doctors' amazement, the biopsy results showed that my hepatitis had been changed, presumably by the prednisone, to chronic steato-hepatitis, a different hepatitis usually associated with great obesity and diabetes in women. My liver now resembled one associated with alcoholism. There were only 11 cases in Australia. The good news was that it was controllable by diet and there was now only a 17 percent chance of getting cirrhosis of the liver. After a two-year battle, my liver function had improved, my chronic active hepatitis had been addressed.

The relief, however, was short-lived. The next week I was passing blood, and the week after that I was outside the operating room. Why had God saved me from chronic active hepatitis only to face cancer two weeks later?

I prayed to God. I did not blame Him, but I asked to understand why this had happened. Reading Job helped. I had served God faithfully over 15 years in a paraministry for disadvantaged children. I had delayed marriage and, as a Christian, had put service to the poor and the downtrodden first in my life. The story of Hezekiah in 2 Kings 20 provided me with hope. Hezekiah was 38 years old (the same age as myself) when he became ill and the prophet Isaiah told him:

> "This is what the Lord says: Put your house in order, because you are going to die; you will not recover." Hezekiah turned his face to the wall and prayed to the Lord, "Remember, O Lord, how I have walked before you faithfully and with wholehearted devotion and have done what is good in your eyes." And Hezekiah wept bitterly (2 Kings 20:1–3).

God's response was swift.

> Before Isaiah had left the middle court, the word of the Lord came to him: "Go back and tell Hezekiah . . . 'I have heard your prayer and seen your tears; I will heal you.' . . . Then Isaiah said, 'Prepare a poultice of figs.' They did so and applied it to the boil, and he recovered (2 Kings 20:4–7).

I related so much to Hezekiah. I prayed to God not because of 15 years of devotion in ministry to emotionally disturbed children and their families, but because of a realization that God favors those who earnestly serve Him. I found myself at the age of 39 years in a nightmare within a nightmare, where I had cancer on top of chronic active hepatitis.

God heard my prayer. My cancer was caught in time. The effects of prednisone wore off eventually some four years later and my chronic steato-hepatitis has stabilized. But every two years, as part of my cancer management, I have to have an exploratory operation to see whether the cancer has returned (there is a 50 percent chance) and relive the nightmare of the same cycle of situations as in the summer of 1992.

Intelligence and reason cannot deal with suffering. Why did I suffer from two serious diseases consecutively starting six weeks after my marriage and the submission of my Ph.D.? I lived in the shadowlands for a further four years because of the inability of my adrenal gland to function normally, and I still get ill from time to time. But God has a sovereign plan, and if my suffering is part of it, then that is what is important. Whatever happens, I have hope today through the God who loved me in my time of need and will love me through eternity.

Two weeks after my cancer operation, I returned to my high school to give the Christmas message to over 1,000 students, of whom only a dozen regularly attended Christian fellowship at the school. A tough audience! I talked on the word "eternity," made famous by Arthur Stace who, up to his death in 1967, was chalking the word "Eternity" on pavements around the streets of Sydney. This was his witness to his conversion to Christianity, which was made famous to a new generation as the symbol on the Sydney Harbor Bridge on January 1, 2000. What we deal with in the Christian message is the question of eternity and an answer to the question of what is beyond our space-time universe. Is there a spiritual conservation principle beyond death? If there is no spiritual dimension to human beings, how does this fit the Christian definition of eternity? The nothingness of evolution and chance has no place within the Christian definition of eternity with God. These questions will not go away by ignoring them. We cannot turn them off like turning a computer off. And even with a computer, if we press "save" and our machine fails, our lost document can still be retrieved as a result of the design by some clever programmer. I believe God will retrieve everyone somehow at the end of time, and what we have typed on our "life screen" and what we acknowledge about Jesus will determine where we are for eternity. My hope, as one chronically ill, is with the verses from Revelation 21:3–4:

Now the dwelling of God is with men, and he will live with them. They will be his people, and God himself will be with them and be their God. He will wipe every tear from their eyes. There will be no more death or mourning or crying or pain, for the old order of things has passed away.

This is a personal view of how I see myself as a Christian. I know suffering but my questions have never been answered by a world view. And I believe an intellectual Christianity is also devoid of meaning, since it paints a superficial and impersonal relationship with Jesus Christ. In my view, God is the simplest solution to a complex problem and Jesus Christ is the only solution to the breakdown of moral law that is increasingly being ignored by the world.

Does God play dice with the universe? I believe the more important question is: Does God love me in the universe? "Yes, through Christ Jesus, the Man-God."

WAYNE W. HUANG

INFORMATION SYSTEMS

Dr. Huang is senior lecturer in information systems in the School of Information Systems, Technology and Management at the University of New South Wales, Australia, and associate professor in management information systems at Ohio University, USA. He holds a B.E. in mechanics from Huazhong University of Science and Technology, an M.B.A. from Xi'an Jiaotong University, an M.Sc. in information systems from the National University of Singapore, and a Ph.D. in information systems as a joint Ph.D. program from the University of Georgia (USA) and the National University of Singapore. Dr. Huang was awarded the Sir Anthony Mason Fellowship for his contribution to research at the University of New South Wales.

How can a scientist believe in God?

Many non-Christians I know, especially younger ones, think that modern society is changing so fast that they simply don't have time to go to church and study the Bible. They are always busy and have to work long hours to earn money to provide for their needs and expenses. This is partly true. I had similar thoughts before I became a Christian. In the following paragraphs I will tell my personal life story, how as a scientist in the field of information systems I became a Christian, and I will share how God helped me to balance my spiritual and material life in this hectic, modern world. You don't need to accept all of what I say. However, I believe a truthful life experience may at least give you some insights relevant to your own journey in life.

I was born in mainland China. Later, my family migrated to Singapore where I started to learn more about Christianity and have some Christian friends. I didn't believe in God and also didn't want to become a Christian. This was mainly because I wanted to have more time to spend following material pursuits such as studying for higher degrees, searching for jobs with higher pay, and buying a new apartment for my family. I thought I simply didn't have time to go to church and study the Bible.

In the early 1990s, I finished my M.Sc. in information systems at the National University of Singapore and started to work as a full-time teaching staff member in the Department of Information Systems and Computer Science at the university. At the same time, I was pursuing my doctoral studies in a joint program between the University of Georgia, USA, and the National University of Singapore. This time period was the most stressful and difficult in my life: teaching full-time on weekdays, doing my doctoral studies, looking after my newly born baby, and financially supporting my newly bought apartment. Obviously, even if I spent 24 hours a day in coping with all these things, there still would not be enough time to fulfil all my family, work, and study commitments properly, let alone to think of going to church and studying the Bible.

During that period, I worked very hard, starting work very early in the morning and coming home late at night. No TV watching and no weekends off at all! However, the worst thing was that, even though I worked so hard, my work on my Ph.D. research project was not satisfactory and little real progress was being made. In addition, I gradually started to lose confidence in my ability to do my studies and to cope with all the stresses of my life. I found it difficult to concentrate on my research, and many times I said to myself, *Maybe I should give up my studies.* I was getting to the point where I couldn't cope with it any more. It was the darkest period of my life.

At this time a Christian, Mr. Owen Liu, came into my life. I had been introduced to him by a friend, Mr. Ke Fan. Owen had a natural, charming personality that really attracted me, even though at that time I did not know he was a Christian. He is the kind of person whom you feel comfortable sharing your real feelings with and whom you feel you can trust. I shared with him about my negative life and working experience. I remember him telling me in a firm voice, "Wayne, I know that there is a real friend who can help you, and all you need to do is to trust Him and pray for His help and let Him dwell in your heart and accept Him. He is God, Jesus Christ. Would you like to have a try?" He said that he would pray for God to help me and also encouraged me to pray for help myself.

I didn't really believe that God could help me because I even doubted the existence of God at that time. However, I thought it wouldn't do any harm to have a try since it was my trusted friend who had suggested it. So I prayed to God (surely with some doubts in my mind) as Owen had suggested, knowing that at the same time Owen was praying for me as well.

To my surprise, one week after I had prayed, I started to notice the difference. I had peace of mind and could concentrate on my research work. Encouraged by this good sign, I continued praying, this time with a more sincere heart. Owen also continued to pray for me and I started to go to church with him.

Two months later, the differences were more obvious. My confidence had recovered — or, perhaps more accurately, I now had confidence in God, who I knew was always there to listen to my prayers and help me with all of my problems. I found that once again I had the ability to concentrate on my research and teaching, and my doctoral studies began to make progress.

However, I still had one big obstacle blocking me from becoming a Christian. I had been trained to be a scientist by my formal education over 20 years or so. I had such a firm belief in science that unless someone could prove the existence of God using the scientific method, I couldn't really believe in His existence. After all, God could be just a made-up idea that was making me feel better by believing it.

Owen and other members in our church and Bible study group all prayed hard for me to overcome this big obstacle. But I was very stubborn and stood firm on my position. A few months passed and still no solution had been found.

One night I had almost fallen asleep when suddenly I heard a voice softly say to me, "Wayne, wake up and I will show you the scientific solution now." A few seconds later, the scientific answer amazingly appeared in my mind. It was an answer that neither my church friends nor myself had come up with over the months we had been praying. We had been striving hard to search for a scientific proof of the existence of God in a direct way, but we had ignored an indirect approach to my question. The solution I was shown is as follows: If we could prove something using the scientific method — for example, the existence of air, which we also cannot see — it would mean that we could repeat the procedure again and again to prove the existence of air whenever we wanted to. This would imply that we had a certain amount of control over air. It would also mean that we had useful knowledge about air and could apply this knowledge to make air do something for us that we would interpret as verifying its existence. This would mean we had become, in a way, the master of the air. The same is true of anything we can prove using the scientific method. Therefore, if someone could prove the existence of God using the scientific method, this person would in a way become the master of God. But God, by definition, is the master of everything. This contradiction indicated to me that it was impossible and illogical to prove the existence of God using the scientific method. When I saw this, the obstacle preventing me from believing was removed and I finally became a Christian.

When I became a Christian, it did not mean that I had no more problems in my life from then on. Rather, the difference was that, because I believed in Him who is always there to respond to our sincere prayers, I knew that no matter how difficult and hard my life and work might become, I would have confidence (coming from God) to overcome the problems. In this way, I successfully finished my Ph.D. studies, and to my further amazement received a job offer to work as a lecturer in one of the top universities in Australia, the University of New South Wales.

Recalling my life since becoming a Christian, I can clearly see a big difference between my life with and without belief in God. Over the last six years, with His blessing, I have been given a chance to study and work in top universities in Singapore, Australia, and Hong Kong. In 1999, my research paper published in one of the international quality journals, the *European Journal of Information Systems*, was awarded the Highest Quality Rating certificate by ANBAR Electronic Intelligence, a partner with British National Library. That same year I was promoted to senior lecturer. Recently, I was given chances to work in American universities as well. I now believe that God wants me to use my achievements in my career and work to glorify His name.

I am just an ordinary person and I have all the weaknesses and shortcomings most normal people have. If God's love and help can make me successful in my studies and my career, I am sure that you also would be able to achieve more after accepting Him into your heart.

Dear friends, if you haven't heard of His name, or still have some doubts about Him, I would like to urge you to give yourself a chance to try God out. Pray for His Holy Spirit to dwell in your heart so that you can feel His presence, and let Him fill your heart with love and joy through all the years ahead.

PAK LIM CHU

ELECTRICAL ENGINEERING

*D*r. Chu is professor of electrical engineering, University of New South Wales, Australia. He holds B.E. with honors, M.E. and Ph.D. degrees in electrical engineering from the University of New South Wales. Dr. Chu specializes in optical fiber research and holds five patents for inventions of optical fiber devices. He served as chairman of the Publications Board of IREE from 1983–90 and has published more than 340 technical papers.

I am an engineer and engineers are supposed to be practical people. We want to make things work. If someone says he has designed a wonderful device but when it is constructed and tested it does not work, we would not accept his design. Similarly, if someone says that he has discovered a fantastic theory about nature, we would not rush to believe him without testing the theory against known phenomena.

As a Christian I also hold the same principle; that is, I want to test God's words. However, it is more than God's words that I want to test. I want to test His reality, His activity, and His love and care for humankind. I do this all the time, when I am happy and when I am sad. The result of each test is always affirmative. God is always real and loving and kindly to me.

How do I carry out these tests? This is done in two directions:

(1) the backward direction, by looking back at my own life; and
(2) the forward direction, by trusting my life to Him.

LOOKING BACK

I was born in China, but when I was an infant, my father went to the United States and toiled as a laundry worker to send back to my mother a small amount of money. It was just sufficient to keep us alive. In 1949, my mother took me to live in Hong Kong and I went to school there. Then in the early 1950s, before I became a teenager, my father applied for my mother and me to migrate to join him in San Francisco, but we were refused by the U.S. consulate in Hong Kong. No reasons were given.

We waited until I finished my high school study and I then applied to study at a U.S. university. The university accepted me but the U.S. consulate once again refused my entry. I next applied to a Canadian university, which accepted me; but this time the Canadian consulate in Hong Kong refused my entry for the reason that I had already been refused entry to the United States. Their argument was that if I could get into Canada, I would be able to get into the United States. In fact, the Canadian consulate suggested that I apply to go to Australia instead because I would not be able to swim to the United States then.

So I took their advice and applied to go to Australia. The process was very easy and I even got into the University of New South Wales a few days after my arrival.

However, I had difficulty with the lectures, as I could not understand the Australian accent. I had come from a Chinese high school in Hong Kong which did not have a very strong English curriculum. The mechanical technology lecturer was particularly boring, to the extent that the Australian student sitting next to me began to talk to me. From then on we became good friends — in fact, he was the only friend I had in Australia in the first year. He was very good to me and took me home to meet his family, who treated me just like one of their members.

More importantly, this was a family of very devout and dedicated Christians. In my final year of high school I had accepted Christianity, but that was more a gesture of gratitude to my alma mater than becoming a true believer. When I lived with this Christian family and observed their behavior, I could not but entrust myself completely to the Lord. In the past, I had lived for myself, wanting to improve myself purely by my own effort. In the second year of my stay in Australia, I realized that I could not do this. What I had achieved was not due to my own effort. It was from Him who had been guiding me silently.

After four years' study I graduated, but I still wanted to go to the United States since my parents were getting on in years and I was their only child. I applied to the U.S. consulate in Sydney for a tourist visa but I was once again refused because they checked up on my records in Hong Kong. So the hope of seeing my parents was cut off. It was not until many years later, after I became an Australian citizen, that I was able to visit my parents — 17 years after I left Hong Kong and about 30 years since I last saw my father in China as a baby.

I discovered my father was a stranger to me. There was very little that we could communicate deeply with each other. We had different beliefs, different educational backgrounds, different cultures, and many other differences. In San Francisco I also met many of my relatives of the same age. I found they had all followed their fathers' footsteps in becoming restaurant workers and laundry workers. They had also followed their forebears' traditions such as ancestor worship, gambling, and drinking. I was really fortunate to have escaped such an influence. I then realized it was really God's purpose that He took me to Australia and kept me there. My fate was quite similar to that of Abraham when God called him out of the city of Ur to go to an unknown destination. From then on, I knew that God had His purpose for me.

TRUSTING GOD NOW

My professional life was also under the guiding hand of God. When I managed to get into the University of New South Wales, I enrolled in mechanical engineering for no apparent reason at all, very much to my own surprise, as I had always wanted to do electrical engineering since I was young. However, it was in mechanical engineering that I met my Australian friend and became a Christian. In the second year, I transferred to electrical engineering. I stayed at the same university to complete all my degrees and continued on to join the academic staff. My head of department started off my academic career by assigning a professional officer to work for me on the newly emerging fiber optics technology. The two of us worked very closely together and our work prospered. We now have a very good-sized research group and enjoy an international reputation.

However, when I look back on my life, I realize that it would not have been possible for me to get where I am through my own effort. "The race is not to the swift or the battle to the strong" (Eccles. 9:11; NIV) — how true that is! My colleague is many times more intelligent than I, yet he has been under me for the past 20 years. In my research group, many of my people are many times better researchers than I, yet they are under my supervision.

My position in the university is very demanding and yet it is flexible. If necessary, I can compress my workload to create a gap to allow me to do something else. For this reason, I have been able to get involved in the Lord's work. I started off with being the secretary of a youth fellowship, then its chairman. For many years I was involved in open-air evangelization in Sydney's Chinatown every Sunday. I became a deacon of many churches and eventually the chairman of a diaconate for many years. I was also for several years the chairman of a combined association of Chinese Christian churches in Sydney. I am now the chairman of a missionary organization which often takes missionary groups to preach the gospel to the Chinese in South Pacific countries such as Fiji, Vanuatu, and the Solomon Islands.

I am not a person who strives for something higher, but somehow I have been moved from one stage to another. The only thing that I really craved was the opportunity to work in the university. The rest was somehow given to me. I was not particularly interested in the missionary work but, for no apparent reasons at all, I was put in the "in-charge" position. Of course, when I am in that position, I dedicate myself to work my best.

On looking at my life, I understand now why I have been placed in Australia. It is God's plan for me. He has been guiding me every step of my life. I am so certain of His presence that whenever I am at a crossroad, I am not afraid or perplexed because He will make the decision of which road to take for me. My motto of life is Romans 8:28: "And we know that in all things God works for the good of those who love him, who have been called according to his purpose."

LINDA S. SCHWAB

CHEMISTRY

*D*r. Schwab is professor of chemistry at Wells College, USA. She holds a B.A. in chemistry from Wells College and an M.S. and a Ph.D., both in organic chemistry, from the University of Rochester. Dr. Schwab served for four years as associate in the Center for Brain Research, School of Medicine and Dentistry, University of Rochester. She specializes in undergraduate chemistry education and natural product research and has published 18 papers and conference abstracts.

"I think it's pretty much agreed that all that God business is out the window." Dismissing the topic as easily as he tipped his chair back from the seminar-room table, our senior colleague continued his brief, articulate review of the leading theories of consciousness.

Who agreed to that? I wondered. Even so, I had no reason to doubt that the offhand remark accurately represented the opinion of most neuroscientists. I had only to look around the room to answer my question. The group assembled for the lunchtime seminar comprised most of the faculty (of whom I was the most junior) and the students of a small, interdisciplinary graduate department within a medical school. Two of us at that table would have disagreed for ourselves, but we couldn't argue with the fact that we were in the minority, even there, and doubtless more so in the scientific world at large. Indeed, from what our senior colleague had been saying just before his casual defenestration of the "God business," Sir John Eccles was the only well-known neuroscientist to think that consciousness is not a purely material phenomenon. In other words, Eccles had the effrontery to believe in something like a soul.

At that time, about 20 years ago, although I was sure I believed in God and identified myself as a Christian, I could hardly have explained why. It has taken me a long time to come to the simple statement that I have found the promises of faith in Jesus Christ to be true in my own experience, especially those promises which I did not previously understand. Furthermore, this view of faith itself — as an active, reciprocal process — goes beyond natural explanations, and therefore might justly be called "supernatural."

Of course, an expression like "the promises of Christ" sounds like the Christian-speak which is so puzzling and irritating to non-Christians, so let me continue the story by way of explanation.

For much of my life, it seemed to me that being a Christian had a lot to do with cultural inheritance. Certainly, it is difficult to be a Christian where the message is not readily accessible! But more than that, I did not realize until I was an adult how important it was to my parents, and to my maternal grandmother, that I should lay hold of that inheritance for myself. Their teaching and example were subtle, powerful, and wide-ranging. I saw spiritual struggles, like my father's with his experiences as a battlefield doctor during World War II and in the illness that killed him at 45, as well as faith's composure and courage, like that of my mother and grandmother, both widowed young.

Seeing the important adults in my life clearly living their lives in the knowledge of God, by about sixth grade I recall having a very strong sense of the presence of Jesus in all my activities, school and home as well as church. In the busy world of high school this sense began to go underground, so to speak. In college, as I became seriously interested in chemistry, I found no clues as to where and how faith related to my developing career plans. At this secular institution, my chemistry professors — all of them men of high and obvious integrity — were deists, as far as I could tell: God started up the great mechanism of nature, which then required no further sustenance. The church I went to dispensed what C.S. Lewis aptly called "Christianity and water," an everything-is-fine faith, with an occasional dash of suspicion directed at technology that spilled over onto science. I wasn't aware of any peer fellowship which could help. So I was caught in a bind familiar to many students: I simply didn't see scientists who self-identified as Christians nor Christians sympathetic to science.

In graduate school in organic chemistry I knew no one else who seemed to have an active Christian faith. Still, on occasion then and later, a book, a poem, or a piece of music brought back my early sense of commitment; phrases of Scripture came to mind with the persistence of an old tune. After the doctorate, a brief post-doc rolled over into a non-tenure-track position in the neuroscience department mentioned above. My research interests brought me into occasional contact with a group in neuroanatomy, and the group's technician was an outspoken Christian. If what I had grown used to was "Christianity and water," her version was straight single-malt! Here was the "zeal" I had read about so long ago. It was fascinating and, at times, puzzling. I was strongly impressed by her courage in asking the dean of the medical school if he could provide theological justification for a new research program using recombinant DNA which he had just proposed as a multidepartment initiative. Much to everyone's surprise, he gave her a very thoughtful, respectful, and sympathetic reply. Clearly, the world of Christians in science was a complicated, and mostly hidden, place. This observation continued to hold as my career developed.

Not long after that, my traineeship in neurochemistry having ended, I moved on to a position at my present institution. I rose through the usual academic ranks in due course, mostly teaching but with time for satisfying research as well. It took 12 years to discover, in the course of a research collaboration, that a colleague in a related department was also Christian; over the next several years, we began to do Lenten readings together, trade books, discuss faith in increasing depth and with increasing enthusiasm, and become more involved at church.

Then came a turning point. I went through yet another administrative shake-up at work, but one which was a particularly bitter personal and professional disappointment. A special assignment I'd been carrying out for several years, with very good results, was reassigned to a committee in a particularly inept and shabby way. With this "last straw," I saw that years of good work and idealistic dedication to the employer which was also, coincidentally, my alma mater had produced no lasting or dependable satisfaction. As the preacher of Ecclesiastes observed so long ago, the race was not to the swift, nor was there any favor to one of skill. Exasperation, anger, and despair closed in on me like a trap: "Therefore I hated life . . . for all is vanity and vexation of spirit" (Eccles. 2:17; KJV).

Having come to the end of what I could do to improve my situation, I recommitted my life to Jesus Christ, first privately, and then publicly before a sympathetic assembly. This choice and these actions were like a seed crystal; what was formerly a collection of apparently random events and interactions crystallized into a change in my perspective that has been profound and surprising.

The surprise came as I realized how incomplete and fragmentary had been my understanding of the transformative role of the Holy Spirit in the life of the individual and of the body of believers. I had confessed Christ early in life; I had struggled, in fits and starts, to understand what this meant; I had been thankful for God's providence in, for example, my recovery from a couple of serious illnesses and an opening to exactly the job I wanted at just the right time; and I had come to some understanding that the existence of evil did not show God lacking in either goodness or power. Still, despite all this, it was as if I had been overlooking the main course at the feast, the one that all the rest of the feast complements — or missing the much-sought host, himself, who planned and provided all, who had been right before my eyes. Scripture was thick with promises of transformation, which I had read one by one, but which now fitted together as a coherent story, of which mine was a part.

A change of perspective of this extent must require the presence of another personality, or person, for what defines a personal encounter but the awareness of a distinctly new and different perspective? And this is precisely the stumbling block for anyone who is adamant that only "natural" explanations are admissible. Such a person might point out that I've told a very typical career story, which I suddenly chose to retell as a transforming spiritual process, with all its crucial encounters and turning points. He or she would add that all of this was organized and reorganized through the integrated action of various neurotransmitters, and occurred in response to a stimulus that's not very precisely identified. In other words, it was "all in my head," although apparently I also "felt better." The conclusions to be drawn? First, no mystery involved; second, Christian faith sounds a lot like mental illness.

Of course, the "naturalist" is unlikely to admit that he or she arrived at such cynicism by exactly the same physiological process! Furthermore, if people could simply talk themselves into understanding things which seemed previously disconnected and only partly clear, teachers would be out of a job.

What strikes me in the stories of people I know, and in the literature which is just beginning to address the role of faith in recovery from addictions, is that transforming changes occur not only intellectually but also psychologically and physically. Indeed, from a chemical standpoint, stories of release from chronic anger, for example, are no less amazing than those of release from dependence on alcohol or drugs. The hypothesis that faith is a sort of self-hypnosis or biofeedback mechanism becomes still less tenable considering the range of temperaments and personalities among those who consider themselves to have been changed.

There are at least two other problems, and even more fundamental ones, with the "naturalistic" oversimplification. One is a misunderstanding about the relationship of a supernatural God to the natural world and natural laws. That God is "supernatural" does not mean He is necessarily only above nature — as if He needed permission to enter nature or operate through as well as outside the logical web that we identify as the way nature works. (Nor will supernatural action necessarily appear "spooky," another common but erroneous association.) Again, C.S. Lewis put it well: "There's no good trying to be more spiritual than God. . . . He *likes* matter. He invented it."[41] The second problem is also a misunderstanding: that faith is something passive, something soaked up gullibly (or perhaps "rammed down your throat") rather than something active and even, in one limited sense, akin to the scientific enterprise.

Most of what we "do" in science is a chain hooked into the unknown. For example, one of the questions that most intrigued me as a beginning student of organic chemistry — and which, as a result, I still particularly like to teach — is how we can say that we know the structure of a complex organic molecule. Composition, properties, and reactions all play a role in the assignment, especially the collection of physical properties provided by spectroscopy. We trust that by this means we "see" in regions of the electromagnetic spectrum far beyond that accessible to our eyes, and "hear" vibrations imperceptible to our ears. Independent evidence amply supports so many of the structural assignments arrived at in this way that we proceed with great confidence in navigating this world of the unseen and unheard. The confidence is so great that we seldom stop to think that when we travel in these regions it is as human beings of limited sensory capacity looking at graphical summaries of data.

Faith is a similarly active process, not passive, blinkered acceptance. Passive acceptance is that of the student who stalls forlornly at "this is the structure because the professor said so"; faith is the application of experiential knowledge for oneself. Those who think that faith in God is a comforting kind of brainwashing which "religious" people have to accept would be very surprised by the most direct biblical definition of faith: "Now faith is the substance of things hoped for, the evidence of things not seen" (Heb. 11:1). Standing alone, this appears to be a slightly enigmatic definition, in whatever translation one chooses: is the unseen "real" only because we believe in it (and, therefore, only for us)? The context, however, makes clear that this definition is a limited one addressing faith *as an experience*: it is a list of the stories of those who took a step into the unknown based on the premise "God is faithful" and who found that confirmed. Faith is the foundation, the jumping-off place, the confidence, for the step into the unknown; the stories of those who took, and still take, the step are the evidence that "He is faithful that promised" (Heb. 10:23). But there is a critical difference between exploring the unknown in nature by reason and reaching into the unknown beyond nature by faith: the former has shortcuts, the latter does not.

A "formal" synthesis or a "formal" proof needs to go only far enough to meet a step which has been carried out or proved by someone else; this isn't true of faith. As my story showed, people of faith play critical roles in supporting and forming one another (as must be the case among fellow members of one body), but no one can experience faith vicariously. Faith is not a program that can be copied from someone else. Another choice which is not available is to decide to try out faith and discard it if it doesn't "work." This amounts to trying to be committed and uncommitted at the same time, "like a wave of the sea driven with the wind and tossed" (James 1:6).

But if faith is a committed reach into the unknown, the results of faith appear to be a direct response into human life. I found that the greater my willingness to commit myself to Jesus Christ, the greater became my awareness of God having worked and continuing to work in my life. This awareness of God's work afforded me a change of perspective which continues to appear in my interests, priorities, and decisions. I find no explanation of this as comprehensive and convincing as this: that at the other end of the chain of experience in my hand is an anchor secured in God.

ROBERT H. ECKEL
MEDICAL RESEARCH

D r. Eckel is professor of medicine, and physiology and biophysics at the Health Sciences Center at the University of Colorado in the USA. He holds a B.S. cum laude in bacteriology from the University of Cincinnati and an M.D. from the University of Cincinnati College of Medicine. He currently serves as vice-chairman, research affairs in the Department of Medicine and as associate director of the Center for Human Nutrition at the University of Colorado Health Sciences Center. Dr. Eckel has published 102 papers, 140 abstracts, and 21 book chapters in the areas of heart disease, obesity, and diabetes research. In 2000 he was presented with the American Heart Association Torch of Hope Award.

I was raised in a traditional American home where church was important to enhance the personal, social, and community aspects of development primarily intended to be provided by the home. Although a moral message was connected to this process, acceptance of the Word of God as infallible proof of the Christian message was never presented by pastors, Sunday school teachers, or members of the congregation. In fact, the majority of peers and adults with whom I interacted saw the church as a means of assembling to discuss the issues of the times, with God in general viewed as too distant and impersonal to respond. Of course, I'm sure there were individual exceptions that I was too ignorant and/or stubborn to notice.

At home a position of equal lack of acceptance was held. Having lost her physician husband (my father) at the early age of 35, my mother became embittered with and distanced from God and felt that His existence was questionable. Thus, an atmosphere of skepticism about God and His workings existed as I entered my college years.

In college, science/medicine was my direction. The image of my long-deceased father, I'm sure, influenced this decision. Understanding the truth about biological systems also motivated me. However, with increasing exposure to agnosticism, atheism, and evolutionary teaching in college, I began accepting the position that if God existed there were many ways to reach Him. This position helped me understand how the many religions of the world could be justified. In fact, a course on the history of India opened up my mind to less familiar manners of approach to things of a spiritual nature. There was no one truth of who God was and what He intended. Fortunately, the girl I was dating in high school and college didn't let my convictions wander too extensively, but maintained in me at least some roots of the Christian tradition. But medical school drove me even further away from the true God, perhaps in part because the commitment to learning and study seemed unending.

After graduation and entrance into internal medicine house staff training, life became more complicated, with a new location, the birth of two daughters in two years, time away from home because of hospital responsibilities, moonlighting to make ends meet, and the temptations of the world around me. After three years, relocation again ensued for a research fellowship in endocrinology/metabolism which would provide the necessary foundation for a career in academic medicine and research in lipid and lipoprotein metabolism. Shortly after the move, my wife and I increasingly struggled with the upbringing of our two girls. In fact, the inconsistencies in our parental skills led to anything but peace and comfort in our marriage and home. *There must be answers somewhere,* my wife thought, and it was back to church we went, and for my wife a local women's Bible study.

Shortly thereafter we were visited by a member of the very liberal, "traditional" church we were attending. He shared with us how an evangelistic seminar he and his daughter had attended had assured him that another recently deceased daughter was now with the Lord. I thought this was impossible for him to know; how could he be so certain? My wife attended the same seminar and for the first time we both learned that we were separated from God by sin and were unable on our own to please God. Moreover, Christ had paid the price for each one of us (and the whole world) — the price we could not pay. My wife shortly thereafter came to salvation.

She then waited patiently for God to reveal himself to me through the evidence of a changed life in her. Although I had dated her for seven years prior to marriage and we had at that time been married for nine years, I was now living with a new woman. Predictable areas of conflict were suddenly lacking and I found myself beginning to ask her questions that I thought no one could comprehend. Nine months after her conversion, we returned to the previously attended seminar and I also accepted the Lord Jesus Christ as my personal Savior. The basis of that acceptance was His grace and the realization that, in the person of Jesus Christ, the truth I had long been seeking in science and medicine, and to a lesser extent spiritually, was before me. The true God-man was He, and over the last 22 years this has been increasingly apparent.

Briefly, three more children followed and a biblical basis became the only way, by His grace, that we could raise our family. The scientific basis of my work in the laboratory and the hospital took on new and enlightened meaning. Creation became a reality and now in my mind He exists, as the Bible states, as the controller of the biological, astronomical, and geological universe. Yes, this is by faith; but it is accepted with more confidence than the results of any of the experiments we carry out in the laboratory or hospital or that we publish.

His sufficiency during trials and hardships has been repeatedly witnessed. This was particularly noteworthy during my late wife's seven-year struggle with breast cancer, which would ultimately prove to be her path to heavenly places. I miss her dearly. But I see the truth stated by Paul in Philippians

1:21, that "for me to live is Christ, and to die is gain." Either way you win! The Lord has now brought me a second wife, and together with the children, mostly raised, we grow by His grace and truth to praise Him in and for all things. He is the way, the truth, and the life. There is no penultimate conclusion to this testimony.

ROBERT WOLFGRAMM

SOCIOLOGY

Dr. Wolfgramm is lecturer in sociology at Monash University, Australia. He holds a B.A. in political studies and applied sociology from the Caulfield Institute of Technology, an M.A. in sociology from the Chisholm Institute of Technology, and a Ph.D. in sociology from La Trobe University. Dr. Wolfgramm has acted as a consultant for a number of minority groups, both in Australia and overseas. He helped prepare submissions for Christian nationalist groups to the 1995 Fiji Constitution Review Committee and presented the keynote opening address to the Strategic Development Planning for East Timor Conference of the National Council of Timorese Resistance in April 1999.

I cannot think of a reason why I should believe in God — at least not a reason which would make sense to someone who does not. I only know I do. The sum total of my experiences of God could be explained away by rational scientific analysis. I have read enough of the social sciences and the greats of my discipline to do that. Karl Marx, for example, understood the social, political, and ideological functions of religion as an "opiate." It was his very useful metaphor for describing the soothing and reality-obscuring effects of religion among classes oppressed by inequalities. Max Weber analyzed the historical bases of religion and described the rise of modern capitalism as consequent upon the development of Protestant Christianity. Emile Durkheim saw religion as merely a face or reflection of the social, that "God" and "society" are interchangeable terms. I think Marx was right, I find Weber's scholarship persuasive, and Durkheim makes some sense, too. But still I believe in God and practice my religion, and though my faith is better informed by these grand social theories, it has not been removed.

Knowing what impact belief in God has in hard times (Marx), knowing the historical roots of an understanding of God (Weber), and recognizing that the social may be seen as a representation of God (Durkheim) is useful reflexivity that satisfies a certain intellectual craving. But even when that is done, when all reasons are accounted for, when it makes sense to be agnostic or even atheistic, my belief still remains. I cannot think of myself as having no belief. Belief is a part of my identity. I cannot know when it started because it feels as if it has always been there — that I was born believing, that I was born *to* believe. Through faith I experience God as a reality which has hold of me.

For sociologists, "socialization" summarizes the process whereby beliefs and identity are shaped within us through our interaction with "the social." Peers, parents, and significant others all help make us what we are. And this is precisely where I have found God — in others.

In 1994 my eldest son — just four years old — died by accidental drowning while we were in Fiji. A taxi driver picking me up after my day's work knew, but did not have the heart to tell me. Instead of taking me home, he dropped me off at the local hospital and told me go in and inquire about my son, and then he just drove off. The thought of death never entered my mind as I entered the emergency ward. And no one there would tell me either; all eyes averted. People walked away as I made for a trolley with a small body under a white sheet. Sticking out the end of it were feet with shoes I recognized as belonging to my son. As I entered the room and saw his lifeless form, my world slowly turned upside down and descended into hell. I began to weep and wail, sobbing hard and loud. I hugged his cold body and asked God, "Why, why, why? Why him and not me?" He was full of promise; I had had a rewarding life. I was full of plans for him and his future was just beginning.

In that moment I realized why some may believe in a god and some will not. I longed for a magical power to bring my boy back to life. I just wanted him back, alive, now. Why couldn't God do that for me? Had He not done it for His own Son? I realized I was powerless and perhaps on the edge of madness. Nothing was going to make any difference and he was going to stay dead and no answer as to "why him" was going to make any sense. It was a moment for faith, and in the months that followed I struggled with all the paradigms of religion, science, and philosophy at my disposal. But I found I still could not banish faith in a loving God.

In fact, I found God again — not as a trite answer to my grief but as the ongoing question, the unfathomed but awesome mystery. I also found that others had faced God in this way. And when they shared this with me, God turned out to be a serenity that I too discovered at the contentious boundary between existence and non-existence, a gift of life and a will to go on in the face of a threatening personal and social madness.

Through the distress and grief of losing my son, God did not appear to me through some private dramatic revelation. He did not draw me out of my bitter silence through some public and mystical experience of nature. Rather, I recognized the divine presence and inspiration in the words and companionship of others, others who had been through parallel experiences. God was in their words and in their arms of comfort. I heard and felt Him from those who came to me in that time of desperate doubt. And I was reminded again that the God of biblical revelation is someone who shares our humanity at its lowest point, and who by doing so can raise our spirits again to their highest.

COLIN W. MITCHELL

GEOGRAPHY

*D*r. Mitchell was formerly lecturer in geography at Reading University, UK. He holds an M.A. with honors in geography from Oxford University, a Master of Civic Design from the University of Liverpool and a Ph.D. in geography from the University of Cambridge. Dr. Mitchell has served for more than 44 years as a soil scientist and land evaluation consultant, with 30 years' specialized experience using remote sensing from both aircraft and satellites, including long-term assignments in Iraq, Sudan, Pakistan, Italy, and Morocco. He is the author of two scientific books, six book chapters and about 50 research papers.

I was born in Chelsea, London, in 1927 when recovery from World War I was shortly to be overtaken by the Depression. My father was an artist who had sold an inherited business in Birmingham to take up his real love, art. He studied painting at the Slade School at the turn of the century under Henry Tonks in the same class as William Orpen and Augustus John. My mother was the daughter of a clergyman, the vicar of East Ham. After a classics degree at London University she also had decided to take up art. They met at a Chelsea party in the early twenties, and with friends made a number of painting trips to the south of France. Although differing in age by 24 years, they married in 1926 and I was born in 1927 and my brother Terence in 1929.

My father had been brought up as a regular churchgoer but the relatively early death of his parents made him doubt the love of God. This was compounded by his contact with the general skepticism current in intellectual circles in the late Victorian period, and by reading Herbert Spencer's popularization of Darwinism. He always remained a non-churchgoer, but we believe he did ultimately find faith. My mother worshiped regularly at Holy Trinity, Sloane Street (called by John Ruskin "the temple of the arts and crafts") for all the rest of her life. Her original reason for going there was that, although it was somewhat farther away from our home than other churches, the services began later in the morning and it lay on a bus route so that she had more time to get ready.

She took Terence and myself to the afternoon children's service, and though it made little impression at the time, I believe we learned more Bible truths then than we realized. During the week we attended Gibbs Primary School in Sloane Street with such distinguished fellow pupils as Bobby and Teddy Kennedy, John Catlin (son of Vera Brittain), and a boy called Armitage whose father was Noel Gay, the composer of the popular song "The Lambeth Walk." Peter Ustinov was an earlier attendee, as he describes in his book *Dear Me*.

The school emphasized the classics, but one of the teachers, Miss Clarice, read Bunyan's *Pilgrim's Progress* to her English classes and this made a lasting impression. At the back of one's mind one wondered about one's own fate if the only characters in the book with a future were Christian and Faithful.

Then came the war. In September 1939, Gibbs School was evacuated to Canford School in Dorset but lost many of its pupils. We enjoyed the year in a rural environment and being almost treated as part of a "big boys" school. My mind is a blank about any religious activities, but I suppose we must have attended the school chapel. Although there had been a few air raids on nearby Southampton necessitating descents to the air raid shelter, this was still the "phony war" until the early summer of 1940 when it ended with the blitzkrieg and the fall of France. The Canford arrangement then ended and Gibbs School closed down.

We had an American cousin, the Reverend Edric Weld, a clergyman who was the headmaster to Holderness, an independent church school in New Hampshire. After the fall of France our parents responded to his repeated invitation to send Terence and myself to them for the duration. In July 1940 we crossed to Montreal in the *Duchess of Atholl*. We were the last ship to evacuate children across the Atlantic, as the one after us was sunk by a submarine, as described by Elspeth Huxley in *Atlantic Ordeal*.[42]

We spent five years in New Hampshire, mainly at the school and at the Welds' home. The Reverend Weld was a fine and generous father and headmaster. He was both theologically and politically liberal. His emphasis in the school was on citizenship, manliness, and social concern. Mrs. Weld was a popular hostess, and hosted a formal and elegant afternoon tea every Sunday in her home for the boys who wished to go. But looking back I have to say that there never was an occasion when the evidences for the Resurrection or the challenge of the gospel were clearly put in a way that a schoolboy could understand. The teachers were dedicated, but only the Reverend Weld brought a specifically Christian orientation to the teaching.

My beliefs became increasingly rationalist and agnostic, and I could see no sense in church, least of all its rituals. However, my long-term roommate, Charlie Dodge, from an old New England family, was a conscientious believer and kept me from being too extreme. I had a year at Harvard from 1944–45, where the pressure of work and late-night smoking and drinking parties in its dominantly secular culture made my life perceptibly downgrade.

I returned to Britain in June 1945 and went to Oxford to read geography in the autumn. I had only one term before His Majesty called me to the colors. But in this term, some old friends from pre-U.S. days, now also undergraduates, pushed me to go to meetings of the Oxford InterCollegiate Christian Union, known as the OICCU, for short. These included *Fact and Faith Films* from the Moody Institute and evangelistic sermons in St. Martin's Church in the High Street (always called "the High"). I felt strongly moved by the appeals, which deepened my feelings of inadequacy and especially made me regret my rebellious and rude behavior to my parents and others. The meetings were followed up by "squashes" and invitations to tea by OICCU members. Squashes are a particularly Oxford institution. Everyone in a college is invited to go to someone's room to hear an invited speaker on an advertised topic. OICCU members pressure their friends to go to theirs. Since the rooms are small and many people come out of interest, it is usually standing room only, and the word "squash" is appropriate. It is a good place to preach the gospel! OICCU members then follow up by inviting attendees to tea and to join college Bible-reading groups. One member of each college group is a representative to the university-wide union. (Incidentally this can give almost the ultimate in acronyms. I remember one girl was defined to me as the "LMH OICCU rep," the LMH standing for Lady Margaret Hall.) They put clearly the case for Jesus' resurrection and the consequences to the individual which followed from an acceptance of His divinity. I thought myself converted, and definitely found a new direction in life.

In December 1945 I was drafted into the RAF for national service, still in the immediate aftermath of the war. This was a shock! The induction center was a wilderness of hutments at Padgate outside Warrington. Draftees were herded around for two weeks before being sent off for basic training. For the first time I was thrown into the society of people whose main interests appeared to be football, beer, and women. Religious convictions tended to be forgotten.

Basic training was for eight weeks at Compton Bassett in Wiltshire. It was winter and I was introduced to such things as drill, route marches, target shooting, and throwing a grenade. I was impressed on one occasion by an army Scripture reader who braved the indifference of man to walk into our billet and talk to us. Most criticized him. Also, I made friends with a Scots boy in the same billet who was a Christian and invited me to go to a church in the nearby town of Calne, where once again I heard the gospel preached. But other feelings intervened and I failed to go on, comforting myself with the reflection that the old minister's view was "too strict."

My RAF career lasted two and a half years in the low rank of aircraft hand. In the UK it included jobs as laborer and cook. I spent the last 18 months overseas, three in Burma and 15 in Malaya, first at Butterworth airport opposite the island of Penang and then in Changi camp, Singapore. In Rangoon I was employed as an assistant military policeman. Some Christian soldiers had organized a church and I went once or twice. Then followed a spell as a clerk at Butterworth airport where there was no Christian influence. The last move was to Changi where my job was in the hygiene section, which involved leading an anti-mosquito spray team and acting as rat catcher (bubonic plague was known in the area). In Singapore I mainly visited the churches on the camp. But it is doubtful if more than one percent of the servicemen at Changi attended services in any regular way. I sought the church out of habit and as a connection with my old life and the cultural values it embodied. But at no time was I moved to make a positive stand, though I did find an affinity with one or two of the soldiers who also attended the services. One of the most appreciated features of Changi was the lending library run by one of the chaplaincies, from which I borrowed a number of books, mainly novels. They made no attempt to offer religion, which was a relief to me.

After my "demob" in 1948 I returned to Oxford and continued my studies for the geography degree. It engaged my interest and I performed the assigned readings in a moderately effective way, but never shone academically. The main reason was divided interests. I had returned to OICCU meetings, but also attended a variety of clubs, all three political ones at different times, the Oxford Union debates (I never spoke), and less well known groups such as the Movement for World Government and the Bridge Club. I even played chess for Brasenose against Jesus College (we won). But I was always aware that the OICCU had something the other clubs did not. I was moved by their intense personal emphasis and went, though mainly out of a feeling of duty, to the college group, the weekly Bible studies in the Northgate Hall, and sermons in St. Martin's. I still had made no definite commitment but had an uncomfortable feeling that a decision was waiting to be made.

The crisis came at a sermon in St. Martin's in the spring of 1949. The speaker was Dr. Basil Atkinson, under-librarian at

Cambridge University. He based his sermon and appeal on a Bible passage which had no apparent relevance to my moral problem. It was the words of Absalom to Hushai when he queried his loyalty to David: "Is this thy kindness to thy friend?" (2 Sam. 16: 17). But this struck home to me in terms of the ingratitude and lack of kindness I had always shown my parents, protectors, and friends. I experienced a strong feeling of guilt and a desire for forgiveness and the removal of this burden. At the end of the meeting we were called to go forward. I can't remember the details, but someone gave me a copy of Dr. D.W. Bromiley's book *Henceforth*. I went back to my college rooms that night with a chastened spirit.

The next day I sat in the Brasenose Library — I can see it in my mind's eye now, looking out on the Radcliffe Camera and All Souls' College — and I read *Henceforth* from beginning to end. This laid out the challenge of the Christian life in practical and unvarnished terms. It was a chastening experience, but something told me I had to go on and not look back. It was there that I decided, despite what might come, that I had to give the Lord the rest of my life, and start in the light of the Holy Spirit. It was not my own doing. All I can say is that the call was overwhelming and the grace sufficient to overcome my resistance. But my old interests still survived, and that same evening I went to the cinema with a friend (at The New Theatre). I cannot remember the film, but I do remember that in spite of watching the entertainment, a moment came when a great feeling of relief surged over me, that a call had been answered, a step taken, a bridge crossed. I felt lighter and happier, despite the worldly surroundings.

Thereafter, OICCU friends asked me to the weekly Bible studies in college and I began to be more regular in attending the weekend meetings in the Northgate Hall and St. Martin's. I had begun to attend St. Aldate's, one of the main churches in the town, but John Billinghurst, a childhood friend then a medical undergraduate, persuaded me to follow other OICCU members in attending St. Ebbe's. This was because Maurice Wood (subsequently Bishop of Norwich) was vicar and had a more conservative and strictly biblical stance. I believe the main doctrinal difference between the churches derived from St. Ebbe's stronger rejection of evolution.

I had started daily Bible study and prayer, though in my unheated bedroom this was usually done under the bed covers. In the Easter vacation of 1949 I attended the annual meeting of the Inter Varsity Fellowship at Swanwick. This introduced us to Christians from other universities in an atmosphere of enthusiastic devotion, exegetical Bible studies and large prayer meetings. I even met Dr. Bromiley, the author of *Henceforth*, who was giving some of the talks. Back in Oxford, I followed the suggestion of Brasenose OICCU colleagues and decided to be confirmed. This involved attending personal preparatory tutorials with Dr. Lee, the vicar of St. Mary's, the university church in the High Street.

Dr. Lee was known as a liberal and had formerly served at St. Martin's in the Fields in London. OICCU colleagues, in the person of Anthony Creery-Hill, subsequently himself to be a clergyman, however, were shocked at my decline from OICCU orthodoxy. They cautioned me about the dangers of non-biblical ministries and persuaded me to withdraw from Dr. Lee's tutorials. He was a little surprised and taken aback when I told him this, but accepted it kindly as a philosopher, as I suspect many clergymen have had to do for reasons which appeared unimportant to them. Instead I went to Dr. Michael Styler, the chaplain of Brasenose, as he appeared to be the obvious choice. His approach was more personal. He came across to my young eyes as somewhat angst-ridden and introspective. I can remember little of what he told me except that "the Adam and Eve story is cogent for man's whole religious problem." When I told Anthony of the change he put up his hands and said, "Oh dear, out of the frying pan into the fire!" However, a short while later he said that he had become reconciled to my continuing with Dr. Styler. I was confirmed in a ceremony by Kenneth Kirk, the Bishop of Oxford, in St. Aldate's, as far as I can remember, in the summer term of 1949.

When I returned to the university for my second year, in October, I continued attendance at OICCU meetings. One of the members of the Brasenose group was an Australian named Adrian Kent, a post-graduate researching into the character of the political assemblies of ancient Rome. I had moved out of college and lived in digs at No. 70 Iffley Road. He lived in Pembroke

Street, off Cowley Road, so we both started our walks home down "The High" as far as Magdalen Bridge. This circumstance brought us together after OICCU meetings. He came from a family which had been involved in a church in Australia for generations and his father was a senior minister. One day he invited me back to his digs and showed me the prophecies of Daniel in the Bible, especially chapters 2 and 7, which give a telescopic view of world history. He also pointed out the importance of keeping the Sabbath day.

Our friendship and discussions continued for a whole year, until finally one evening in my digs I decided that as the fourth commandment about keeping the Sabbath day was part of the Ten Commandments of the Bible (see Exod. 20:8–11 and Deut. 5:12–15) and as I had already committed myself to full acceptance of Bible authority, I must start to observe it.

So began my life as a Sabbath-keeping Christian. After graduation I started to attend a church in Chiswick, the nearest to our Chelsea home. There followed two years at Liverpool University on a post-graduate course in town and country planning. After this time I was baptized into the Christian faith by immersion in July 1951.

It may be of interest to readers to hear of the struggles of one individual over the issue of biblical authority. To a geographer with some training in geology the key problem is of course the validity of the early chapters of Genesis in the light of evolution theory. In my case it was the spiritual experience that determined the intellectual stance. I believe biblical authority rests on unshakeable ground and so must take precedence over any other consideration, however apparently scientific. As a result of taking this stand, one seeks to understand, from a *scientific* perspective, the supreme biblical authority. I believe the prayerful pursuit of this investigation leads one to understand how very weak many of the evolutionary arguments are and how much evidence supports special creation, a young earth, and a geological column largely formed by a single universal flood.

The completion of my university studies led to the necessity of finding a job. After a disappointing six months of trying, I accepted a job advertised in the *Times* as a soil surveyor in the Sudan. I flew out to Khartoum in October 1952. This was a new world. It faced me with many new challenges. It was a fascinating job intellectually but a dry one spiritually. I was removed completely from OICCU-type Christian fellowship and did not observe the Sabbath for the whole two-and-a-half years I worked there. The Christian contact was the church at Wad Medani where I attended services when back at base. But much of the time was spent with teams of Sudanese in remote areas. I acquired some knowledge of Arabic and a fascination with the scientific problems of soil survey for irrigation development. I served under two bosses, Dr. Tom Jewitt at base in Wad Medani, and Stanley Willimott in the southern research center of Yambio for four months in the summer of 1953.

I resigned from the Sudan in 1955 to do a one-year course in soil science at Aberdeen University. I rejoined the church there, and a fine Christian girl, Clemency Phillips, who six years later became my wife, arrived to study medicine that same autumn. There were so few young people in the church that we naturally gravitated together. But while her course lasted six years, mine ended in 1956, and I was faced with the same challenge as before — to find a job, especially now that I was specialized, with the Sabbath off. I was accepted by Hunting Surveys to be a team leader in soil survey in Iraq. When I arrived there I went through a week of spiritual agony such as I don't remember before or since. Should I make a stand for the day in this Muslim country? Could I? Something told me that I must and this resolution was strengthened by a letter I received from an old friend from Liverpool who was baptized with me, Roy Atkinson. Finally I asked Tom Jewitt if I could have Sabbaths off and work Fridays instead. I can still remember his reply: "Well, I think you're bloody silly, but okay." The relief was immediate, and from then on I was able to arrange my work so that I never had to go to office or field on Sabbath days.

I left Hunting Surveys in 1963; Clemency and I married in the same year. After a spell on a doctorate at Cambridge, I became a geography lecturer at Reading University in 1968.

Among my duties at Reading, I organized and executed a field class to southern Morocco in 1969 to study a desert environment. This became an annual event.

The move to Reading was our final career move. We have felt God's leading hand on us and that our earlier lives were a divinely ordained foundation for the relatively settled life of the lecturer and doctor with a family of four children in middle age and retirement. Our central focus has been a deepening commitment to the Lord's work, to helping in the church, seeking to win our friends and relatives, and helping in the community in various ways.

It is perhaps of interest to summarize some things that my life has taught me. First, the Lord seeks us even when we resist and performs the whole miracle of conversion in the midst of our doubts and fears. Thereafter, He leads us in ways that are often unexpected, but in retrospect we understand. Secondly, we can only progress spiritually when we are willing to obey His voice. Further knowledge is only given after we have obeyed earlier leading. I have been brought back to "square one" to surrender before ever being able to progress in the Christian life. Finally, God holds us. Once we have been born again, the Holy Spirit guides and strengthens us so that we are able to continue. We suffer if we resist or disobey. The revelation of God's love as shown in Christ overwhelms all other considerations and increasingly fills our hearts with joy and deepens our desire for commitment.

PETER H. BARRY

PHYSIOLOGY

Dr. Barry is a professor of physiology in the School of Physiology and Pharmacology at the University of New South Wales, Australia. He holds a B.Sc. with honors in physics and a Ph.D. in biophysics from the University of Sydney, and a D.Sc. in membrane biophysics from the University of New South Wales. He serves as a reviewer for a number of international journals and has published 65 papers and reviews, together with 120 conference abstracts and eight book chapters in the area of physiology and biophysics.

Although I came from a background sympathetic to Christian values, it was only when I started at the University of Sydney as a young student doing geology and physics that I really began to understand properly what the Christian faith was all about. It was towards the end of my first year that I really started to question what were the ultimate values in life. What was the point in trying to live an ethical life if there was no God out there? Was Christianity the answer to such questions? I went along to one of the Christian groups on campus and was quite impressed by a talk that Billy Graham gave at the university during his 1959 Sydney crusade. This was all helpful preparation for what was to follow.

Close to the beginning of my second year of study, while on a geography excursion, I met a group of Christian students, including one, Humphrey Babbage, who was to be of particular influence on me later on. It so happened that these students all attended a church close to where I lived, even though it was in one of the distant northern suburbs and other students came from all over Sydney. At their invitation, I started going to that church and to one of their Bible study groups. I was very impressed by the obvious sincerity of their faith and the way those members lived it out. However, I wanted to make sure that the Christian faith really was intellectually rigorous and authentic, and so, in addition to reading the Bible, I started to read some books on Christianity (C.S. Lewis's *Mere Christianity*, *Surprised by Joy* and *Screwtape Letters*, as well as books by J.B. Phillips and various other authors). Later I went along to meetings of the Evangelical Union at the university and found them especially helpful.

Humphrey Babbage had dinner with me from time to time at the University Union, and one particular evening after one of those dinners, I reached the point where I had become convinced that the Christian faith was authentic and true and that Jesus Christ had died on my behalf on the cross. The only remaining significant question became one of my response. I remember going up alone after dinner on to the balcony outside the University Union and being absolutely overwhelmed with the conviction that I really had no choice but to accept God's forgiveness and seek to endeavor to live for Him. And that is what I did.

As a science student, I also wanted to relate my studies in science to my newly discovered faith. I found especially helpful a book by Professor C.A. Coulson, professor of mathematics at the University of Oxford, entitled *Science and Christian Belief*.

When I had completed my B.Sc. (Hons) degree in physics, the question became one of seeking God's leading for a future career. There was a possibility of doing a Ph.D. in plasma physics, in which I had done my honors year. As I thought through the implications of some of the possible career options open to me and prayed about my future, I was still uncertain. Perhaps, it was a lack of faith in my own ability to make a decision, but like Gideon in the Bible, I prayed that God would make it very clear to me with a sign. In my case, the sign was this: that if He wanted me to do a doctorate in physics I would get a scholarship to do this. When the Commonwealth Scholarship results came out, it turned out that I had just missed out. I was told I could still do a Ph.D. in plasma physics on a tutorship and was given a couple of hours to make a decision as to whether to accept this alternative. For me the decision was very clear-cut and, after a short time in prayer, I turned the offer down.

Shortly after this I commented to another physics student on my failure to get the Commonwealth Scholarship. He informed me he himself was doing an M.Sc. in biophysics in the CSIRO Plant Physiology Unit of the School of Botany at the University of Sydney, and he understood there was a special CSIRO Ph.D. scholarship available to do a doctorate in membrane biophysics in that unit. When I approached the head of the unit, I was told that although there had been no other applicants, the deadline for the scholarship had passed. Nevertheless, he suggested I apply for it anyway. Some weeks later I heard I had been successful.

In thinking the whole decision-making issue through, it was clear to me that if God had withheld a scholarship from me, and therefore from other students with similar marks to mine, because of my need for some sort of sign, this was a bit problematic. It was therefore with amazement some time after this that I was informed that some more Commonwealth Scholarship positions were available and I was now eligible for one. But, of course, I already had a scholarship and no longer needed to accept this new offer. This all reinforced my strong sense of God's gracious answer to my prayer. In retrospect, this career pathway via plant cell biophysics turned out for me to be an excellent way to eventually get into biomedical research. I should add that other future critical decisions were generally reached more with a careful thinking through of issues and a resultant sense of conviction following prayer to God for guidance.

I later completed my Ph.D. research with a year and a half at the new Flinders University of South Australia, since my supervisor had moved there. This was followed by three years of post-doctoral work in animal physiology at the University of California in Los Angeles (UCLA). It was here that I met my future wife at the Graduate Christian Fellowship group I was involved with at the time. We were married before leaving North America and moving on to the University of Cambridge, where I spent a further year doing post-doctoral research.

I returned to Australia with my wife and took up a Queen Elizabeth II fellowship in 1972 to work in the School of Physiology and Pharmacology at the University of New South Wales. This was followed by a lectureship, and finally I reached the position of professor of physiology in 1994.

Currently my research group, with quite an international mix of doctoral students and post-doctoral fellows, is investigating the properties of ion channels, including an inhibitory neurotransmitter glycine receptor, in cell membranes, and of ion channels involved in olfactory transduction. Parts of our projects include working with some molecular biologists, who are able to mutate single amino acid groups within those protein channels. We then investigate the resultant effects of those mutations on the functioning of those channels within the cells. I have also for a long time had an interest in unstirred-layer effects near membranes and problems of liquid junction potentials as they affect electrophysiological measurements. In addition, I have over the years developed some computer programs to aid both in research and in the teaching of electrophysiology.

From a scientific perspective, has being a Christian helped my research? Apart from being able to bring research problems to God in prayer, the knowledge that the universe has been created by a God of order and reliability makes it a much easier framework within which to experiment and test scientific models. I have also had the great privilege to work in a number of outstanding university departments for over 30 years, and I have been impressed by the surprising number of scientists who are either Christians or at least sympathetic to Christian (or Jewish) values.

From a Christian perspective, one thing I have found especially helpful over the years as strong evidence for the authenticity of the claims of Jesus Christ and the historicity of His resurrection has been the change in Jesus' disciples after the resurrection. They were transformed from being a group of frightened fishermen to a band of leaders who turned the known world of their time upside-down. They were now prepared to be tortured and killed, as indeed many of them finally were, for their belief that Jesus was God's Son, who had risen again from the dead. My faith has also been strengthened over the years by God's answers to my prayers, both spoken and unspoken, in personal, family, and professional matters.

ERIC BARRETT

METEOROLOGY AND REMOTE SENSING

*D*r. Barrett is senior research fellow at the University of Bristol in the UK. He holds a B.Sc. in geography, an M.Sc. in applied climatology from the University of Sheffield, and a Ph.D. in satellite meteorology and a D.Sc. in applied climatology from the University of Bristol. Dr. Barrett has taught at the UK Universities of Sheffield and Leicester and for over 30 years at Bristol, where he became the founding director of the University Research Centre in Remote Sensing. He has served as consultant to both UK and foreign government departments and organizations, including the European Commission, NASA, and several United Nations agencies, including FAO, UNDP, UNEP, UNESCO, and WMO. Dr. Barrett has authored or edited nearly 20 books and more than 250 scientific papers and reports and has been honored with a medal and prize by the Royal Meteorological Society.

QUESTS AND DISCOVERIES

In the mid-1980s I received unexpected yet highly encouraging news. For nearly two decades I had served, in my spare time, an international Christian mission interested primarily in Slavic countries. In those days Christianity was militantly opposed by their prevailing atheistic governments, especially in the USSR. A mission colleague had been monitoring Soviet newspapers and magazines in respect of their lines of attack on churches and

Christians. Though articles denouncing the Christian faith on the grounds that it was "unscientific" had long been epidemic in their number and intensity, my friend suddenly realized they had *completely ceased.*

This was particularly encouraging for me because I had long exercised a special concern for Russian-speaking people, and had come to believe that my scientific career had been purposed by God not so much to see the frontiers of knowledge pushed back a little further, but to equip me to work out that concern in some quite specialized and specific ways.

Trained initially as a geographer, then as a climatologist, when I had gained my bachelor's and master's degrees I began to travel widely behind the old Iron Curtain. My aim? To become personally familiar with one of the less-known major world regions, and so develop a competitive edge over others for academic staff vacancies in geography or environmental science departments of British universities. In those days, the Cold War was at its most intense. Few others, I surmised, could lecture on central and eastern Europe and beyond with true authority.

I still remember vividly the USSR I found on my first visit in 1965. Clearly, that gigantic land was unusually strongly organized. On the credit side, it was actively addressing social deprivation and economic inequalities: no one was begging on the streets, and unemployment was unknown. Also, as I was to discover for myself when my digestive system revolted in response to local food, the state cared for people in need to levels rarely rivaled even in the world today: although, to put it mildly, the UK and USSR were not friends at the time, I was given free hospital treatment as an in-patient until I had recovered. Indeed, I was even given compensation for the hotel food I had not eaten while away on the ward! But what impressed me most was the progress the Soviet Union was making in science and technology. Less than a decade had passed since the USSR had startled everyone by placing Sputnik 1, the first-ever artificial satellite, into orbit around the earth.

Unfortunately, though, it became quickly obvious that there was also a huge debit side to life in Russia. The first problem hit me at the border. Even in those pre-mass travel days, customs inspections at most international frontiers were far less draconian than mine was at that oh-so-sleepy border post between the then Czechoslovakia to the west and the Soviet Republic of Ukraine to the east. All my possessions were raked by the proverbial fine-toothed comb — and all the papers in my luggage (and as an academic I had many!) were leafed through virtually page by page.

But my Bible came in for the closest scrutiny. "What's *this* for?" I was brusquely asked. When I replied, "For personal use," the retort rifled back that, although it was an English Bible, I must list it separately on my customs declaration form — and show it to the officers on my way home.

Strikingly, too, the next time I visited the Soviet Union I found the standard questions being put to all my fellow-passengers were: "Have you any pornography? . . . Have you any Bibles?" Amazingly, these literary antipodeans were officially considered as bad as one another.

Such acid antipathy to anything Christian was evident all across the USSR. Among the most eye-catching expressions of this were the tall roadside banners, even in central Moscow itself, proclaiming stridently: SCIENCE HAS PROVED 100 TIMES THERE IS NO GOD! This indefensible assertion was joined by others affirming urgently, yet so inappropriately: OUR ASTRONAUTS HAVE TOURED THE HEAVENS, BUT DID NOT SEE GOD!

In the USSR in those years, freedom from poverty and progress in science and technology, were being purchased at a high price indeed. Freedom of thought was discouraged, there was little freedom of worship, and virtually no freedom to share one's personal beliefs with others. Nor was there intellectual freedom of the kind honored and espoused in the West.

Yet, despite all the official pressure on those without a faith in God to never even begin thinking of trusting Him, plus all the overt persecution of those who had come to believe in Him already, many educated people clearly did not find satisfactory the foundational assertions of atheism that there is no God and that the universe came about by chance. On one memorable occasion I found myself talking with an undergraduate of Moscow University. Like all Soviet students of her time, part of Svetlana's curriculum at both secondary and tertiary levels had been lectures in atheism. And yet, when she learned I was a Christian, she was full of curiosity.

"Who is God?" Svetlana urged. "What is He like? How do you speak to Him? How do you know the Bible is the 'Word of God'?" I wondered what more fundamental questions anyone could ask than these.

Certainly, though, I had no inkling at the time that, just 12 years later, I would be granted an unusual and extended opportunity to address these and many more related questions asked by thinking people, not only across the USSR itself, but literally all around the world. In an interesting way, which I have subsequently recognized to have been God's plan for my life (so clearly overwriting any I might have thought I was developing for myself), I was soon to find that my growing, hard-earned knowledge of communist Europe and Asia was never to benefit my academic career at all. After my first visit to Moscow I quickly found myself appointed to a permanent post in the School of Geographical Sciences in the University of Bristol. Almost uniquely in those days, this prided itself on a systematic, not regional, approach to teaching and research about the surface of the earth, so I never got to lecture in those Soviet countries in a professional capacity. But since becoming involved with our mission in 1967, knowledge of them has been indispensable on the innumerable occasions I have been asked in public meetings to describe what our organization seeks to do in the Slavic world, and why.

Knowledge of this region became specially valuable in 1977 when our mission's general director invited me to develop a new magazine-style radio program to be broadcast to the USSR in Russian from several Christian shortwave radio stations around the globe. The program series would have four basic purposes: first, to confirm that the Christian faith is held to be tenable even by objective, highly educated people; second, to explain why science cannot prove even once that God does not exist, much less "100 times"; third, to share widely the personal experiences of many from the fields of science who have become convinced that God does exist, and wants people everywhere to enjoy personal relationships with Him; and last but not least, to help persecuted Christians in the USSR and elsewhere defend their faith in discussions, arguments, or worse, against antagonists.

The 30-minute weekly program that resulted — dubbed "Radio Academy of Science" in English, "Quests and Discoveries" in Russian — was first transmitted on January 1, 1980. It continued to be broadcast several times a week, across each of the time zones of the former Soviet Union, until 1993. By that time atheism had long since lost the support of many governments, and the sympathy of many people. As we saw at the beginning of this chapter, it was around 1985 that clear signs of that great change of attitude first became evident in the USSR. What part our programs played in the process of change we cannot tell; but we are certain that the information provided in them, the explanations given, and the insights and experiences shared from Christian viewpoints by scientists and technologists of many nationalities helped make a fundamental difference to the attitudes and lives of many individuals, both Russians and non-Russians (for eventually the program was broadcast in other languages to many other countries). Because in the post-communist era, Russians now have the freedom to debate matters of faith openly in their new Commonwealth of Independent States, and because Christian programs are recorded today in studios even in Moscow itself, our program is no longer in production. But its message lives on. Two books have been published from it, telling how in total nearly 50 of our program's contributors have triumphed in their personal quests for truth and reality by discovering God for themselves. At the time of writing both are still in print. [43]

My Life-Changing Discovery

Meanwhile, what of my own journey to faith in God? As I have explained above, I can now see major ways in which He was directing pivotal personal decisions of mine long before I knew how or why. And it is clear that all of these life-changing decisions depended on one early "quest" and one fundamental "discovery" that I made on my own. I was not quite a teenager at the time. No one of that age could fairly be described as a scientist. But, with the wisdom of hindsight, it is now intriguingly evident that my path from being a natural, often wayward lad to a born-again believer in Jesus Christ followed the steps of what we broadly know as "the scientific method."

Let me explain.

The first step of the scientific method involves the observation of events and situations: without data, science would be a baseless sham. What, then, did I observe when 11 years old that first set me thinking about spiritual things? Many children of that age are quite capable of sharp observation, careful thought, and apt reasoning. I was one of these.

I had served for two years as a choirboy in the established church in my country. In my church the services were very formal and ritualistic. I had observed nothing in them to make me think that churchgoers were any different from other people, except for their strange desire to spend time in church for no visible reward. As a choirboy I was in a different category: I was *paid* (although not very much!) for my attendance at practices, services, and — best of all — weddings. Why, I wondered, should ordinary churchgoers bother?

Then, suddenly, events in my family arrested my attention. First, my mother's whole demeanor visibly changed. Virtually overnight she became a calmer, happier, kinder person. She herself had never been a regular churchgoer, but she now announced that she had been "born again" through a seemingly chance attendance at a church I did not know. The change in her life was easy to observe because it was so obvious.

I thought this must be in some way a once-off event, so I was nonplussed when, soon afterwards, my older sister's behavior also changed likewise. Apparently, the reasons were the same.

To say that I was very puzzled by these developments would be an enormous understatement. After careful thought, I reckoned that closer study might clarify the issues. So one evening when I was particularly unwilling to go to my own church, despite the loss of pocket-money I knew I would incur as a result, I agreed to go to the other church with Mother and Sheila. There, and thereafter (for I never went back to my old church again), I took the second step in the scientific method: after observing, I *analyzed* what I saw and heard.

What struck me most in the simple but seemingly more sincere services was that I found myself hearing clearly and directly, for the first time in my life, that without God we are incomplete, and totally unable to realize our full potential by our own efforts or "good works." I further learned that, by ourselves, we cannot please God — and that eternal separation from God is the penalty for incurring His displeasure. Happily, I discovered too that God has always loved us — so much so, in fact, that He has provided, through His own Son, Jesus Christ, a substitute to suffer for our sin. This was all good news indeed. It seemed odd to me at the time that, if these things were true, I had never heard of them through years of attendance at my other church. However, as I looked around at other people in this new congregation, there was no doubt about it: whatever, or *whoever*, had changed two members of my family had clearly changed most of these other folk as well. In general demeanor they were nearly all alike — and different from almost everyone else I knew. After this realization I paid even more careful and critical attention to all they said and did.

My analysis led me to this simple conclusion: apparently two things were necessary to change me, too. The first requirement was that I should repent before God for all I had done wrong. It was clear I needed to do this; like most other boys of 11 or 12, my conscience was acute. The second requirement was that I should believe in Jesus Christ as God's Son, the One who had been punished in my place at Calvary, and request forgiveness in His name.

One Sunday, without warning, I suddenly felt the urge to progress one step further. I wondered, could faith in God really make a difference in me, too? Instinctively I knew I could only find out by *experiment*. To my great surprise, but also enormous pleasure, I instantly found that, as I tried to trust in God, so I could: the very moment I reached out to Him, He gave me the assurance He is real and loved me in a special, individual way.

So surprised was I by the overwhelming sense I immediately received of God's presence in me and beside me, that at first I forgot to ask Him to forgive me for the years I had neglected and disobeyed Him. Then I remembered that was what I also had to do. My relief was palpable. And, despite all the years that have followed, I am still able to enjoy the feeling of euphoria I felt as I walked home that summer evening knowing that my inner self had been reborn and my whole life redirected. The first, fundamental experiments of my Christian life had been a huge success!

After that, just as scientists who make new discoveries in their work have the urge to publish what they have found, I just had to tell others what had happened, and I have been glad to do so ever since.

Now, there often comes a time when a scientist has completed enough observation, analysis, and experimentation to be able to model his findings into scientific theories and laws. So it has been in my Christian life. As I got to know God better through my teenage years, enjoying many of the activities of my newly adopted local church, so my confidence in the Bible as the inspired word of God continually grew. In the meantime, my interests at school were increasingly focused on the sciences. As I appreciated more and more the debt we owe to earlier scientists for bringing us to our present level of knowledge, so I recognized more and more that the Bible, God's textbook for life on earth, is a means of boosting rapidly our understanding of Him. I became interested in the great doctrines of the Christian faith — models of the nature and activity of God, the states and positions of men before and after they trust in Him, and His plans and purposes for the world. I learned more, too, of the laws of God — His immutable guidelines laid down for the good of everyone to whom He has given life.

Faith Applied

For many of my scientific colleagues, the scientific method — observation, analysis, experimentation, model building and development through hypotheses, theories, and laws — is quite sufficient in itself. They see no need to do more with their science. We know them as "pure" scientists. But many of us see things differently. We are more concerned with the use of science in everyday problem solving than we are with the solving of problems for the sake of advancing scientific knowledge alone. We are dubbed "applied" scientists.

Of course, it is natural for all scientists to learn the essence of their chosen field of study before they can put it to proper use, for pure science is the springboard into the pool of applications. So, in my own case, my early scientific work was more pure than applied. My M.Sc. research represented a purely academic study of the influence of cities on climatic change. And few could find a ready application for my discursive Ph.D. thesis on "The Contribution of Meteorological Satellites to Dynamic Climatology." It was not until later, from the early 1970s on, that my interests began to change and my work became much more practical. Since then they have included applications as diverse as desert locust monitoring and control for the United Nations . . . assessment of weather and soil conditions influencing cocoa palm productivity for the chocolate manufacturing industry . . . and modeling inshore wind and wave conditions to help keep naval ships "off the rocks"!

Again, my experience as a Christian has paralleled this principle of "learn then use." Pure science pursues knowledge for its own sake. It neither presumes nor seeks uses for its findings: it reckons that the world of matter is worth exploring for its own sake alone. Similarly, the life of the Christian also involves a quest, or search, and for some that exploration of God and the meaning of His Word is enough.

On the other hand, just as there is great scope to apply the findings of science to help and serve others, so the Bible says that God's people are generally set free from our naturally godless ways "so that we may serve the living God" (Heb. 9:14; NIV). And anything the believer learns of God could be of value to his fellow human beings. So for many Christian believers "pure" and "applied" Christianity are co-equal partners.

In my own case, therefore, it was a particularly fulfilling thing to be asked in the mid–1970s to design, and with others write for, that new radio program which came to share the quests and discoveries of many scientists who are Christians. Indeed, for me this activity has seemed to be the most important single reason why I became and have remained a professional scientist. Without my scientific knowledge and worldwide travels, I could not have fronted the program and perhaps it might never have gone to air. And I believe a general principle is evident here, too. In the providence and economy of God, some Christians are called to occupy solely Christian jobs. For others the call is to occupations for which a Christian faith is not a prerequisite; but the skills they develop in these so-called "secular" jobs specially fit them to serve God in other, complementary ways. I am in this latter group. And it has been encouraging indeed to feel that the work I have been paid to do has brought its greatest benefits through the work I have considered so much more vital: serving God, and sharing with many my understanding of Him and what He has done.

Why do I think this task is so important? Because of its link with the final goal — and the toughest test — of science: *the prediction of the future*. Scientists say, "If we have the data we need, and we understand a type of situation well enough, we must be able to predict the outcome of related experiments or natural events."

As a Christian, I have *data* on the spiritual situation. In the world today, crucially there are many people who do not know God for themselves. Yet I *understand* that He remains the Lord of life. So, not surprisingly, my firm prediction — and that of the Bible — is that the day is coming when God will say to each of us, "Enough! Give me an account of all that you have or have not done!" His judgment will not be on the basis of the New Age, postmodernist creed which claims that so long as what people do seems right for them, and not too wrong for others, it is acceptable. Rather, it will be on the basis of God's unchanging law, within which basic rights and wrongs are absolutely clear and immutable.

It is in this crucial area that the parallels I see between science and the Christian faith finally break down. I have often remarked to my students (to keep us all humble!) that, as scientists, we do the things we do today so that someone else may be able to do them better tomorrow. But, in the spiritual realm I know that there are things God requires each of us to do that can never be done for us by another person. Most important of these are honoring and obeying Him: He holds us individually responsible for these. Furthermore, and this is one of the Bible's most solemn warnings, for each of us there may be no tomorrow in which we might do them if we fail to do so today.

So what must our general conclusions be? Science and Christianity are so compatible that they can both be approached by a common method, whose hub is *experimentation* — the testing, in faith, of an initial notion or hypothesis. The Bible puts it like this: "Taste and see that the Lord is good" (Ps. 34:8; NIV), and "call on him while he is near" (Isa. 55:6; NIV). As such, the experiment to find and know God for ourselves is something every one of us can perform, whether our training lies in science or not, for the "scientific method" may also be dubbed, less pretentiously perhaps, "practical common sense."

ANDREW RUYS

CERAMIC ENGINEERING

*D*r. Ruys is a QE2 fellow, mechanical and mechatronic engineering at the University of Sydney, Australia. He holds a B.E. with first class honors in ceramic engineering and a Ph.D. in materials science and engineering from the University of New South Wales. Dr. Ruys is the founding editor of International Ceramic Monographs and serves on the editorial board of Interceram — International Ceramic Review (Germany). He specializes in composite bioceramics research for bone and tooth replacement and has edited seven books and published six book chapters, 34 research papers, and 38 conference papers.

When you ask somebody about their Christian experience, often you get an account of a conversion event that happened to them some decades ago, but not what is happening now. I had a conversion experience two decades ago, but what is of equal or greater importance is my walk with God over the subsequent two decades, and what preceded my conversion experience.

I was raised in a very religious family. We attended church every Sunday, and it was a long session, beginning at 8:30 a.m. when we departed for Sunday school and continuing with a long, stern church service that ended at midday. None of my school friends attended church and I received significant ribbing in the schoolyard for my church attendance. While Sunday school was usually fun, the church services were interminable. I remember resolving at a relatively young age that when I was old enough to make my own decisions, I would not attend church.

Many years later, in my final year of school, I began studying astronomy as a physics elective. It became a passion for me. The infinity of the night sky, and the awesome natural forces involved brought a new dimension to my life that took me out of my drab Monday to Friday existence and into a deeper metaphysical experience of reality. My father, himself a scientist (clinical biochemist) and a keen amateur astronomer, fostered my interest, and we spent many a long hour talking astronomy and metaphysics, peering at the night sky through binoculars and later a six-inch Newtonian telescope we built together.

As it turned out, this backdrop of astronomy and meta-physical discussions with my father led to my conversion. Leighton Ford, an evangelist in the Billy Graham mold, held a two-week crusade at a nearby showground that year, and I went along with my school friends, partly for the evening social event, and partly because my parents always let me borrow the car if it was for religious activities. When the altar call was made, I found myself challenged by it. I wanted this salvation. But I was very mindful that if I took it, it would change my life and there would be things I would have to leave behind. It was quite a struggle, but in the end I went forward, and my life did indeed change dramatically.

What was my conversion like? C.S. Lewis put it very well in the title of one of his books: "surprised by joy." One day, I was mostly preoccupied with whether I could borrow the car; the next day, I was completely bowled over by an encounter with the living God in which I received an assurance of my salvation, genuine peace of mind for the first time in my life, and a very real and personal experience of God. I never understood before that eternal life was an offer as a free gift and all I had to do was accept it. Having done so, I was suddenly in touch, in a very real and tangible way, with a benevolent mystical being, the Holy Spirit.

In the next few weeks, I had two powerful mystical en-counters with God. It is difficult to describe these experiences, just as it is difficult to explain to somebody who has never been head-over-heels in love what that is like. Suffice to say that it was very real, very powerful, and the memory of it remains with me two decades later. I have had many such experiences since, but none of such magnitude.

I Am a Scientist yet Still a Christian. Why?

I became a Christian before I became a scientist. Therefore, for my reader, probably the more important question is: Why am I, now a scientist, still a Christian two decades later?

Firstly, because of my *subjective* experience of God. God is as real to me today, in a personal, subjective, experiential way, as He was during that dramatic first encounter two decades ago. Indeed, God and God's love are as real to me in a personal, experiential, and emotional way today as my family members and close friends. This is not surprising when you consider my personal relationship with God now spans two decades.

Secondly, because of my *objective* experience of God, my walk with God has directly paralleled my progression over the last two decades from a final-year school student to a professionally trained and experienced scientist. In this time, evidence of the "mind of God" from the sciences, and historical evidence of the activities of God from the Bible, have increased in their relevance and importance to me.

Science is about the objective approach to the world around us, testable in a quantifiable sense. Personal relationships and love are part of the subjective experience of life, fulfilling and meaningful, but often difficult to define. Both the objective and the subjective are valid, and both are important for a balanced experience of life. Life without the objective is a vapid, rudderless existence. Life without the subjective is a cold, meaningless, and lonely existence, like the materialist robot-like existence found in some of the more chilling examples of futuristic fiction. Put more bluntly, without the objective, the subjective would lose its foundation, and without the subjective, the objective would lose its meaning.

With regard to the subjective, a double standard is often applied. If you say you love your child or your spouse in a real, personal, and mutual way, few people would question the reality of that love experience. If you say you love God in a real, personal, and mutual way, that statement has significant shock value when expressed in the company of certain non-believers. Intriguingly, in my life experience as a Christian and a scientist, and in my experience as a public speaker on the topic of science and God, it is usually non-scientists who are shocked by this statement. This is not surprising considering that a survey published in the scientific journal *Nature* in 1997[44] showed that 40 percent of American scientists believe in a God who answers prayer.

There are a lot more scientists who are Christians than the general public might suppose. I am obviously not alone in the viewpoint that the more I see through science, the more I see God. In my experience, it is not usually science that causes people to make a decision to become an atheist. Usually, it is a subjective reason, for example, a negative response to a repressively religious church, school, or upbringing.

Before I became a Christian, it was the objective that laid the foundation: astronomy gave me my first glimpse into the "mind of God." The historical evidence from the Bible gave a second objective perspective: Jesus, a man who said He was the Son of God, who said He would die and rise again, did so. And thirdly, the evidence of history. Jesus reset our calendar; He changed the course of history, and 2,000 years later there are two billion Christians, making it the largest religion in the world today. These are objective realities. But though it was the objective that laid the foundation for me, it was the subjective that prompted the conversion event and cemented the relationship with God.

My Two-Decade-Long Walk with God

My conversion was only the beginning. It is interesting to now reflect upon where I went from there, and how it is that I have kept the faith for so long.

The year after my conversion, I went to a university far from my school friends and began a new life studying the applied sciences in the hedonistic, anti-Christian environment of an early 1980s Australian tertiary campus. For the first five years of my Christian life, I only read the New Testament. I was afraid of the Old Testament, and especially Genesis, because I feared that it may contain material that would cause for me a crisis of faith as a scientist. It was not until I was doing my doctorate that I had the courage to face up to this issue. I enrolled in an evening diploma course in a mainstream theological college. I tackled Old Testament 1 first, and to my pleasant surprise, I felt that there was no real conflict at all.

Unfortunately, reading for pleasure on the science and God topic is an indulgence I never have enough time for, because my own scientific career has increasingly dominated my life as the years have gone by. I gradually evolved into a mere "pew warmer" in a mainstream church, reading on the science and God theme purely as a hobby, but working 70 hours a week or more in my scientific career. My area of specialization is composite bioceramics. I currently run a number of research projects concerning nanostructural and microstructural design of spinal implants, dental implants and bone-substitute materials. I have been involved in such research since the mid-1980s, working long hours publishing papers, speaking at conferences, writing grant proposals, and so on. This became an all-consuming task.

Though my private relationship with God was in good shape, my public life as a Christian was in a holding pattern for a long time. Then, a few years ago, I had a brush with death. It prompted me to ask myself a few probing questions about the purpose of my life. What had I achieved by devoting myself heart, mind, and soul to my career in bioceramics for so many years?

Humanitarian benefits to society? My contributions to bioceramics research have provided benefits in terms of potential orthopedic and dental surgical improvements.

A place in posterity? My children and grandchildren can one day look me up in *Chemical Abstracts, Science Citation Index* and so on.

Providing employment and training? I have employed researchers and trained students.

Paying the bills? The income from my work earns a living.

None of these answers seemed to justify my being spared. God's answer to my question did not come in the form of the powerful mystical experiences of my late teens. Instead, it was a growing conviction that I could, and should, do more to serve

God with the abilities and training that God had given me. After six months of pondering, I wrote an article on the theological significance of the fine tuning of the universe. I wrote it for a popular audience, based on my years of reading on the science and God topic, and published it in *Alive*, a widely distributed mainstream Australian Christian magazine. I put a little footnote at the end of the article that I would be prepared to speak in churches or schools on the topic if invited. It was more of a throwaway line at the time and I never imagined where it might lead.

Four years later I have given about 100 public seminars on the topic in churches and state schools. Weekends, lunchtimes, I fit them in whenever I can, even though it is often very difficult and inconvenient. Addressing a group of several hundred high school students does fully utilize all of my professional training and applied Christianity training, and brings into sharp focus the practical relevance of science and God. I simply tell the students that for me, two decades on from school, and two decades since my dramatic conversion in my final year of school, Christ is still central in my life, and science is no obstacle to the faith. Indeed, in my personal experience, the evidence from science points to God and therefore my scientific training is a strengthener for my faith, not a stumbling block.

It was science (astronomy) that laid the backdrop for my Christian conversion, and it is science that gives an extra dimension to my Christian experience now. I am not alone in being an objective scientist who is convinced. I stand with the 40 per cent of American scientists who, today, believe in a personal God who answers prayer.

Science and God? I find no conflict, only harmony.

Author's note: I would like to thank my father, Jan Ruys (clinical biochemist), for valuable discussion on this chapter.

CURT WAGNER

PHYSICS

*D*r. Wagner is professor of physics (retired), Southwest (Minnesota) State University. He holds a B.A. summa cum laude in physics from the University of Wisconsin (Madison), an M.S. in physics and astronomy and a Ph.D. in theoretical physics, both from the University of Illinois (Urbana). Dr. Wagner was a recipient of a National Science Foundation Fellowship and undertook research in the area of chaotic non-linear mechanics. Subsequent academic research covered a wide range of areas, including non-linear mathematical mappings and properties of various black hole solutions to Einstein's field equations of general relativity, computer modeling of various chaotic systems, artificial intelligence, biophysics, acoustics, cloud physics, and high-temperature superconductivity.

As I sit in one of my favorite spots on earth, hearing a bubbling streamlet at my side and looking through the pines and aspen across the narrow Kootenay Lake in southeastern British Columbia, Canada, I am drawn back in time 33 years to when I first set eyes on this beautiful, peaceful valley. Gretchen, my wife-to-be, and I had just responded to a lone climber's request to leave the Bugaboo Mountains and join him for some first ascents on the West Kootenay side of the Purcell Mountains. This seemingly insignificant decision marked a major fork in my life in a year that contained several life-changing forks.

In February of that year, 1967, I had fallen deeply in love with Gretchen, whom I had met on the 14,431-foot summit of Mt. Elbert in Colorado on August 13 of the previous year. Without understanding this newly discovered phenomenon of love, I nonetheless sensed I would spend the rest of my life with her. So it was only reasonable to ask her to join me and a group of students from the University of Illinois climbing club on a summer climbing expedition. After a warm-up climb in Colorado we arrived at the Grand Teton National Park in Wyoming. The next morning, Sunday, June 25, I accompanied Gretchen to a simple church service in the Chapel of the Transfiguration nearby. Though Gretchen had been a Christian for many years and I had been a Buddhist for nine years, I naively ignored this difference in world views. After the service we sat outside talking, and suddenly I found myself asking her to marry me. To the surprise of both of us, she agreed!

With my heart now in orbit around Gretchen we returned to camp. Five days later I led three novices on a climb, but surface avalanching forced us onto rock ledges where we had to bivouac for the night. Early next morning we started an arduous seven-hour roped descent of the steep frozen snow. That evening Gretchen told me she had worried constantly about me and realized she loved me so deeply she didn't know what she would have done if I hadn't come back alive.

We traveled next to Mt. Robson Provincial Park in British Columbia and then on to Bugaboo Provincial Park to climb several major peaks. After a couple of weeks of backpacking and climbing we met Bruce, a stranger, who asked me to join him for some first ascents in the West Kootenay Mountains. (There began that fork in the road of my life that 33 years later would lead us back to the place where I am writing now.) After two successful climbs Gretchen and I returned to Illinois, where I went back to my eighth and final year of graduate studies in theoretical (non-linear) physics at the University of Illinois and Gretchen and her mother prepared for a November wedding. I had wanted to get married on top of Mt. McKinley in Alaska, but our mothers plus Gretchen's common sense prevailed and the wedding was held in Gretchen's home church. My Buddhist beliefs would not allow me to participate in the Christian prayers or communion, but Gretchen and I were joined together before God all the same, even though I didn't believe in Him.

The final significant incident of that eventful year began innocently enough with a winter mountaineering trip to Colorado to climb 14,100-foot Mt. Yale. This was our honeymoon trip, albeit with about a dozen other students from the U of I climbing club! Backpacking to a base camp at 10,000 feet and then snowshoeing and skiing up to a high camp at around 11,500 feet, we settled in to send various small teams to the summit. Because of a cold I was grounded at first, but in a few days Gretchen and I were ready to go. Ascending the easy northwest ridge we arrived at a false summit at around 13,000 feet. I was thrilled to see the summit perhaps a mile away along a wind-swept ridge. But when I looked at my new mountaineering bride I could see she was tired and cold, in no condition to continue the climb. I put my parka on her, and as I looked at her huddled behind some rocks to break the icy wind, I (unknowingly) was at another major fork in the road of my life. The enticing summit ridge was beckoning to my mind (soul), but Gretchen's tired face was tugging on my heart (spirit). I then made a most important decision, a very uncharacteristic choice of heart over head. I knew I must forsake the summit to help my beloved wife.

As we slowly descended the barren ridge with the wind-driven snow biting into our faces, a strange thing happened. I suddenly stopped in my tracks and began to sob. The tears ran down my face and froze to my moustache and beard. Though the snowy wind whipped around my windbreaker, I did not notice the cold. I was filled with an incredible joy I had never known before — a joy far deeper than any of the abundant happiness I had known growing up. For 15 minutes that seemed like an eternity, I stood looking at the almost Himalayan panorama before me, the snowy winds nearly sweeping me away, and wept profusely with that unearthly joy. Then the tears abruptly ceased.

In the months following that mystical experience I wrestled with what had happened and why. This was not the world of orthodox physics I was researching but the shadowy world of metaphysics to which I was no stranger as a Buddhist. Eventually I concluded that one cause of what occurred was my wilfully sacrificing something very important to me in order to care for the needs of someone I loved. But precisely what had happened to me on the mountain, and what primal cause had led me to make such an uncharacteristic (though free) choice of heart over mind, remained unclear.

After finally receiving my Ph.D. in June of 1968 I accepted a temporary position to teach physics full-time at Central Washington State College, so we packed up and headed west. There I began to explore the many ramifications of my fascination with Tibetan Buddhism, including some of the psychic and occult arts. I even co-taught an "Advanced Psychology Seminar" class in "parapsychology." This sparked my interest in developing more rigorous scientific testing of psychic phenomena. Implementing this desire required a series of rather amazing apparent coincidences.

In the early summer of 1969 bad weather forced my wife, our baby daughter, and me to sit out the rains in an Alpine Club of Canada hut. There we met a climber from the University of Wisconsin. When we shared with him our plans for another first-ascent expedition into the West Kootenays, he told us of a University of Wisconsin chemistry professor who planned to climb the same peaks several months later. The following winter, during a Christmas trip home to my family in Wisconsin, we met Professor Bob West and shared stories about our summer climbs. When I also shared some of my somewhat unorthodox philosophies about teaching physics, Bob told me that one of his graduate students had just taken a faculty position at Southwest Minnesota State College (SMSC), a new college open to innovative teaching methods. After returning to Washington I was surprised to receive a letter from the physics chairman at SMSC asking me to apply for one of three new physics positions. I really hoped to find a permanent position in the west, close to the mountains, but I reluctantly sent in my application to the new college anyway. Soon I received a phone call to come to Minnesota for an interview, after which I was offered a position. Though it meant postponing my dream of teaching in the mountains, I accepted the offer, intending to stay in Minnesota only until I could find a permanent position in the western United States. Little did I realize I would remain at SMSC for 29 years, walking down the road that forked off at that "insignificant" 1967 decision to go climbing first ascents with a total stranger and that led us to the man who introduced us to SMSC.

Teaching physics at a small, three-year-old, innovative undergraduate liberal arts/technical college immediately proved exciting, challenging, and rewarding. Research was unofficially encouraged but not required; excellence in undergraduate teaching was the basis for hiring and promotion. I continued to develop my unorthodox methods of personalized general education and apprenticeship-style specialized education for our physics majors, with experimental and even some theoretical physics research open to any student. I also continued my own research into the non-linear mapping properties of the field equations for various kinds of black holes, as a forerunner of a general relativistic approach to a non-linear unified field theory (research which continues even today). On the extracurricular side, Gretchen and I were immediately conscripted as founding members of the Southwest Minnesota Orchestra, leading the first and second violins. Together with a physical education faculty member, I co-developed a Wilderness Encounter Program to teach students climbing and wilderness survival skills. Soon all thoughts of relocating to some college in the western United States simply vanished. I was happy and fulfilled where I was.

Concurrent with all these exciting pursuits I also had the opportunity at SMSC to investigate scientifically the intriguing realm of the paranormal. I reasoned that if only a tiny percentage of reported psychic and occult phenomena were valid, physicists should nonetheless research the physical properties and dynamics of those phenomena to learn the laws that govern them. Some of the alleged paranormal phenomena seemed to violate the established laws of matter, energy, and space-time. On the other hand, as a Buddhist especially interested in Tibetan models of reality, this would complement my personal faith and world view. From the first academic year of 1970–71 I was able to find students who wanted to do directed studies and/or directed research in what I termed "paraphysics," the physical study of the paranormal.

In the beginning the students and I tried to study, replicate, and model the classic work of J.B. Rhine and others, especially in the areas of clairvoyance and telepathy. After occasional astounding successes we expanded the research into precognition and telekinesis. It was then a logical step to investigate specific sub-cases of these four basic areas of so-called ESP. By the second year we were investigating radiesthesia (dowsing or witching), the Backster Effect on plants (psychically influencing the biophysical properties of plants or simple organisms), and scientific astrology (linking astrophysical causes to astrological predictions). From this I developed a new introductory physics course called "Paraphysics," which quickly grew to become our most popular physics course.

One of the earliest students in the course told of his personal experiences with spirits during seances. It sounded rather strange (though not uncommon), so in order to be objective and thorough I decided that this controversial phenomenon also needed to be investigated. Using physiological measurements of pulse rate, skin resistance, skin temperature, and even brainwaves (using EEG techniques), I began to investigate the physiological correlates of altered states of consciousness (ASCs), including trance states during seances and various types of meditation and yogic exercises. As a result of these tests I was able to select which students would make the best candidates for future mediums of paranormal phenomena.

Because these techniques were so effective, our research activities increased in proportion to the number of newly trained mediums. By the third year (1972–73) I had to add an "Advanced Paraphysics" course to the curriculum as well as expand the offerings of the introductory course. At the advanced paraphysics seminars students shared the results not only of their seance activities but also their Edgar Cayce-style psychic readings, traditional (ancient) astrology and tarot card readings, ouija board sessions, out-of-body experiences or astral projections, and even some white witchcraft experiences.

I planned and attended most of these experiments, using physiological and other electronic measuring equipment to get hard data. For example, to evaluate mediums' claims of feeling cold during seances or readings, we did a controlled ASC in my lab with complete audio and thermal documentation of our most adept medium. After establishing a thermal baseline record we monitored the medium as she slipped easily into the ASC. From the moment her spirit guide began to take control, as evidenced aurally, her forehead surface temperature plummeted 5.5 degrees C in one to two minutes. In the course of this controlled psychic reading her forehead temperature slowly returned to normal. But when her spirit guide suddenly departed, her forehead temperature shot up by 5.5 degrees C in less than one minute. The next day we had the same medium try to produce these results using any meditation or mental technique she knew in conjunction with the thermal biofeedback equipment with which she was familiar. Her best performance was less than +/– 0.5 degrees C.

Similar measurements were made at uncontrolled (normal) seances, where similar results were obtained, thus demonstrating the objective nature of mediums' reports of feeling cold. Some measurements of room temperature were also made without finding any significant changes in temperature, which indicated that the phenomenon was personal and biophysical in its effects. At most of the uncontrolled seances the standard equipment used was portable reel-to-reel tape recorders. I was always the interested but detached external observer, asking questions and cross-examining any drop-in communicators who used the mediums' vocal chords and lips, tongues, cheeks, and lungs as transducers of their spirit communications. Seances were held in many diverse locations: physics and mathematics labs, the planetarium, the theatre main stage, dorm rooms, private homes, and even haunted farmhouses. All sites were approximately equally effective, again demonstrating that the phenomenon was personal and biophysical in its effects.

By the beginning of the fourth year of research another new phenomenon was added to our list: psychic healing. One morning one of the core-group mediums came to my office, saying her spirit guide had instructed her to come to me to be healed of her advanced bronchitis. I was puzzled because the spirits hadn't revealed how I or anyone could heal. Not having any idea what to do, I simply put my hand on her head and mentally (silently) hoped she would recover. To my utter surprise, the next morning she came bounding into my office, apparently totally cured!

I might have dismissed this as a one-time coincidence, but some time later the main medium came to see me, having missed three days of classes and looking terrible. Her spirit guide had also sent her to me for psychic healing. Still unenlightened, I simply used the same method I had used with the other medium. Two days later she came back to school, not yet totally healed, but much improved.

About the same time as this, several of the core mediums began to receive personal revelations from their spirit guides that they should be prepared to abruptly flee the area as a group and move west to the mountains to await further revelations about the ultimate purpose of the group. All of this was somehow linked to an impending cosmic omen, the predicted December 1973 arrival of a potentially spectacular comet named Kohoutek. But something considerably more spectacular was about to happen for the core group, and especially for me — something that no one in their wildest imagination could have anticipated.

Wednesday, October 10, 1973, was just another normal day for me, teaching my usual classes and attending the weekly divisional meeting in the late afternoon. Yes, there was a psychic reading scheduled for late in the day with our main male medium, Dan (not his real name). But I didn't normally attend all the routine, private psychic readings anyway, so I gave little thought to missing it. When I returned to my office/lab after the divisional meeting, I found five or six of the core group of mediums gathered around Dan. This too was not especially unusual because often the advanced students debriefed each other after seances or readings. But when I looked into Dan's face I knew something was seriously wrong. In broken sentences he eventually told us what happened during the reading. Everything proceeded normally until the very end, when his spirit guide left him explosively. In his body he said it felt like an explosion of millions of tiny, sharp needles penetrating his skin from the inside out. But in his head he said the psychic explosion left his mind in a total whiteout state.

Dan was completely wasted, body and soul, so it was only reasonable he should have a psychic healing. Out of compassion, and as I had done before, I laid my hand on his head while the other mediums laid their hands on his shoulders. But this time, rather than just hoping, I unexpectedly began to analyze the situation. Here I was, a professor of physics, trying to heal someone without knowing in the least how to do it! Merely hoping for healing seemed ludicrous at best. But then suddenly a completely unpredictable event occurred. Out of nowhere a simple thought dropped into my mind, softly and lovingly: *Why don't you ask Jesus Christ into this situation?*

My immediate reaction was amazement. *Where did that come from?* I thought. The idea was so bizarre. As a physicist I tried to think logically and carefully, and this strange idea I *knew* was definitely not one of my own thoughts. Though I was raised by a Christian mother (and a good father who was silent about religion), as a teenager I rejected Christianity as hypocritical at best. I viewed Christians (except my wife, because I loved her) as emotional cripples and mental weaklings, easily duped and manipulated. As far as Jesus was concerned, I wasn't even sure if He had really existed or was merely the invention of religious charlatans.

But then as I reflected on that thought which had seemingly come from nowhere, I remembered that the spirits had been strangely silent about how to heal. So my mental response was this: *Okay, Jesus, if You're real — and I don't believe You are — but just in case You are — do something!* The next moment I began to weep, softly but deeply. These tears were not expressing any emotions of my mind but rather came from deeper within me, from my spirit. It seemed as if someone had put a spiritual funnel into my heart and was pouring in an unending stream of transcendent love and joy, deeper and more deeply refreshing than any human love or happiness I had ever known. Furthermore, I knew without doubt that this gently overwhelming love was from an infinite personal source who was loving me personally with a perfect love. My mind seemed to know immediately that the source of this great love was the very Creator of the universe! I continued to weep softly and silently in stunned awe at the peace that enveloped my being.

After what seemed like an eternity, I abruptly stopped weeping and looked up. The others had taken their hands away from Dan and seemed to be standing around in awkward silence. Finally someone remarked that Dan seemed to be looking a little better. Then everyone quietly drifted away.

I was still so peacefully stunned that I went home for supper without saying anything to Gretchen. Not until the next morning, as I looked out our apartment window before heading off to college, did I really ponder what had happened. I knew that psychologists tell us that if we believe in something or someone long enough and strongly enough, that something or someone will take on some measure of reality to us. Since I had knowingly believed in Buddhism for about 15 years, I had always assumed that if I ever had a mystical experience it would probably involve the Buddha appearing to me in some way. But the one who had come to me personally and rationally was someone I didn't even believe had existed at all! Trying to explain this apparent paradox, I reasoned that perhaps Buddha wasn't personally interested in his disciples after all these years. Or perhaps he had died years ago and was still dead in his tomb, whereas Jesus had come to me because in some way He was still alive! What that way was, and why Jesus would come to me, an unbeliever and a Buddhist at that, was truly a puzzle.

Then I remembered the similar puzzle of what happened to me on the snowy, wind-blown ridge of Mt. Yale almost six years before. Suddenly I realized that the two puzzles were the same. Exactly what had happened and why was still hazy, but now I knew that the ultimate source of what had happened was the infinite, transcendent yet personal God. Why I was touched by God had something to do with infinite, powerful yet gentle love. And how I was touched had something to do with that Jesus person who had revealed himself to me. I realized that I simply had to find out more about this enigmatic Jesus who held the key to my puzzles.

When I returned home from college that evening I asked Gretchen if we could read the Bible together. (For her this was truly a miracle!) I knew only that the Bible had an old part and a new part, and that the new part was about this Jesus person, and that the first four portions of the new part were about the life of Jesus. I sized up those portions and saw that the second one, the Book of Mark, was the thinnest, so I chose that one so I could get the main points about this Jesus person as quickly as possible! We read together only the first chapter that night, but that left me in suspense. I hurried home from college the next day, and could hardly wait to finish supper so we could go further. After reading the second chapter together, Gretchen stopped, but I simply had to go on. By the time I got to the fifth chapter, which records Jesus' authority over the legion of evil spirits in the Gadarene demoniac, I was absolutely amazed. If that account were true, then this Jesus person was the most amazing person who had ever lived! His authority and wisdom were simply incredible!

As I read on I also began to see the obvious similarities between the evil spirits that Jesus commanded and the spirit guides and drop-in communicators of my paraphysics research. These parallels became increasingly disturbing. I began to sense that I would eventually have to terminate my paraphysics research.

About a month into this daily Bible-reading pattern I told Gretchen I wouldn't mind going to church with her again. (After our wedding I tried going but it was too boring and meaningless.) On our sixth wedding anniversary I found myself in her church being surprised by joy all over again as passages from the Old and New Testament Scriptures were read. I wept quietly as my heart bore witness to the truth of what I was hearing. Surprisingly, my mind also knew without doubt that what I was hearing was absolute truth — the truth I had been searching for ever since as a child of eight I had decided I wanted to be a scientist. This breaking into deep, uncontrollable tears of unfathomable joy simply on hearing the words of Scripture continued for the next three Sundays.

Then on the fourth Sunday morning of spontaneous weeping, December 2, 1973, another totally unexpected event occurred that connected and explained the puzzle of the two previous supernatural events (1967 and October 1973). I began to weep again on hearing the Word of God, but my profuse tears of joy were abruptly transformed into tears of guilt and shame as the Creator God revealed to me the bleak and desolate landscape of my sins set against the backdrop of the sinfulness of all humankind. I was overcome by humiliation and grief, disgust, and despair. For the first time since beginning to read the Bible, I realized that I too was a sinner to the core and personally needed a Savior. I recoiled in horror as God showed me how I had grieved Him by forsaking Him years ago as a spiritual rebel and by going my own way. From deep within I knew that the absolutely reasonable and just judgment on my sin was not the easy solution of mere physical death, but total banishment from the presence of God (the state usually referred to as "hell"). I felt like a miserable worm wishing God would be mercifully quick in squishing me out of existence. But I now knew that God was not in the business of squishing out miserable worms. Instead, His desire was that not one worm should be lost! Furthermore, He had provided a unique way for any and all sinners to be pardoned: the way of the infinitely self-sacrificial death of His sinless Son, Jesus the Messiah, on the cross, followed by His victory over sin, death, and Satan through His glorious resurrection from the grave.

Recalling these liberating truths which I had already read in the Scriptures, I cried out in my heart to God to forgive me for my sins of rebellion and pride and receive me back as His child. As I asked this with faith that was a pure gift, I felt a heavy load (which I hadn't even realized was there) suddenly lift off me, leaving me feeling much lighter and changing my tears of despair back into those original tears of joy. I continued to weep quietly with thanksgiving to God because I had perfect assurance that as a prodigal son I had been forgiven and received back by my Father.

But God's revelation continued. In my mind's eye I saw Jesus walking with me through a desolate wilderness. When I gazed across the landscape I saw a snow-capped mountain peak which I immediately wanted to climb. When I bolted away from Jesus toward the mountain I suddenly fell into a deep pit. I cried out, "Help me, Jesus!" and Jesus came over, pulled me out, and brushed me off. Continuing on, I looked up again and saw a billboard advertising a new book about the latest scientific discoveries. When I moved away from Jesus to read the details, I again fell into a pit and the previous scenario was repeated. Walking on with Jesus again, I looked up once more and seemed to see a mirage of a rustic cabin near a bubbling brook flowing through an idyllic mountain valley. Such a peaceful scene had been my dream for the future, but I did not do as before and try to embrace it. Rather, I found myself looking into Jesus' face and humbly asking Him, "Lord, is this for me?" "No, my son," He answered. I simply answered, "Okay, Lord," and kept walking side-by-side with Jesus. This time I did not fall into another pit!

Returning abruptly to the mortal stream of time, I realized that Jesus had just shown me the simple, practical meaning of His lordship. This so resonated with my deepest desires that I again cried out, this time to Jesus, asking Him to come into my heart and be the true Lord of my life forever. I then and there surrendered my right to myself to Jesus.

Returning home from church that morning, I reflected on the amazing grace I had just experienced, and on my desire and commitment to serve the living Lord for the rest of my life. Naturally, I first thought of resigning my teaching position at SMSC and entering a seminary. But in time the Lord showed me that He had me where He wanted me for the time being, in one of the most difficult mission fields in the world — the spiritual jungle of academia.

The next day in my office at the college I got an urgent message from the main medium. Her spirit guide had directed her to gather a few core mediums in my office for a reading or revelation from him. I had told no one, not even my wife, about what had happened to me, yet the group's spirit guides obviously knew something had occurred that displeased or even threatened them. During the reading her spirit guide warned us of terrible troubles immediately ahead for our group. He then spoke a specific prophecy: "Your group is going to be broken up soon, and by someone in the inner core group." Another gentle thought dropped into my mind: *Yes, and it is going to be by you.* Though I knew this thought was from the Spirit of God, my instantaneous reaction was, "But that's my research work!" No sooner had this response flared up than I knew the unbidden thought was from God because He filled me completely with His peace.

The next two weeks of classes were exceedingly difficult for me, especially the paraphysics classes and regular seances and readings. I dutifully attended one of the seances, but the spiritual atmosphere was so oppressive I had to excuse myself early and then find reasons to not attend further sessions. Christmas break finally came and I could at last immerse myself in the Scriptures and prayer to get the mind of the Lord. By the time classes resumed in January I knew I could no longer "serve two masters" and would have to terminate the research as soon as possible, even though eight more weeks of classes remained.

I decided to tell my advanced paraphysics class first, but that Tuesday only a few of the core mediums were present and they were talking about a book they had read, *The Passover Plot,* that mocked the cross of Christ. After class a Jewish student asked me what I thought of the book. I proceeded to explain how Christ's death on the cross and resurrection were essential to the gospel of salvation from sin and death. While I was speaking I could tell he was coming under attack from an evil spirit trying to prevent him hearing my words (a phenomenon we had encountered before and called "psychic screening"). When he finally broke free he told me what he had just experienced. Suddenly his eyes seemed to turn yellowish, and evil so thick you could almost cut it with a knife seemed to ooze from them. My teeth began to chatter uncontrollably because of the instant cold I felt and the terror that tried to overcome me. As a one-month-old babe in Christ, all I could get out was "Jesus, help!" Immediately the chattering stopped as the cold and terror were replaced by the exquisite presence of the Lord. I began to weep quietly with the same unfathomable joy as before, and I was amazed to see that the student's eyes were no longer yellow and that he too was weeping. He then told me about the times he had been thrown to the floor of his apartment by the same entity that had tried to control him just minutes earlier, and how he had been forced to try to choke himself to death using his own hands around his neck.

After that close encounter between good and evil I realized I was now in a life and death struggle, not against flesh and blood, but against the powers of darkness. I couldn't straddle this razor blade divide between God and Satan any longer; I simply had to terminate all the research immediately. Two days later, when every student in my advanced paraphysics class was present, along with some students from previous classes who just dropped in "to see what was new," I spent two hours sharing my story. I announced I could no longer serve Satan's kingdom through the paraphysics research, which I was now terminating permanently. I gave students the option to continue their own research instead of class and write it up in a research paper, or continue to attend class as a forum to discuss the controversial nature of paraphysics and related topics, writing a term paper about that instead. Thankfully, most students elected the latter option, and some were so moved they decided to stop dabbling in the occult. Some later became believers in Jesus.

When I told my colleagues that I could no longer teach the paraphysics classes they were surprised and disappointed, but understanding. One colleague suggested I try to share what I had discovered in the research, even if it had been totally unexpected, so in 1974 I began to teach classes in "Good and Evil" and "What Is Reality?" I also taught a new course entitled "Creation and Cosmology," which tackled the controversial subject of origins, and an independent studies class on "Spiritual Laws and Dynamics." Some faculty members felt I had just flipped "from ghost chaser to Jesus freak"! One professor told me he knew I must have been "frightened into Christianity" by fire and brimstone religious propaganda, but his jaw dropped when I told him, "No, I was loved into God's kingdom by the Lord Jesus himself!"

Over the nearly 27 years since that day of amazing grace, God has sharpened my mind to do orthodox physics research in more efficient and insightful ways. He has taught me especially about creation as a mirror of His character as Creator and Redeemer. He has given me insights concerning the spiritual principles governing the dynamics of the unseen realm of spirits, demons, and angels. He has begun to teach me the rudiments of what I've called "theophysics" — the physics of the living God as revealed in His eternal Word, as well as in the redeemed and sustained lives of His people. He has made me more compassionate and created in me a tender shepherd's heart to love and serve others. In fact, as I look back over the time-mural of my life beginning on August 13, 1966, when I met Gretchen on a mountaintop, I see the hand of my Creator gently changing me to experience and understand, and then to demonstrate, the most powerful yet delicate force in the universe: the sacrificial agape love of the Lord of all.

ARIE VAN NIEUW AMERONGEN

MEDICAL RESEARCH

Dr. van Nieuw Amerongen is professor and chairman of the combined dental school within the faculty of medicine at Vrije University in Amsterdam, Holland. He holds a masters degree and Ph.D. in biochemistry from Vrije University. Dr. van Nieuw Amerongen also currently chairs the sub-department of Oral Microbiology, Oral Cell Biology, Oral Anatomy and Material Sciences within the School of Dentistry. He is the author of 170 research papers and three textbooks and holds five patents in the area of dentistry.

I was born in the last year of World War II (1944) in an orthodox Protestant family, living in a small Christian village. I received a Christian education both at home and at local schools. During this time I heard several Christians speaking on the holiness of the Lord and of the way of reconciliation for the sinner only by the blood of Jesus Christ. Nevertheless, when I became a student at a university in Amsterdam, I did not participate in the Christian faith with my whole heart. I was convinced that I could make the right decisions and the right choices in the world using my natural understanding and insight. Therefore, I thought that it could be possible to combine both service of the Lord and participation in the pleasures and entertainment of the world. On Sundays I attended church for worship and the rest of the week I spent in my own pursuits of studying, visiting movies and theater, and student festivities.

During this time I became somewhat restless, seeing the idleness and vanity in myself and in the world around me. Sometimes reading the Bible gave me some peace, but I still did not see the radicality of the Christian faith: "Trust in the Lord with all thine heart; and lean not unto thine own understanding" (Prov. 3:5). On looking back, my beliefs were swinging to and fro like the pendulum of a clock. Gradually I felt I was not on the right track, and I was in doubt about my salvation many times during my first two years at university.

In the third year of my study I accepted the invitation of a Christian girl to accompany her to a student night dancing festival. But in the last week before the date I saw more and more that visiting this student festivity was not in accordance with the holiness of the Lord. In the holy service of the last Sunday before the festivity, the sermon was on the history of the prophet Elijah, King Ahab, and the prophets of Baal on Mount Carmel, where Elijah said to the children of Israel, "How long halt ye between two opinions? if the Lord be God, follow him: but if Baal, then follow him" (1 Kings 18:21). This scriptural Word showed me clearly that I had been holding onto two opinions up to that point: serving in part both the Lord and the devil and his world. In that worship service the radical choice was made to follow only the Lord and to leave the world. For the first time I was aware that "all that is in the world, the lust of the flesh, and the lust of the eyes, and the pride of life, is not of the Father, but is of the world" (1 John 2:16).

In making the good choice, like Ruth the Moabitess, for the God of Israel, I had to leave behind me a great number of things in my student lifestyle and also several friends. Later on I found new Christian friends who were very helpful and supportive to me as I started my new life as a Christian. I became a member of a Christian student association where we studied several books of the Bible together. These studies were encouraging and helped me to understand the foundations of the Christian faith and to distinguish the essentials from the matters of secondary importance and from tradition. I came to understand my need of a relationship with my Lord, just as Naomi, in Old Testament times, had seen the need for her widowed daughter-in-law, Ruth, to have a relationship with Boaz. Ruth had made the right choice of following the God of Israel; however, she remained a Moabitess as long as she was not the bride of Boaz. Up to that point Ruth could not participate in the Jewish right of succession and continued being an outsider. But after her wedding to Boaz she became one of the Children of Israel and even one of the ancestors of Jesus Christ.

SERVING THE LORD

At that time I was confirmed, confessed my faith, and became a full member of our church. On that occasion our minister gave me a personal text from the Scriptures as a guide for my life. It was 1 John 2:17: "And the world passeth away, and the lust thereof: but he that doeth the will of God abideth for ever." Again, I felt the Lord was showing me to follow Him only and completely and to separate with my whole heart from the world.

Although I knew I had made the right choice, I did not enjoy peace with God the Father. I spent more and more time studying the Scriptures but I still felt I was not reconciled with the Father. My sins still stood between me and God, although I knew objectively that His Son had died on the cross to pay for all the sins of His children. This restlessness remained in my mind and heart.

Then one night, when I was in prayer, the Lord showed me that the risen Son, sitting at His right hand, was also my advocate, my intercessor with the Father. I had the personal experience that all my sins were covered by His blood, that His death substituted for my death and that He had paid for all my sins. A deep peace came over me, as is described by the apostle Paul in Philippians 4:7: "And the peace of God, which passeth all understanding, shall keep your hearts and minds through Christ Jesus." I received the assurance that I was reconciled with the Father and that He had adopted me as His child. A new world was opened to me, and I knew I had to follow Him wherever He wanted me to go. On the other hand, the Lord left me dependent on His grace, so that every time my faith had to be reconfirmed and was strengthened. The Lord showed me that the word of

Zephaniah 3:12 should remain as a daily guide to me: "I will also leave in the midst of thee an afflicted and poor people, and they shall trust in the name of the Lord."

HIS WAY'S HIGHER THAN OURS

A new intention came into my heart: to serve the Lord wherever He appointed me. A short time later an opportunity came to take a one-year part-time course in missionary training. At the end of my university study, I had the opportunity to meet with the missionary board of our church. There appeared to be an opening to go to Indonesia as a teacher in chemistry and bioscience at a secondary school in Rante Pao on the isle of Sulawesi-Selatan. For a whole year, 1969, I prepared myself to go abroad by attending the missionary high school, where I learned the Indonesian language and became more acquainted with Indonesian culture. However, at the end of that year Indonesia closed its frontiers to all Dutch missionary workers. Since I had to wait for another opening, I decided to go back for a short time to the university to learn more and to do research in brain biochemistry. I started my Ph.D. degree, expecting that I could go to Indonesia within a year. But the frontiers remained closed, and I finished my doctoral thesis in 1974.

I planned to become a full-time teacher in chemistry at a Dutch Christian secondary school. However, unexpectedly a tenure position at the university, in the faculty of dentistry, became vacant and I was urged to take it up. Although I had not intended to have a university career, I saw this opportunity as the leading of the Lord.

Ten years later new financial pressures were imposed on universities, and whole dental faculties had to be closed in the 1980s. Our faculty, part of a Christian university, was amalgamated with a secular dental faculty. The chairman of our department retired at this time, and I was appointed vice-chairman of the department of oral biochemistry.

However, the Lord opened new opportunities for me in this new agnostic environment. In 1990 I was appointed as a full professor in oral biochemistry, in spite of strong competition from other candidates. In that period I was encouraged and strengthened by my readings of the Scriptures. One time I was encouraged by the question of John the Baptist to Jesus when he was imprisoned and disappointed about the way of the Lord: "Art thou he that should come? or look we for another" (Luke 7:20). But the Lord answered: "Go your way, and tell John what things ye have seen and heard. . . . And blessed is he, whosoever shall not be offended in me" (Luke 7:22–23). On other occasions I received personal encouragement from the Book of Psalms, for example, the words written by King David: "Thou hast put gladness in my heart, more than in the time that their corn and their wine increased. I will both lay me down in peace, and sleep: for thou, Lord, only makest me dwell in safety" (Ps. 4:7–8). And another time from Psalm 84:5–6: "Blessed is the man whose strength is in thee; in whose heart are the ways of them; Who passing through the valley of Baca make it a well; the rain also filleth the pools."

During that time I came to understand more clearly that the Lord's ways are always higher than our ways, as the heavens are higher than the earth, and His Word will not return to Him void but will accomplish what He pleases (Isa. 55:9–11).

THE WONDER OF MOLECULAR PROCESSES

As a biochemist I have learned to analyze biological processes on a molecular level. From the very beginning of my study I was impressed by the regulation of complex physiological processes. The first example I studied was the hormonal regulation of the level of blood glucose with several agonists and antagonists. During my doctoral research I studied specific brain proteins and the neuronal regulation of many physiological processes in our body.

Later, when I moved to the faculty of dentistry, I studied the regulation of the secretory processes of the salivary glands so that these processes could be elucidated in molecular terms. I found it remarkable that peripherally the autonomous nervous system regulates differentially the secretory processes. Stimulation of the parasympathetic nerves results in more watery saliva, whereas sympathetic stimulation induces more viscous saliva, and these physical properties are based on differences in protein composition of the various types of saliva. Even a body fluid as simple-looking as saliva is so complex and variable that each type of stimulus results in saliva with appropriate characteristics. Stressful situations also are immediately reflected in variation of the composition and properties of saliva. After many years of study we were able to mimic this fluid only partially because its functions are so wide and complex. A whole team of researchers could spend their lifetimes in studying a simple body fluid like saliva and still not understand it completely.

From my scientific work I am deeply impressed by the wisdom and knowledge of the almighty God as Creator and supporter of His creation. The most clever researcher understands only a small part of the Lord's creation. I believe the creation points to the Creator, so that "they [people] are without excuse" (Rom. 1:20). It has been a great privilege for me to have the Lord call me back from the world of the flesh and to open my eyes both to His creation and to His Holy Scriptures. I am deeply impressed that the Lord "has quickened me, who was dead in trespasses and sins; Wherein in time past I walked. . . . For by grace I have been saved through faith; and that not of myself: it is a gift of God" (Eph. 2:1–8, adapted).

GRAHAM R. EVEREST

MATHEMATICS

D r. Everest is professor of mathematics at the University of East Anglia in the UK. He holds a B.Sc. with first class honors in mathematics from Bedford College, University of London, and a Ph.D. in mathematics from Kings College, University of London. Dr. Everest has published 50 research papers and one book relating to various areas of number theory. He has been an invited speaker at several mathematics conferences in both the UK and abroad.

The words of the Lord are pure words even as the silver, which from the earth is tried, and purified seven times in the fire (Ps. 12:7).[45]

The New Testament contains many details about the way men and women came to be converted and called Christians. But to what extent can we expect conversion today to mirror the experiences of these early believers? Can we take the words in the Bible and expect to apply them to ourselves in a straightforward and simple way? In this chapter I am going to argue from personal experience that we can. One of the challenges in my life has been daring to trust the words of Scripture, and seeing them fulfilled.

I came to the Christian faith with few preconceptions, not having been brought up in a traditional Christian family. Having said that, I have been very grateful for loving parents who provided me with a secure and happy home. When I came to hear later of God's love, I could at least say I knew something about what those words ought to imply. Without the hope that Christ provides, my teenage life quickly slid into cynicism and despair, so examples of Christian living manifested in a college friend made quite an impression. I have often thought that the honesty (and sometimes raw courage) he showed easily compensated for any failures in his persuasive powers.

My resistance to God's love really began to crumble several years later when I was appointed to a lectureship at the University of East Anglia. Needing to find some accommodation quite quickly, we came to the rural Norfolk village where we now live. This was quite a shock after life in the center of London; we thought we would die! In a sense we were right, but in a way we could hardly begin to imagine. Here we got to know the local vicar. This man (bless him) was a bit on the crusty side and not that popular in the village. But his rugged determination to stand by God's Word was just what I needed, and he helped me to understand the essentials of the Christian faith.

At the same time, I experienced a familiar discrepancy between what I believed with my mind and the way I lived my life. I learned the importance of repentance and faith in the death and resurrection of the Lord Jesus Christ and tried my best to copy the example of the early disciples, but I fell dismally short. I was helped enormously at that time by the friendship of believers who encouraged me to experience the fullness of the Holy Spirit, as it is recorded in the New Testament. At last I could say that my initiation into Christianity, after several years of seeking, matched up with that of the early believers. To me, it did not matter that the various components of baptism, repentance, faith in Jesus, and the receipt of the Holy Spirit came at different times. After all, there are several similar instances in the New Testament.

Just about everybody agrees that a person who claims to have become a Christian should provide proof of that claim. I could be quite certain within myself that I had changed. For one thing, I simply could not get enough of the Bible, digesting it in great chunks. There also came a great assurance that Jesus had truly died for me and that I now stood forgiven. With this assurance came a great boldness to share Jesus with others, and this was one way in which it appeared to others that I had changed.

Christians often say that God talks to them and I would agree that He does. Soon after these things began to happen to me, I began to form a strong impression that God wanted me to take this new life into my home. To be honest, cracks had started to appear in our marriage even at an early stage and I felt God was telling me I should work things out from there. I was greatly encouraged that my wife noticed how my interest in the Bible and early morning prayer meetings seemed to be leading to some kind of payoff for her!

It was in those days that I began to form the impression that my life was being worked out according to some kind of plan. What I mean is that my life as a mathematician, living in rural Norfolk, no longer seemed to be the product of merely random forces. It seemed as though these aspects of my life, where I worked and where I lived, had a meaning, too. Of course, this was an enormously challenging thought. While it was true that I had begun on a new path, a lot of my life was still shaped by my past. But I can say that I have lived at home and at work in the knowledge that what I do matters in God's eyes. Many of my attempts to live in this kind of faith have been flawed, but I can say that God has showed amazing faithfulness.

DO MIRACLES HAPPEN TODAY?

Much of what I have said already bears testimony to the supernatural. However, when the question above is usually asked, what is meant is whether biblical-style miracles happen today: miracles of healing or provision, that kind of thing. Due to my acquaintance with quite a large circle of Christian friends, my faith in a God of miracles began to be seriously challenged. It is one thing to say you believe God can do miracles, but quite another to pray for one and actually expect to see it happen. I am now going to relate two stories of things that really happened and leave you to make up your mind about the reality of miracles today.

Around this time, I was asked to give a short talk at a Full Gospel Businessmen meeting. These meetings take place in a fairly informal setting and consist of a common meal followed by an opportunity for people to talk about their experience of Christ. At the time I was suffering from a chest infection, a problem that had been recurring for several years; the infections would come on during winter and last for weeks or even months. They were quite painful and antibiotics did not seem to help. It occurred to me that I should pray and ask God if He would heal me. I can tell you that in the intervening period between being asked to speak and actually speaking, about one week, I wrestled very hard with this. The infection showed no signs of relenting and, right up until the evening of my talk, my prayer seemed to have made no difference. Outside the meeting hall, in my car, I prayed again, almost impudently declaring that as Jesus healed once, so He would heal today. And He did. The infection left me and I have not been troubled with it since.

For the second story, you need to know that in my profession your career begins quite late, the salary scale is long, and it can be quite a few years before you earn anything like a professional salary. We had two children fairly quickly in our marriage, a mortgage, a car, and bills to pay. You will believe me that our finances balanced precariously close to the edge. I suppose that if you looked at our money management you would say we could have been more careful and you would probably be right. However, we were not careless and we did make real efforts to manage. But we started to get into serious trouble. Now I have always been suspicious of Christian testimonies about money, preferring to believe that talk of money is rather embarrassing, even believing that God himself is rather embarrassed by the topic. So I kept our problems to ourselves and would have gone on doing so until something happened that changed it all.

In those days I was attending a men's prayer meeting every month. I cannot really explain how this meeting differed from others I have attended, but I have sensed this kind of difference several times. There seemed to be a quality of power and love and faith that was almost tangible. When we praised God at those meetings, we seemed to be lifted into another realm. At the end of one such meeting, the leader asked if there was anybody present who had any needs. Without stopping to think, I blurted out that we had a few financial difficulties at home. I started to regret saying this when the leader asked me to come and stand in the middle of the floor while the men gathered around me and laid their hands on my head. The experience took me back to my days playing rugby, of which my only solid memory is of about 20 sweaty hands placed on my head all at once! For the next few days, I kept the experience at the front of my mind, and I was amazed when one of my wife's aunts sent us a check through the mail because she thought we could use it. The sum was not small and did just enough to set us back on a right course. Nobody (on earth) had told her about our situation, and she had never done anything like that before and has not since.

I could tell of similar occurrences I have been involved with, but I have limited my account to these because they really happened in that way and they do not rely upon hearsay at all. I know critics can raise philosophical queries. Why should Jesus heal me when infants are dying every day, and why should He help my financial difficulties when millions live in poverty? I cannot answer these questions except to say that the Scriptures do show a similar instance of God's particularity. God chooses to bless people not on account of their merits but simply on account of His grace.

Do Miracles Happen All the Time?

Perhaps you are wondering if these events have affected my understanding of God's will and whether I now go hunting for miracles all the time. Let me answer this first with a question: should we *expect* miracles to happen all the time?

The answer to this question is not as easy as it sounds. Jesus certainly challenged His disciples to believe in God for everything while at the same time teaching them to work and live within the created order. Paul, even though he was an agent for miracles, clearly did not expect them to happen on request. My attitude is that we need to exercise some holy common sense. As

I write, I am still getting over the death of a Christian friend, a lovely young lady who was the mother of three young children. My prayer throughout her long and painful illness was for physical healing, but it did not come.

Another wrong impression would be that my own life is now one long blissful joy ride and I never have any problems that cannot be settled immediately by waving the prayer wand. This is simply not true. As it happens, I spent several painful years in the throes of burnout after years of exhausting work at home, at the university, and in the ministry. But I can honestly say that everything has worked together for good, even the painful things. Perhaps that is one of the most profound mysteries of Christianity, the power to transform suffering into glory. The death and resurrection of Jesus is the paradigm, and I have been privileged to witness this mystery at work in the lives of others.

In the Beginning (Again)

I have made it clear that Scripture has played an important part in my growth as a Christian. Inevitably, the question will be asked about just how literally, or simply, I believe it. For example, do I believe the Book of Genesis, or do I try to harmonize my belief in Scripture with the teaching of evolution?

At first I must say the question did not trouble me a lot, although I was aware of the profundity of Genesis and was not inclined to dismiss it. As I looked into the subject more, I began to realize that evolution is simply not the scientific fact that the popular media proclaim it to be. It is unlikely and certainly unproven. Also, I began to realize that the simple reading of Genesis is important because it is the foundation for the gospel. In particular, the fall of humanity with the consequent entry of death into the world is the only logical foundation for the gospel of Christ. More than that, evolution is such a cuckoo in the nest that, once accepted, it starts to edge out the other great doctrines of Christianity. For example, if evolution is true, then death is natural, something which undermines the whole biblical thrust of redemption.

Finally, let me say something about God in my life as a mathematician. I said that I have tried to serve Him in my professional life and I can say that He has blessed me. I am not saying my theorems are better than those of other mathematicians; there are many who do far better work than me who never pray at all. All I can say is that God guides me and I thank Him for His guidance.

I have never seen any contradiction between being a mathematician, working in a highly sophisticated area of thought, and exercising simple trust in God. On the contrary, everywhere you look in mathematics you see beauty, and, although it is a highly technical subject, you will find universal agreement among mathematicians that at the heart of the best theorems lie the simplest ideas. I would reckon this to be a universal principle in science generally and it points gloriously to God's ordinance.

ANDREW G. BOSANQUET

MEDICAL RESEARCH

*D*r. Bosanquet is director of the Bath Cancer Research Unit and honorary senior lecturer in the School of Postgraduate Medicine at the University of Bath, UK. He holds a B.Sc. in biochemistry from the University of Bristol and a Ph.D. in biochemistry from the University of Canterbury, New Zealand. Dr. Bosanquet has published over 65 research papers and book chapters and 70 research abstracts, and is a Fellow of the Royal Society of Chemistry.*

I cannot remember a time when science did not fascinate me. As a child, my father told me how scientists now knew enough to create the molecules of life. To a boy's mind this awesome prospect fueled my respect for science, the cradle of wisdom and knowledge that would empower humankind to improve and progress. Forty years on, President Clinton's flattering eulogy apropos the genome project "revealing the secret of life" provoked a less flattering reaction. I had been a scientist involved in medical research for nearly 30 years and was only too well aware that rhetoric may advance careers and gain kudos, but the more we learn the more we realize how little we know. Paradoxically, increased knowledge leads to increased awareness of how much more remains to be discovered.

In the 1950s and 1960s, confident academics proclaimed, "God is dead." Society had matured. We no longer needed childish myths embodied in religious doctrines. We had science.

In common with many growing up through that time, I imbibed religion as a neat but separate compartment to life, more to do with being good according to the prevailing cultural ethos than with relationship, experience, and study. With a talent for chemistry and math and a careers guidance report suggesting medical research, I went to the university to study biochemistry.

It was exciting to be taught to the limits of current knowledge — the third year included lectures correcting the previous year's "knowledge" in the light of latest findings. And not only in the academic field was this happening. I was meeting fellow students who studied the Bible seriously as the Word of God and talked about being born again and knowing God personally. Impressed by their lives and what they were saying, by the beginning of the second year I gave up my safe middle-class English value system and became a disciple of Jesus, convinced against all prevailing wisdom that the Bible was the source of knowledge and wisdom and that God, having created the universe from nothing, was actively at work on planet Earth.

Leaving the university, faith in God seemed hugely more important than a degree in biochemistry, and I imagined Bible college and a life of "Christian" work. However, a wise pastor suggested that God might want me to be a biochemist, and after 18 months in medical research I enrolled for a Ph.D. in New Zealand, where the family of my wife, Margaret, lived. This was my first opportunity to embark on research undertaken with prayer for God to guide. A "glitch" in early results became the subject of my thesis that two-and-a-half years later earned a doctorate.

Equally important was the lesson that "problems" can be springboards, in scientific research and in other parts of life. Margaret was going to teach during my post-graduate studies and provide for us financially, but an oversupply of teachers led to job shortages. Having exhausted normal income-generating avenues, our joint meager incomes were insufficient. But God was not. Regularly, we brought our needs to God, believing He was our Father and would take care of us. We did not discuss our situation with people. Week by week, the right amount of money would turn up or God would provide our needs. One week we found cash in our post-box. Another time we invited friends for Sunday lunch, emptied the fridge for the first course and were just saying we had no pudding when a neighbor knocked on the door and walked in with an apple pie hot from the oven. Even a car knocking into our fence helped the finances. Despite the driver giving a false number plate, the police found the culprit and suggested he pay us for the damage. Estimated by a friend who was a builder, these costs supplied another few weeks' finances, since everything needed to repair the wall and fence was already at hand. Not only did we read in the Bible that God intervened in lives, but we experienced it repeatedly.

By now Britain was in the throws of recession, and as we contemplated our return to the UK and job hunting, friends were on hand to assure us that jobs in science were scarce. Faith is a wonderfully protective shield when surrounded by "Job's comforters." Four interviews and four job offers later, I took the least likely post (humanly speaking) because reading the Bible and praying the morning of the interview, we were confident this was where God was leading. Having turned down a prestigious post in London and its huge grant, I arrived in Bath to an empty lab and no support, and without relevant background — my doctorate was in heart disease and this post was in cancer research.

A mundane research topic led me four years down the road to seriously look for guidance about the direction to take. I was investigating anti-cancer drug metabolism and drug combinations, but what really interested me was how to help patients receive the best treatment. Commonly, treatment is by protocols derived from clinical trial results. But the best drugs for most patients in a select group were not optimum for many individuals, and the only way to assess a patient's response was to treat and monitor response. Performing the experiment in the patient in this way means that many times toxic treatment, with unpleasant side effects and leading to increased resistance, is ineffective. I explored how to test individual patient cells in the test tube to assess relative effectiveness of drugs so that patients could receive effective therapy and be spared ineffective drugs with their concomitant toxicity.

I had personal experience of the frustrations of drug therapy. My eldest son had a series of ear infections requiring repeated courses of antibiotic. At eight months old, David was not hearing well and grommets were planned to avoid problems in language development and prevent further bouts of pain and distress. He regularly woke in the night or early morning screaming with pain, and no sooner had antibiotics tackled the infection than the next one started. We were desperate and prayed frequently for healing.

Leaving church one evening, the rector said he would come and pray and suggested that the problem might be the house. I mentioned this to Margaret. Although she had dismissed it at the time, she recalled that during the week two other people had suggested to her that David's ear infections were somehow linked to the house. The next evening the rector arrived late, between meetings, and briefly prayed in David's room and for David. Although encouraged by his kindness, the visit, as far as the problem was concerned, seemed a non-event. The next morning we overslept — no screaming baby as an alarm call. At 8.30 a.m. Margaret woke me feeling very anxious because the house was so quiet. Was David alright? I went in to find him gurgling happily in his cot. At the next hospital appointment the consultant cancelled his operation, and he has not had an ear infection in the 17 years since. A little research revealed that our house had been owned by a sect and under the nameplate was a dubious name of cultic origins. There was a spiritual dimension to this world that scientific reductionism could not explain.

I was increasingly convinced that God's guidance and help were necessary and available in every area of life; faith was not taking part in church services so much as following God's way through each day. And this must include scientific research. I could not claim to be a disciple of Jesus and then act as if He were irrelevant to a large proportion of life. However, many influential experts believe such faith is not only irrational but inappropriate for a scientist, as I was to discover.

In the meantime, attending a conference in Florence, I heard Dr. Larry Weisenthal talk about a test to screen patients' cells for drug response before cancer therapy was chosen. I had one of those "eureka" moments when I knew this was the research I would do. What I didn't know then was how unpopular this line of research was with the establishment. The fashion was very much for sophistication and complexity — molecular biology, monoclonal antibodies, gene research — rather than simple concepts like testing patient cells in the test tube to predict individual drug sensitivity. I could not get funding for this work. I was vilified publicly and privately. I found it inordinately difficult to get work published. But the results I was seeing were suggesting that drug sensitivity testing could be a great benefit in choosing treatment for cancer patients — not the Holy Grail, but a relatively cheap and accessible technology that could benefit patients immediately.

The conviction that patients could benefit and God had guided me to this research kept me going. Grants were not forthcoming, but individuals began to support the work. We published a leaflet to inform supporters how their money was spent and held "open days" to show them our laboratories and talk about our work in layperson's terms. A ready-formed fundraising committee approached me and offered its support. The work and support grew and Bath Cancer Research was born. I had not planned this, but I was greatly encouraged by this support which enabled me to continue this line of research. Twenty years on, we have an eminent scientific committee, papers published in top journals, involvement with the latest national clinical trial in chronic lymphocytic leukemia, and a growing volume of requests from cancer specialists worldwide to teach them the work — to say nothing of requests from patients from Australia to Canada, South Africa to Scandinavia, to test their cells for drug sensitivity.

As the 20th century was drawing to a close, I was invited to present my results to a U.S. government hearing in Baltimore. Drug sensitivity testing had been commercialized for a decade in America and Medicare had received an application from companies involved to be reimbursed for tests performed for people over 65 years old. A panel of eminent specialists from across the country met to hear evidence from people in the field and experts from relevant government agencies. The panel sat for two days and considered the evidence for and against drug sensitivity testing. They concluded that my work showed clinical utility — no other work was ratified although it showed promise. Bath Cancer Research, with a staff of seven and a turnover of just £150,000 a year, had achieved what companies with 60+ staff and $10 million annual turnovers had not. The difference — the God factor. You can spend your life chasing money and power and success, embrace the current deities of pleasure and materialism, or even, dare I say, knowledge. But the narrow road, although less traveled, arrives more surely at the destination, and you have God's company and blessing along the way.

After nearly 50 years on planet Earth, what can I say about the God factor? I have met many people more clever and knowledgeable than I am. I have seen scientific research from the inside, warts and all. I still derive great pleasure from science and research — it's an interesting and rewarding subject. But it comes a poor second to the value I would put on wisdom. Solomon wrote, "The fear of the Lord is the beginning of wisdom," and the apostle Paul, "The cross is a stumbling block to Jews and foolishness to Gentiles." My experience echoes the apostle's conclusion, "The foolishness of God is wiser than man's wisdom" (Prov. 9:10; 1 Cor. 1:23, 35; NIV). Professionally, in family life, health, finance, and many other ways, I have experienced the God factor and can report that He is alive and at work in lives committed to Him on planet Earth in the 21st century. And the greatest research project around is accessible to all — to seek first His kingdom and experience His care, provision, and guidance in every part of life. You don't need a grant for this research, but you have to give your life.

1 Ben Carson, *Think Big* (Grand Rapids, MI: Zondervan Publishing House, 1992), p. 242–243.

2 E.J. Larson and L. Witham, "Scientists Are Still Keeping the Faith," *Nature,* vol. 386, 1997, p. 435–436.

3 http://www.serve.com/herrmann/main.html

4 Clarence Rufus Rorem, Encyclopaedia Britannica (1956), Vol. 11, p. 791.

5 These diagrams and a wealth of other information about Fibonacci numbers can be found at http://www.mcs.surrey.ac.UK/Personal/R.Knott/Fibonacci/fibnat.html

6 F.F. Bruce, *The New Testament Documents: Are They Reliable?* (London: Intervarsity Fellowship, 1960), 5th rev. ed., p. 15.

7 The Greek pronoun translated "one" is in the neuter gender, as opposed to the masculine, indicating oneness in will, not in personhood.

8 Bertrand Russell, *Why I Am Not a Christian, and Other Essays on Religion and Related Subjects* (New York, NY: Simon and Schuster, 1957).

Bertrand Russell, *The ABC of Relativity* (London: Harper & Brothers, 1925).

Bertrand Russell, *An Inquiry into Meaning and Truth* (London: Allen and Unwin, 1940).

Bertrand Russell, *Human Knowledge: Its Scope and Limits* (New York, NY: Simon and Schuster, 1948).

Also see: Bertrand Russell, *Our Knowledge of the External World as a Field for Scientific Method in Philosophy,* The Lowell Institute Lectures of 1914 (London: Allen & Unwin, 1914).

9 Alfred North Whitehead and Bertrand Russell, *Principia Mathematica* (Cambridge, England: The University Press, 1910–12).

10 Bertrand Russell, *A Free Man's Worship* (Portland, ME: Thomas Bird Mosher, 1923).

11 Abraham Adolf Frankl, *Foundations of Set Theory*, second revised edition (Amsterdam: North-Holland Publishing Company, 1973).

12 Gottfried Willhelm Leibniz, *Discourse on Metaphysics* (c. 1700), re-issued in English in 1953 in Manchester, England, by Manchester University Press.

13 B. Hoffer, *The 22nd Linguistic Association of Canada and the United States (LACUS) Forum, 1995,* "How Grammatical Relations Are Determined," J.W. Oller Jr. (Chapel Hill, NC: Linguistic Association of Canada and the United States, 1996), p. 37–88.

14 J.W. Oller Jr., "Adding Abstract to Formal and Content Schemata: Results of Recent Work in Peircean Semiotics," *Applied Linguistics*, 16 (3), 1995: p. 273–306.

   J.W. Oller Jr., "Semiotic Theory Applied to Free Will, Relativity, and Determinacy: Or Why the Unified Field Theory Sought by Einstein Could Not Be Found," *Semiotica*, 108 (3/4), 1996: p. 199–244.

   Lewis Pyenson, editor, *Word and Icon: Saying and Seeing*, "Word and Icon: The Indispensable Connection As Seen From a General Theory of Signs" J.W. Oller Jr. (Lafayette, LA: The Center for Louisiana Studies, University of Southwestern Louisiana, 1998), p. 50–62.

15 P.A. Schilpp, editor, *The Philosophy of Bertrand Russell*, "Remarks on Bertrand Russell's Theory of Knowledge," Albert Einstein (New York, NY: Tudor Publishing, 1944), p. 279–291.

16 Fred Hoyle, *The Intelligent Universe* (London: Michael Joseph, 1983).

17 Stephen J. Gould, "This View of Life: Evolution's Erratic Pace," *Natural History*, 86 (5), 1977: p. 12, 14, 16.

   Stephen J. Gould, "This View of Life: The Return of Hopeful Monsters," *Natural History*, 86(6), 1977: p. 22, 24, 28, 30.

   T.J.M. Schopf, editor, *Models in Paleobiology*, "Punctuated Equilibria: An Alternative to Phyletic Gradualism," Niles Eldridge and Stephen Jay Gould (San Francisco, CA: Freeman Cooper, 1972), p. 82–115.

18 Graham Maddox, *Religion and the Rise of Democracy* (London: Routledge, 1996).

19 Perry Miller and Thomas Johnson, editors, *The Puritans*, "A Modell of Christian Charity," John Winthrop (1630), 2 Vols, 2nd edition, (New York, NY: Harper & Row, 1963), Vol. 1, p. 198.

20 See John D. Barrow, *Impossibility: The Limits of Science and the Science of Limits* (Oxford: Oxford University Press, 1998), p. 51–53.

21 Eric Laithwaite, *Why Does a Glow-Worm Glow?* (London: Beaver Books, 1977).

22 B. Carson, with Gregg Lewis, *The Big Picture: Getting Perspective on What's Really Important in Life* (Grand Rapids, MI: Zondervan, 1999), p. 51–52.

23 J.A. Tucker and P. Tucker, *Glimpses of God's Love* (Washington, DC: Review & Herald, 1983).

24 Barrow, *Impossibility: The Limits of Science and the Science of Limits*, p. 22.

25 Ibid., p. 96.

26 Carson, *The Big Picture: Getting Perspective on What's Really Important in Life*, p. 270.

27 Josh McDowell, *The New Evidence that Demands a Verdict* (Nashville, TN: Thomas Nelson Publishers, 1999).

28 Ibid.

29 E.J. Larson and L. Witham, "Leading Scientists Still Reject God," *Nature*, vol. 394, 1998: p. 313.

30 Henry Morris, *That Their Words May Be Used Against Them* (Green Forest, AR: Master Books, 1997), p. 417.

31 David J. Tyler, "The Crisis in Radiocarbon Calibration," *Creation Research Society Quarterly,* 14(2), 1977: p. 92–99.

32 David J. Tyler, "Radiocarbon Calibration — Revised," *Creation Research Society Quarterly*, 15(1), 1978: p. 1–23.

33 David J. Tyler, "Megaliths and Neolithic Man," *Creation Research Society Quarterly,* 16(1), 1979: p. 47–58.

34 Edward Young, *Studies in Genesis One* (Philadelphia, PA: Presbyterian and Reformed Publishing Company, 1964).

35 R.E. Walsh, editor, *Proceedings of the Third International Conference on Creationism,* "Tectonic Controls on Sedimentation in Rocks from the Jurassic Series (Yorkshire, England)," David J. Tyler (Pittsburgh, PA: Creation Science Fellowship, Inc., 1994), Vol. II, p. 535–545.

36 David J. Tyler, "A Post-Flood Solution to the Chalk Problem," *EN Tech. Journal*, 10(1), 1996: p. 107–113.

37 R.E. Walsh and C.L. Brooks, editors, *Proceedings of the Second International Conference on Creationism*, "A Tectonically-controlled Rock Cycle," David J. Tyler (Pittsburgh, PA: Creation Science Fellowship, Inc., 1990), Vol. II, p. 293–301.

38 W. Gitt, *In the Beginning Was Information* (Bielefeld, Germany: Christliche Literatur-Verbreitung e.V., 1997), English edition, p. 160–61.

39 Delores Kreiger, "Therapeutic Touch, the Imprimatur of Nursing," *American Journal of Nursing*, May 1975: p. 784–787.

40 James Fowler, *Stages of Faith: the Psychology of Human Development and the Quest for Meaning* (New York, NY: Harper and Row, 1981).

41 C.S. Lewis, *The Case for Christianity* (New York, NY: Simon & Schuster, Touchstone Edition, 1996), p. 54–55.

42 Elspeth Huxley, *Atlantic Ordeal* (New York, NY: Harper & Brothers, 1942).

43 E.C. Barrett and D.F. Fisher, editors, *Scientists Who Believe* (Chicago, IL: Moody Press, 1984); and E.C. Barrett, editor, *Scientists Who Find God* (Eastbourne, UK, and Loves Park, Illinois: Slavic Gospel Association, 1997).

44 E.J. Larson and L. Witham, "Scientists Are Still Keeping the Faith," *Nature*, vol. 386, 1997: p. 435–436.

45 From the 1662 *Anglican Book of Common Prayer*. This verse appears as verse 6 in other translations.

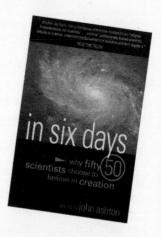